Human Intelligence

Perspectives on Its Theory and Measurement

edited by

Robert J. Sternberg

Yale University

Douglas K. Detterman

Case Western Reserve University

 Ablex Publishing Corporation
Norwood, New Jersey 07648

Library of Congress Cataloging in Publication Data
Main entry under title:

Human intelligence.

  Proceedinngs of two symposiums held at the 1978 and
1979 annual meetings of the American Educational
Research Association in Toronto and San Francisco,
respectively, and published in the 2d and 3d volumes of Intelligence.
  Includes bibliographies and index.
  1. Intellect-Congresses. 2. Intelligence tests—
Congresses. I. Sternberg, Robert J. II. Detterman,
Douglas K. III. American Educational Research Associa-
tion. IV. Intelligence. [DNLM: 1. Intelligence—
Collected works. 2. Intelligence tests—Collected works.
BF431 H921]
BF431.H796   153.9′3   79-17994
ISBN 0-89391-030-9

ABLEX Publishing Corporation
355 Chestnut Street
Norwood, New Jersey 07648

Contents

iii

Preface

Several years ago, one of us (D.K.D.) decided that the time was ripe for the creation of a multidisciplinary journal devoted exclusively to articles concerning human intelligence. The idea was to bring together in the pages of a single journal the theory and research of investigators from a wide range of disciplines. It seemed that the range was wide enough that many of these investigators would not read each other's work unless some common outlet of publication were provided. But it was clear that these investigators *should* be reading each other's work. A new journal, *Intelligence,* was instituted in 1977 to fulfill the need for a common outlet. The journal is now in its third volume of quarterly issues.

The other of us (R.J.S.) joined the project during its first year, initially as a member of the editorial board, and later as Associate Editor. During this year, the two of us decided to supplement the regular submitted papers with solicited papers that would help steer the field in what we hoped would be productive directions. The field of intelligence has had more than its share of garden paths, and we believed that by soliciting some of the best talent in the field to comment upon directions in which the field should go, some of these and other garden paths might be averted in the future. The solicitations took two forms: guest editorials and invited symposia.

Beginning with Volume 2, Number 2, each issue of *Intelligence* has contained a guest editorial by an individual prominent in the field of intelligence. Guest editors were asked to write on any matter of concern to them, so long as the matter concerned intelligence in some way. The chosen individuals have varied widely in their theoretical perspectives, methodological preferences, and substantive areas of research. But they have been united in their concern with the field of intelligence, and the directions in which it is going.

Beginning with the second volume, we also instituted a series of annual symposia dealing with what we have believed to be timely and significant topics in the field of intelligence. The first symposium, "The Reunification of the Two Disciplines of Scientific Psychology," dealt with the sudden wave of responses that had belatedly been made to Cronbach's 1957 plea to bring together experimental and differential research. The symposium was held at the 1978 annual meeting of the American Educational Research Association in Toronto, and the proceedings were published in the second and third numbers of the second volume of *Intelligence*. The second symposium, "Intelligence Tests in the Year 2000: What Forms Will They Take and What Purposes Will They Serve?" dealt with the not-too-distant future of intelligence testing. This symposium was held at the 1979 annual meeting of the American Educational Research Association in San Francisco, and the proceedings were published in the third number of the third volume of *Intelligence*. Next year's symposium, dealing with how and how much intelligence can be modified, will be held at the 1980 annual meeting of the American Educational Research Association in Boston, and will subsequently be published in *Intelligence*.

Early during 1979, we decided to compile a volume that we originally entitled, tongue-in-cheek, *Intelligence on Intelligence: The Best of Intelligence*. We didn't want a frivolous title to conceal some serious goals, however, and so we have switched to a more serious title. Our goals for the proposed volume—this volume—were twofold. First, we wanted to publish as a separate volume a collection of papers whose function was to point the way toward future research on the theory and measurement of intelligence. Selections from the papers we had solicited seemed naturally to group into two categories—those concerned with the future direction of the theory of intelligence, and those concerned with the future direction of the measurement of intelligence. The dual collective function of these papers was not clear to us when we solicited the articles, nor was it clear when they appeared in the journal, in many cases, scattered throughout a number of different issues. We believe that the collection of papers published together here can serve a guiding function that could be provided only partially by their journal publication. We have therefore grouped the papers into two collections, one dealing with perspectives on the theory of intelligence, the other dealing with perspectives on the measurement of intelligence. The papers in the first collection deal with both the present and the future of research on intelligence. The papers in the second collection deal specifically with the future of the measurement of intelligence. We have written introductions to and discussions of the papers in each collection in order to highlight the unities among them, and also to highlight certain differences in points of view among the various authors. Second, and stated in the frankest possible way, we hoped through this book to acquaint readers with the caliber of work presently being published in *Intelligence*. We are well aware of the multiplicity of journals that have become "required" reading in today's psychological world. We hope that a reading of this book will convince at least some students of intelligence to add *Intelligence* to their list of required reading.

R. J. S.

D. K. D.

I

PERSPECTIVES ON THEORY

In his influential presidential address to the American Psychological Association in 1957 Cronbach suggested that there were two separate disciplines of scientific psychology: the correlational approach and the experimental method. His major point was: "A true federation of the disciplines is required. Kept independent, they can give only wrong answers or no answers at all regarding certain important problems." The final form of this federation was also specified: "Correlational psychology studies only variance among organisms; experimental psychology studies only variance among treatments. A united discipline will study both of these, but it will also be concerned with the otherwise neglected interactions between organismic and treatment variables." The following papers examine the various extant methodological approaches to determine if such a unification has taken place or, indeed, if one is necessary.

Carroll begins on a pessimistic note by documenting his contention that the attempt to account for traits in terms of more basic psychological processes from information processing models has had little success. He finds two basic problems with this research. The first is that methodological shortcomings abound. The second problem concerns the speculative nature of the hypothesized theoretical processes. More optimistically, Carroll points to some approaches which he believes have considerable potential. Sternberg gives a more detailed account of one of the approaches favored by Carroll: componential analysis. He first describes guidelines for the selection of an appropriate methodology and then applies these to research in intelligence. Pellegrino and Glaser argue that the cognitive component approach advocated by Sternberg and Carroll is superior to the cognitive correlates approach. They present a number of reasons for favoring this approach. Chief among these, however, is that they believe that the cognitive

1

components approach has been more productive. They support this contention by comparing the results of recent research using one or the other of these approaches.

Campione and Brown describe an extensive research program with mentally retarded subjects using the cognitive correlates approach. They argue that this approach has identified a major component of intelligence, namely the ability to generalize across situations. The deficits displayed by retarded subjects in this domain seem to result from faulty control processes.

Snow is the least certain of all of the authors concerning the best methodology for studying individual differences in human intelligence. After an analysis of the problems faced by individual differences researchers in human intelligence he presents an integrative framework incorporating the best aspects of several different approaches. He is of the opinion that such multifaceted approaches will be essential to an understanding of human intelligence.

Hunt and MacLeod present the rebel's point of view. They believe that individual differences research and cognitive psychology will never be united. The best that can be hoped for is a synergistic parallel development. In support of their position, they identify four basic incompatabilities between the two areas.

In view of the wide variety of methodological preferences, Detterman suggests that the best approach might be to learn to tolerate differences in approach. He contends that this diversity may be the real strength of individual differences research in human intelligence.

1

How Shall We Study Individual Differences in Cognitive Abilities?—Methodological and Theoretical Perspectives

JOHN B. CARROLL

University of North Carolina at Chapel Hill

Selected studies in recent research literature are examined with regard to (a) their methodological adequacy in establishing dimensions of individual differences in information-processing abilities, and (b) the theoretical problems involved in inferring psychological processes from individual difference dimensions. Many methodological inadequacies are noted, including use of small Ns, questionable procedures in establishing variables (e.g., use of raw difference scores), improper or inadequate use of factor analysis and other multivariate statistical techniques, and poor presentation of results. On the whole, little progress has been made thus far in identifying psychological processes through research in individual differences, even though this research approach is viable and potentially useful. Serious theoretical difficulties arise in attempting to infer the nature and operation of psychological processes merely from the identification of individual difference trait dimensions. Promising research, however, is represented by studies in which an effort is made to analyze tasks into their components, to vary task characteristics, and/or to consider the strategies that individuals can employ in performing the tasks.

"How shall we study individual differences?" This was the question considered by S. S. Sargent in a paper of that title published in the *Psychological Review* in 1942. It is a question that needs to be asked again and again, for it is one that has no final answer. Certainly Sargent was not the first to have raised it—the problem goes back to the time of Galton, James McKeen Cattell, Edward L. Thorndike, and other founders of psychometrics. The particular concerns addressed by Sargent in his 1942 article, however, were somewhat novel at the time, and they are particularly pertinent to our current interest in the analysis of "intelligence" in the light of information-processing theories. Sargent was pointing out that:

> ... quantitative approaches do not give an accurate picture of individual differences. ... quantitative treatment, per se, does not describe the methods of work used by a subject as he performs a task; ... it does not depict adequately the pattern of behavioral processes involved;

'Preparation of this article was supported in part by the Personnel and Training Research Programs, Psychological Sciences Division, Office of Naval Research, under Contract No. N00014-77-C-0722, Contract Authority Identification Number, NR 150-406.

[and] preoccupation with quantitative method causes one to lose sight of important aspects of individual personalities and therefore of differences between personalities. (p. 171)

"Information-processing" had not become the catch phrase it is today, but we can assume that Sargent was thinking of what we now call information processing when he wrote about "methods of work" and "behavioral processes." And when he mentioned "important aspects of personalities," perhaps he was thinking of what we would now call "cognitive styles." In this paper I will not concern myself with cognitive styles, but I will address the question of how we can get at the methods of work and the behavioral processes that presumably underlie individual differences in cognitive abilities.

Let us remind ourselves that Thurstone (1940), in his use of factor analysis, was much concerned with the explanation of mental abilities in terms of psychological processes. This will be evident from the most casual examination of his attempts to infer the psychological meanings of the factors he identified. But Thurstone was dissatisfied with purely intuitive interpretations of factors. At one point he stated that his preference would be "to head as soon as possible to direct forms of laboratory experiments in terms of which the primary factors may eventually be better understood" (p. 204).

Within the last few years, psychologists have gone into the laboratory in droves to look at possible relations between mental abilities and variables in the kinds of experimental tasks that are characteristically studied in cognitive psychology. How are these psychologists faring in arriving at a better understanding of mental abilities?

Currently, I am engaged in preparing a review of individual difference research for the 1979 volume of the *Annual Review of Psychology*. This work has prompted me to assemble a large parcel of recent psychological research literature pertinent to an information-processing view of mental abilities. Surveying and carefully examining this literature has caused me to conclude that little progress has been made thus far in understanding mental abilities in terms of processes. It can be argued, to be sure, that there has been some success in identifying psychological processes, but the interpretation of these processes often stands or falls depending upon whether one can accept the information-processing models on which the identification of a particular process is based. Further, the experimental identification of a process often depends chiefly upon the finding of individual differences in the parameters of the process, which in turn are frequently quite specific to that process. This has led, in effect, to the identification of a whole new series of individual "traits" that are little related to the mental abilities isolated in classical psychometric studies. Even if the relations are found to be of substantial magnitude, it is not very revealing or informative merely to establish correspondences between traits and processes that are defined largely on the basis of those traits. There is an obvious danger of circularity in all this.

In what follows, I want to expand this point of view and offer some thoughts on how we can avoid circularity and make independent determinations of processes and individual difference variables. In preparing my review, however, I have been disturbed to discover that information-processing psychologists, and even some psychometrically oriented psychologists, have in many cases misapplied traditional psychometric methodologies and have drawn inferences and conclusions that I believe are unjustified or at least questionable. Before I discuss problems of studying psychological processes, I aim to clear the ground by offering an extensive critique of the statistical methodologies that are now being utilized in the attempt to study individual differences in mental abilities from an information-processing point of view.

STATISTICAL METHODOLOGIES IN INDIVIDUAL DIFFERENCES RESEARCH

For many years, statistical methodology in studying individual differences has been essentially correlational, resting usually on bivariate or multivariate linear models. Perhaps it is inevitable that this methodology is correlational, for a first approach to the study of individual differences is to examine the generality of those differences over sets of observed variables, leaving aside the effects of differential treatments or manipulated conditions. Since the time of Spearman and Pearson, it has been assumed that if two measures taken on a given sample are significantly associated, they may be regarded as to some extent measuring "the same thing"; further, that if two acceptably reliable measures are not significantly associated, they are measuring "different things." If the observations are taken over a sample of persons, these "same" and "different" things are often assumed to represent attributes, characteristics, or "traits" of the persons. Such an assumption lies at the base of factor-analytic methodology, which is claimed to permit a detailed analysis of the multiple determination of observed variables by inferred latent traits. The theory of mental tests makes appeal to such an assumption in its postulation of "true scores" on latent traits that underlie observed measurements. A persisting source of controversy in psychometrics is over whether such latent traits are mere statistical artifacts or, rather, represent real entities in the makeup of individuals. Let us for the moment leave this controversy aside and focus on purely statistical aspects of individual difference methodology.

Simple Correlations

The literature of research in individual differences provides countless examples of the use of simple correlation to support the claim of a common element existing between two observed variables. It is tempting to assume that this common source of variance is a single entity. It is often overlooked that a single correlation could reflect the common operation (or lack of operation) of numerous sources of variance—sources of variance that could, presumably, be teased out only by some appropriate multivariate design.

I will cite and comment on two examples of the use of simple, zero-order correlations in current literature, chosen because they well illustrate certain points I wish to make.

Cohen and Sandberg (1977) were concerned with the relation between intelligence and short-term memory (STM). Their method was, essentially, to dissect the supraspan memory test into certain components, searching for those one or more components that showed correlations with IQ as measured by a certain intelligence scale constructed for Swedish children. A typical finding was a correlation of .68, highly significant, between IQ and performance on probed recall of the last three digits of a 9-digit sequence, but a correlation of .06, not significant with $N = 38$, between IQ and probed recall of the first three digits. Actually, their paper includes replication of this finding on a number of groups in a variety of conditions, and I am not doubting its reliability. I merely wish to point out that (except in plotting trends by score categories to demonstrate "continuity" of the function) they did not go beyond the use of simple correlations to explore further implications. The significant correlations could have reflected a number of different sources of variance. Since the "IQ" test actually consisted of six subtests, it might have been fruitful to inquire whether the correlations were higher for certain subtests than others. One could question whether the subtests are truly measures of IQ; as described, the subtests were "designed to measure verbal performance (synonyms and antonyms), abstract-logical (inductive) reasoning, and spatial performance" (Cohen & Sandberg, 1977, p. 538). Some of the subtests, therefore, could have reflected special kinds of learning.

My second example comes from a series of investigations by Hock and various coauthors. In the first of these, Hock (1973) reported a correlation of .60, $p < .05$, between what he called a "symmetry effect" and a "rotation effect" in a study of individuals' reaction times (RTs) in a same–different comparison task involving dot patterns. Hock interpreted this result as reflecting individual differences in modes of processing the stimuli. Individuals whose RTs were affected by asymmetry and by rotation of the stimuli were said to be using "structural processing," whereas individuals whose RTs were not affected by these variables were thought to be using an "analytic" mode of processing. It must be pointed out, however, that the reported correlation was based on only twelve cases; furthermore, if we examine the scatterplot of scores on the two variables, it is evident that the correlation arises mainly from the presence of one or two strikingly outlying cases; omitting the most extreme of these reduces the correlation to .34, and omitting the next most extreme reduces it to .28, neither value being significant with $p < .05$. Hock himself did not comment on the unusual distribution of cases in the scatterplot (or in the underlying distributions), but he did recognize that the correlation might have been due to an "artifact of performance level"; partialing out mean RTs to familiar, symmetrical patterns as measures of overall performance level, the resulting correlation between the symmetry effect and the rotation effect was still .60, according to Hock (1973, fn. 4). However, both these effects were measured as *differences* between mean RTs; one can question the meaning of a partial correlation between difference variables when the partialed-out variable is a variable that enters into the computation of the differences.

It should be observed, also, that RTs are themselves notoriously unreliable and variable, and their distributions are often quite skewed and loaded with outliers. My experience with RTs has been that it is wise to transform them before taking means; my preference (which for lack of space I will not attempt to justify here) is to use the reciprocal transformation, and to report mean reciprocals or the inverse of the mean reciprocal (in effect, the harmonic mean). (See Wainer, 1977, for further comment on this matter.) When *differences* between means are taken, and especially when this is done for individual subjects, one is creating variables whose reliability must be carefully examined. Even though in his later studies (e.g., Hock, Gordon, & Corcoran, 1976; Hock & Ross, 1975) Hock used slightly larger sample sizes in attempting to support his claim of an individual difference variable contrasting "structural" and "analytical" modes of processing, there are persisting methodological problems of the types mentioned here. Furthermore, in none of these studies has Hock attempted to identify an independent measure of the individual difference variable he claims.

Factor-Analytic Methodology

Factor analysis has been the classical method of choice in the study of individual differences, and increasingly, experimental psychologists are turning to its use. Despite its many virtues, factor analysis is a very tricky technique; in some ways it depends more on art than science, that is, more on intuition and judgment than on formal rules of procedure. People who do factor analysis by uncritical use of programs in computer packages run the risk of making fools of themselves. One can even be misled by misspellings in computer programs; I do not know how many times, in published literature, that I have seen *principal components* spelled "princip*le* components," presumably because several widely-used computer programs happen to spell it that way in their printouts. I assure you that the correct spelling is *principal* (Hotelling, 1933). But there are also a host of methodological problems that beset the unwary factor analyst. Many of these were discussed in an article by Thurstone (1940), but apparently this article is seldom read any more. I will cite some of the problems by commenting on the factor-analytic methodology used by Jarman and Das (1977) in an article that is almost fresh off the press in a new and, hopefully, prestigious journal. If I single out this study for comment, I do so only because it is a small, concise study that is easy to present and discuss. Many of my remarks could be directed equally well to various other recent studies in the literature.

Jarman and Das were concerned with establishing an "alternative model of mental abilities'' that appeals to information-processing theories that claim information can be processed either by ''simultaneous syntheses'' or by ''successive syntheses.'' They made separate factor analyses of seven psychometric and experimental variables obtained on 60 4th-grade boys in each of three ranges of IQ as determined by the Lorge–Thorndike Intelligence Test—Low, Average (''Normal''), and High. Principal component analysis with varimax rotation yielded three factors for the Low and High groups, and two factors for the ''Normal'' group. In each case, one factor was identified as representing the operation of ''simultaneous syntheses''; the one or two other factors were identified with ''successive syntheses'' and speed, or some combination thereof. Let me make a number of observations about the methodology and presentation of these results.

1. *The small Ns*. Jarman and Das (1977) state: ''The selection of a group size of 60 was based on the requirement that there be a sufficiently large sample to perform within-group principal component and common factor analyses'' (p. 154). Certainly an N of 60 is a bare minimum for establishing reliable results. It is better than the Ns of around 20 to 40 that are being used by many experimenters in the individual differences field, to be sure, but one would still wish for a large sample size. I am afraid that this matter of sample size is going to plague the field for quite a time, for the kinds of experimental learning or performance tasks that we want to study in an information-processing mode require much more time to conduct or administer than the brief group paper-and-pencil tests that have traditionally been used in psychometric studies. The problem is compounded when one wants to study a large number of variables. Sometimes the number of variables actually approaches or even exceeds the sample size (e.g., Favero, Dombrower, Michael, & Richards, 1975). As a rule of thumb (for which I can give a certain justification), I recommend that to establish m factors, the sample size be at least as great as the quantity $(2m + 2^m)$. On this basis, Jarman and Das's sample sizes were large enough to establish something like five factors, but they did not have enough variables to do so. This leads me to the next observation.

2. *The small number of variables*. Since Jarman and Das were interested only in establishing *two* factors, it could be argued that seven variables were sufficient. This is, for example, larger than what would be required by Thurstone's (1947, p. 293) criterion $n \geq [(2m + 1) + (8m + 1)^{\frac{1}{2}}]/2$ for the minimum number (n) of variables required for the determination of m factors. On the other hand, experience has shown that restricting oneself to small numbers of tests in a factor battery does not permit the kind of variation and sampling of factor domains that is desirable to provide persuasive evidence for the interpretation of any factors that may be found. Certainly Jarman and Das would be encouraged to explore the nature of their factors with a wider selection of variables.

3. *Failure to reflect variables*. One of the most bothersome things, I find, in the inspection of factor analytic results is authors' failure to orient all their

variables in some consistent direction, i.e., preferably with the positive (algebraically greater) side being toward the more correct, desirable, fast, efficient, etc., kind of behavior. In Jarman and Das's factor matrices, we find a number of large negative values. One immediately wonders whether the matrices fail to exhibit what Thurstone (1947, p. 341) called positive manifold, i.e., a condition where all the loadings are positive or vanishingly zero after rotation for simple structure. It turns out, in the Jarman and Das data, that two of the variables were entered into the correlation matrices in what I call negative orientation, i.e., high values were associated with error or slowness. For one of the tests (Memory for Designs) the score was the number of errors, and for another test (Word Reading) the score was time for the subject to read 40 words. If I had been reporting and analyzing these data, I would have replaced the error score by a "number correct" score, and I would have converted the time score to a rate-of-performance score (by using some multiple of the reciprocal of the time score; e.g., words per minute). (Usually, such a transformation produces a more symmetrical distribution.) As it is, one can try to remedy the situation only by reflecting signs in selected rows of the factor matrices.

All this is mostly a matter of nicety and clarity in presentation: of course nothing is really changed in the results (except when one reverses orientation by making a reciprocal transformation, as in the case of the time score). The problem becomes particularly acute in connection with difference scores. Authors sometimes fail to report the direction in which they take differences. For example, Lunneborg (1977) reported a "Stroop Difference" score as "the average difference in 'reading times' between the name and asterisk conditions" (p. 311). I am unaware of any convention whereby such a statement would convey whether the score was computed as $(N - A)$ or as $(A - N)$, and one cannot decide which it was on the basis of any other statement in Lunneborg's paper. (From Hunt, Lunneborg, and Lewis's, 1975, report on the same data, one finds that the Stroop difference score was computed as $N - A$.) Of course, sometimes, one is not able to assess in advance how a difference score is best oriented, but this matter can usually be decided in terms of the configuration of factor loadings and taken care of at the time of preparing the final results.

4. *Failure to reflect factors.* Here is another matter that I find bothersome. In some studies we can find columns in factor matrices with most of their large loadings negative. Or sometimes we see them with some high positive loadings, and some negative. Often this situation arises because of the failure to reflect variables, as just mentioned. But even after reflecting variables appropriately, one can still have a large number of negative loadings. Again, one immediately raises the question of a possibly nonpositive manifold. In nearly every instance in my experience, the large number of negative loadings arises simply because the computer knows nothing about positive manifolds; it can make the loadings for a factor mostly all positive, or mostly all negative, depending upon certain conditions in the computation of eigenvectors or in the process

of analytic rotation. The orientation of a factor is entirely arbitrary, as far as the mathematics is concerned. Regardless of whether a factor vector is oriented positively or negatively, it will make the same contribution to the reproduced correlation matrix, because, in reproducing the correlation matrix, one is multiplying entries pairwise within a vector; in matrix notation, these multiplications (for uncorrelated factors) are represented as $R_r = FF'$, where F is the factor matrix (variables $\times$ factors) and R_r is the reproduced correlation matrix. The situation is quite analogous to the computation of a square root, which can be either positive or negative: computers are "trained" to report positive square roots, normally, and they can be "trained" or programed to report positively oriented factor vectors. I recommend to all authors of factor analysis computer programs that they program in such a way as to change all the signs of any factor vector (either in eigenvector or in analytic rotation routines) that fails to have a positive algebraic sum. Many currently available computer package programs fail to do this. The remedy, short of changing these programs, is to change the signs by hand.

When appropriate reflections of variables and factors are made for the Jarman and Das matrices, they exhibit generally positive manifold. Even then, the matrices are of doubtful value because of another unwise procedure of analysis that these authors followed:

5. *Separate factor analyses by ability strata.* As noted, Jarman and Das reported separate factor matrices for three groups defined by IQ. To be sure, IQ was not one of the variables included in the matrices, although one of the variables (Raven's Progressive Matrices) is often regarded as a measure of IQ, and indeed Jarman and Das's Table 2 (showing means of all variables for subgroups) suggests that all the variables were correlated with IQ to at least an appreciable extent. Now, doing separate factor analyses by ability strata is a very risky procedure. Obviously, it entails restrictions of range and the consequent attenuation of correlations. It can also entail the creation of peculiar distributions of variables, even if there are no ceiling or floor effects in the tests themselves, because one is selecting from different portions of approximately Gaussian distributions. These peculiar distributions can affect the correlations in various somewhat unpredictable ways, as I have pointed out in an earlier publication (Carroll, 1961). And, of course, the sample sizes are automatically much reduced, with consequent loss of statistical power. Jarman and Das opted for the analyses by strata on the basis of their supposition that "different levels of intelligence . . . may be characterized by different uses of simultaneous and successive syntheses for particular tasks," and their statement of the purpose of their study as being "to identify the similarities and differences, if any, in the employment of simultaneous and successive syntheses by groups of children differing in IQ" (p. 153). Unfortunately, because of the limitations just noted, factor analysis by ability strata is not in general a sufficiently reliable and effective tool to investigate hypotheses concerning differential use of processes at different

levels of ability. Such hypotheses, I would suggest, could better be investigated at the level of particular correlations, e.g., by testing equality of regression slopes over ability groups for particular sets of variables, or by using contingency tables and other nonparametric techniques. Possibly Jöreskog's (1970) methods of covariance structure analysis would be useful. But for a preliminary evaluation of a set of data, I would recommend factor analysis based on a single group pooled from the several strata, even if the single group is not completely representative of some population because of gaps in the distributions, as where, for example, "high" and "low" tails or segments of some stratification variable are pooled (Hunt, Frost, & Lunneborg, 1973; Hunt, 1975).

6. *Use of principal component analysis.* On this matter there is, I acknowledge, a difference of opinion among experts, and some will say that it does not make much difference what factoring method is used. Jarman and Das used a principal components model (that is, I assume, an eigenvector factoring of a correlation matrix with unities in the diagonal) with varimax rotation, "for reasons of comparability to previous research" (p. 161). They also report that "high correspondence" was found between the principal components analysis and an alpha factor analysis that was also computed. There could indeed have been high correspondence in *patterns* of results, but principal components analysis tends to yield factor loadings that are considerably inflated over those of alpha and other types of common factor analysis, leading to overgenerous factor interpretations. I find principal components analysis useful chiefly in helping to decide on the number of factors to be used in subsequent communality estimations and common factor analyses. I much prefer some form of *common* factor analysis that avoids the intrusion of variance uniquely associated with each variable into the common factor space.

7. *Problems of factor rotation: orthogonal vs. oblique factors.* This is another controversial problem. It happened not to present itself in the Jarman and Das data, because the factors exhibited a more or less satisfactory simple structure on orthogonal coordinates. Nevertheless, if one pools the data over the groups (as I have done, with the accuracy permitted by what these authors report, and doing the pooling on the basis of the reported group means and standard deviations and the correlations reproduced by the reported factor matrices), and if one uses a common factor analysis, the data are satisfactorily fit by two factors. A graphical rotation of these factors to simple structure suggests that the factors are to some extent correlated. The resulting analysis is given as Table 1, which also shows a Schmid–Leiman (Schmid & Leiman, 1957) orthogonalization of the data in such a way as to exhibit a "general" factor and two group factors. (I do not mean to identify this general factor with Spearman's "g," although it may well be highly correlated with it. The "general" factor is general only in the sense that it has substantial loadings on all seven variables.) The Schmid–Leiman factor matrix produces the same reproduced correlation matrix as the orthogonal two-factor solution does; that is, it accounts for the data equally well, although less par-

TABLE 1
Reanalysis of Data from a Study by Jarman and Das (1977)

Estimated correlation matrix for pooled groups $(N = 180)^a$

		1	2	3	4	5	6	7
Raven's Progressive Matrices	1	1.000						
Figure copying	2	.503	1.000					
Memory for designs[b]	3	.545	.547	1.000				
Serial recall	4	.218	.206	.202	1.000			
Visual short-term memory	5	.207	.185	.193	.510	1.000		
Word reading (speed)[c]	6	.206	−.022	.022	.503	.446	1.000	
Auditory–visual matching	7	.442	.433	.410	.489	.360	.149	1.000

Solutions with two factors

	Common factor orthogonal varimax			Oblique simple structure		Schmid–Leiman hierarchical orthogonalization		
	A	B	h^2	A'	B'	G	A''	B''
Raven's Progressive Matrices	1	.672	.178	.483	.615	.083	.447	.527	.071
Figure copying	2	.741	.042	.551	.713	−.062	.418	.611	−.053
Memory for designs[b]	3	.748	.058	.563	.716	−.047	.429	.614	−.040
Serial recall	4	.216	.770	.640	.037	.732	.494	.032	.628
Visual short-term memory	5	.189	.640	.445	.040	.608	.415	.034	.521
Word reading (speed)[c]	6	−.023	.661	.437	−.171	.658	.312	−.147	.564
Auditory–visual matching	7	.558	.384	.459	.457	.303	.487	.392	.260

Λ

| | A | .974 | −.139 |
| | B | −.225 | .990 |

R

| | A' | 1.000 | .358 |
| | B' | .358 | 1.000 |

[a] These correlations were estimated by pooling correlation matrices for the Low, Normal, and High IQ groups as reproduced from the factor matrices presented by Jarman and Das, using also the data given for means and SDs of each variable for each group.

[b] This variable was reflected from the original variable, which was in terms of error scores. Here, the variables may be thought of as number correct.

[c] This variable was reflected from the original variable, which was in terms of time to read 40 words.

simoniously. The Schmid–Leiman "hierarchical" procedure has been too little employed in factor-analytic studies; it provides one way of resolving the perennial controversy between those who argue for simple structure, correlated factors (when necessary), and parsimony, and those who argue for orthogonal factors because of their ease of interpretation.

In general, of course, the problem of rotation to simple structure is a very tricky one. As an old hand in factor analysis, I would still prefer rotations done completely by hand, i.e., by graphical techniques, but I have not done one of these messy jobs for any large study in about 20 years, now that analytic rotations by computer are available. My current practice is to use the Kaiser normal varimax method to produce an orthogonal solution, followed by any graphical adjustments to obliqueness that may seem desirable. In this I often use a "semianalytical" Procrustes rotation to the oblique structure suggested by the pattern of varimax results, using a method developed by Tucker (1944). The direct oblimin method (Jennrich & Sampson, 1966) is also to be recommended. I have not taken any extensive opportunity to experiment with Jöreskog's methods (1967, 1970), but they have much appeal because they include tests of statistical significance.

While we are on the matter of rotation, however, let me mention some possibilities that might be considered. One of the more interesting factor analysis studies that I have encountered was that of Underwood, Boruch, and Malmi (1977). These investigators factored correlations of 22 scores from nine verbal learning and memory tasks, hoping to find factors associated with particular "attributes" of memory items such as concreteness/abstractness, meaningfulness, and time. In this they were largely unsuccessful, concluding that "associative memory" variance was so prominent as to swamp any effects of memory attributes, also pointing out that apparently subjects adapt themselves to use whatever attributes are relevant for a particular task. Nevertheless, the final factor analysis data are of interest, even though the five factors are all largely task-specific. That is, there is a factor that loads on scores from paired-associate and serial-learning tasks, one that loads on scores from free-recall tasks, and so on. The N of 200 was respectable, and the factor analysis was performed in a sophisticated way, using Jöreskog's (1967) maximum likelihood method, among others. If one plots the factor loadings for Factor 1 (the "paired-associate" factor) and Factor 2 (the "free-recall" factor) that are shown in their orthogonal factor matrix (Table 4, p. 59), an obvious oblique simple structure rotation is possible, as shown in Fig. 1. The normals to the two hyperplanes are separated by an angle of about 138°, and this would correspond to a correlation of about .743 between rotated primary factors. (I ignore any other possible rotations.) Thus we could have a strong second-order factor underlying *both* the paired-associate and free-recall scores; one might interpret it as an "associative memory" factor and identify it with the associative memory factor (often symbolized as *Ma*; see Harman, Ekstrom, & French, 1976) that has been found by Thurstone and many others in the psychometric tradition. A Schmid–Leiman orthogonalization would yield this "associative memory" factor as a group factor, plus separate factors for the paired-associate and free-recall tasks. In this case, the Schmid–Leiman procedure would be neither parsimonious nor very informative. Another kind of analysis might be more useful: let us pass a primary vector through the centroid of *both* the paired-associate and free-recall test vec-

CARROLL

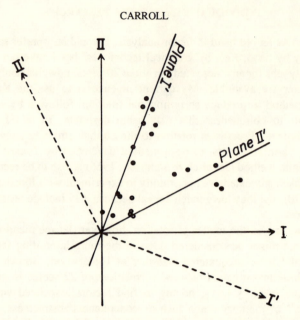

FIG. 1 Plot of 22 task vectors on orthogonal rotated Factors I and II, with suggested oblique simple structure rotations. Data are from a study by Underwood, Boruch, and Malmi (1977, Table 4, p. 59).

tors, letting this represent an associative memory factor, *AM*, underlying these two types of tasks. Orthogonal to this vector, as shown in Fig. 2, we could establish a bipolar vector that would represent the *difference* between paired-associate and free-recall performances. Arbitrarily, let the positive pole represent the performance of those who are better at free-recall, relatively, than they are at paired-associates. Surely with all the information we now have about the similarities and differences of these two types of tasks, we ought to be able to make an interpretation of this vector that would appeal to the processes differentially involved in them. This illustrates a rotational maneuver that may often be desirable in studies of individual differences in an information-processing mode. (This maneuver, incidentally, preserves orthogonality in the matrix as a whole, provided factors are always rotated pairwise and orthogonally.)

In continuing this critique of factor-analytic methodology, I will refer to various studies other than those of Jarman and Das and of Underwood and his colleagues. Certain subtle methodological problems are illustrated in studies conducted by the group at the University of Washington (Hunt et al., 1973; Hunt et al., 1975).

8. *The problem of experimental dependence.* In the theory of matrices, it is shown that if any variable or linear combination of variables can be perfectly predicted from another variable or linear combination of variables, the matrix of correlations among the variables is "singular," with no inverse. In factor-

analytic computations with matrices that are singular or approximately so, the effect of the singularity can show up as spurious common factor variance (i.e., common factor variance that would be unique variance if it were not for the singularities). In many cases, one finds common factors that are associated solely with the source of the singularity, but a partially spurious common factor could be one that is associated with the variables producing a singularity plus any variables that are substantially correlated with them.

In the light of these considerations, it has sometimes been argued that one should avoid any potential source of singularity (even approximate) at all costs, even to the extent of avoiding measuring two or more variables from the same experimental task. Such variables are said to be experimentally dependent. In the light of experience, however, I believe the rule of avoiding multiple measurements from a single task is too stringent. There are many instances where one can derive a number of logically independent variables from the same task. By "logically independent," I mean "conceivably having a correlation of zero." For example, the rate at which a task is performed can be logically independent of the accuracy with which it is performed. Of course, speed and accuracy may in fact be substantially correlated, either positively or negatively, but if they are not

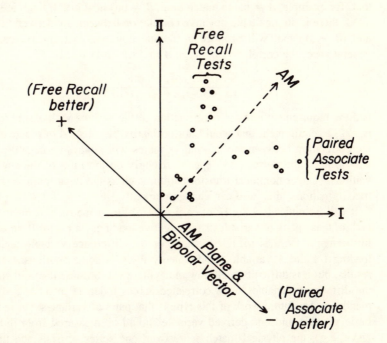

FIG. 2   Plot of data as in Fig. 1, but with a suggested orthogonal rotation to yield a general associative memory (AM) factor and a bipolar factor representing relative abilities in free-recall and paired-associate tasks.

highly correlated, and if there are independent measures of each of them from a variety of other tasks, the risk of obtaining spurious common factors is minimized.

One source of singularity, however, should be carefully avoided: the use of sum and difference scores when these sum and difference scores are perfectly predictable from other variables that are used in the correlation matrix. (The lower bound communality estimates for such variables would be unity.) It is an egregious error, for example, to use such sets of variables as $(A, B, A + B)$ or $(A, B, B - A)$. Such an error is illustrated by the use of a series of part scores on a test along with the total of these part scores. It is better, in such a case, to use only the part scores, or only the total score, but not both. But what about the situation in which it is desired to use variables $(A, B - A)$? This is exemplified at least twice in the Hunt et al. (1975) factor analysis of psychometric and experimental tasks. One pair of variables was derived from a modified Stroop task: "asterisk reading time," and "color name minus asterisk reading time." Another pair of variables was derived from the Posner task: "physical match time" and "name minus physical match time." Now, the variables in such pairs are logically independent, and they could be completely uncorrelated in the data. But notice that if the basic variables (which might be symbolized as A and B, so that, for example, A = name match time, B = physical match time) are uncorrelated, there is an inevitable negative correlation between the derived variables A and $(B - A)$ that will produce artifactual common factor variance. For the general case, the correlation between A and $(B - A)$ will be

$$\frac{r_{AB}\sigma_B - \sigma_A}{(\sigma_A{}^2 + \sigma_B{}^2 - 2r_{AB}\sigma_A\sigma_B)^{\frac{1}{2}}}$$

and the requirement on a zero correlation of the derived variables is that $r_{AB} = \sigma_A/\sigma_B$, a requirement that would not ordinarily be satisfied in practice. In fact, the correlation between the derived variables will always be negative if $r_{AB} < \sigma_A/\sigma_B$; thus, the correlation depends strongly on the ratio of the standard deviations. (Under nonlinear transformation, such as the logarithmic or reciprocal transformations, this ratio can change markedly.)

It will be noticed in the Hunt et al. (1975) factor matrix just mentioned that both of these pairs of variables have negative loadings on Factor II; in each case, furthermore, there is a high loading for the difference variable and a lower loading for the A variable. Undoubtedly there is some spuriousness in these results, but it is difficult to tell how much there was because it would appear that the difference variables were correlated across independent tasks. My recommendation for future work of this type is that pairs of variables that include one basic variable and one derived variable should be measured from independent tasks, e.g., the physical match score from one series of trials and the name–physical match difference from another series of trials, even at the cost of lessened reliability. Even so, the difference score variables might have been correlated over tasks spuriously, i.e., on the basis of an overall RT factor. The problem is similar to that encountered in the Hock (1973) study mentioned earlier. A possible solution is to compute the derived variables in terms of standardized scores of basic variables.

9. *The design of a factor analysis.* Ideally, a set of variables entered into a factor analysis should conform to a hypothesized structure in which each factor has at least three or four significant loadings that are not accompanied by significant loadings on other factors, and in which each variable has a minimum of nonzero loadings—preferably, only one, unless the variable is regarded as impure ex hypothesi. It is not generally good science to factor-analyze any arbitrarily selected series of variables. It is not necessarily good science to frame a factor analysis according to the question "To what extent do the psychometric and the information-processing variables measure the same abilities?" To this extent the Hunt et al. studies could be faulted. In these studies there is little evidence either that the information-processing variables were selected specifically to coordinate with the psychometric tasks, or conversely. Furthermore, the specific primary factors that are known to be measured by the several psychometric tests (Space, Number, Verbal, etc.) were not separately represented by adequate marker tests in the battery design, so that it is not surprising that the significant loadings for the psychometric tests came out chiefly on a single factor, Factor I (Hunt et al., 1975, p. 222), which had experimental task loadings chiefly on scores derived from a complex mental arithmetic task, the "Sunday + Tuesday" task—surely a task that would have counterparts in the numerical and verbal reasoning psychometric tasks.

In fact, the irony of the Hunt, Lunneborg, and Lewis study is that although it claims to find common variance between the psychometric tests and the information-processing tasks, such variance is only weakly apparent in the factor-analytic results. In general, the two sets of variables have significant loadings on *different* factors; in particular, the purely "verbal" tests had no significant loadings on the factors that were chiefly associated with the information-processing tasks. It is difficult to square this observation with the generally significant contrasts between "high verbals" and "low verbals" that are reported in the descriptions of results for specific tasks, and that are supposed to tell us "what it means to be high verbal." I can possibly reconcile these sets of results by assuming that the factor analysis was not done by proper common-factor techniques, and not carried to the point of oblique rotation, second-order analysis, or hierarchical analysis. The high–low verbal contrast might have appeared at the level of a weak but significant second-order factor.

If indeed one wants to ask the question that Hunt, Lunneborg, and Lewis asked, "To what extent do the psychometric and information-processing tests measure the same abilities?", there are variants of factor analysis, and other multivariate techniques, that would be more appropriate than classical factor analysis. One of these is Tucker's (1958) interbattery factor analysis; the use of this method is well illustrated in a study reported by Hundal and Horn (1977). They administered a series of "psychometric" tests, as one battery, and a series of learning and memory tests, as another battery, to 265 14-year-old school children in India. Tucker's method was used to determine what kinds of variance were common to the two batteries. They identified two such types of variance: a "*Gf*" or fluid intelligence factor in the psychometric tests that was related to the primary memory storage aspects of the memory battery, and a "*Gc*" or crystallized intelligence factor that was more related to those aspects of the memory battery that relied on what they regarded as a "secondary acquisition process."

Canonical Correlation Analysis

One might also use canonical correlation analysis to identify sources of variance common to two sets of measures. In effect, one finds linear composites in one set of measures, say the psychometric tests, that correlate optimally with linear composites of the other set of measures, say the information-processing tasks. This technique was in fact used by Lunneborg (1977), but I do not recommend it for this purpose because canonical weights are generally difficult to interpret. The technique is highly subject to problems of collinearity, and canonical weights have the undesirable sampling characteristics of beta-weights in multiple-regression analysis. Indeed, canonical correlation analysis is a generalization of multiple-regression analysis. If canonical correlation analysis is to be used at all, it should be followed by rotation of the canonical variates and computation of correlations between each variable and the canonical variates (see Cliff & Krus, 1976; Wood & Erskine, 1976). In this case, however, the results will probably resemble those of Tucker's interbattery factor analysis, which could have been used in the first place.

Multiple-Regression Analysis

Multiple regression is, of course, a popular technique, particularly for prediction studies. I believe, however, that it should be used only very cautiously in basic studies of individual differences. The problem of collinearity among predictor variables is especially to be attended to in the interpretation of either raw or standardized regression weights. This problem was encountered, for example, by Sternberg (1977, p. 219) in his attempt to determine "structural regressions" relating "component scores" from analogical reasoning tasks to overall scores on these tasks and reference ability measures. If multiple correlation techniques are to be used, I would warn particularly against the popular forward stepwise solution, which can be very misleading. It can even fail to produce the optimal subset of variables for predicting a criterion variable, by stopping short of taking account of some significant *combination* of variables at a point when no *single* variable adds significant variance. I recommend the use of a complete regression system, followed by a backward stepwise elimination technique, if perchance one wants to reduce the number of variables in the prediction. With care, one can usually make some acceptable interpretations of multiple regression weights.

Having completed my catalogue of the major statistical sins that can be committed in individual difference studies, let me now turn to the more psychological side of the question: How shall we study individual differences?

I said earlier in this paper that I believe we have made little progress, thus far, in identifying psychological processes, at least through individual difference research. In most of the individual difference research I have surveyed, it seems that whenever one tries to find a process, one really finds a trait. That is, in simple terms, one sets up a study involving certain tasks. One notices that individuals differ in their success, speed, or efficiency in performing these tasks. Through factor analysis or other techniques, one tries to pin down the types of tasks, or components of those tasks, in which the individual differences can be observed, and then to determine, if possible, to what range of other tasks (or components of tasks) these individual differences generalize. Even if one is successful in such a venture—and there are relatively few success stories—the final data comprise the following: a description of certain tasks, or components of tasks, and a statement that individuals (in defined populations, presumably) exhibit characteristic differences in their performance of these tasks. To the extent that the differences are truly characteristic of the individuals in terms of relative stability and permanence, the individual differences comprise what we call a trait. Actually, the stability of individual differences in most of the information-processing traits found thus far has hardly been investigated, unless one assumes that correlated performances spaced a few hours or days apart signify a degree of stability. How much do we know, for example, about the long-term stability of simple or choice reaction time measures, or about the types of measures taken, to say, in the Posner physical versus name match paradigm? Not much, I fear.

The important point, however, is that inferences from individual difference traits concerning underlying psychological processes, even when studied in an information-processing mode, seem speculative at best. Perhaps I am asking for too much, or wanting too much, in a description of a psychological process, but most "descriptions" of psychological process that I have seen seem to boil down to descriptions of tasks—perhaps in terms of the stimuli, the instructions, and the responses, with speculations about what kinds of information are involved, and how the information is transferred and manipulated. There is little talk of different strategies that individuals might employ.

Let us review some of the data that come out of the studies I have referred to in my statistical critique, to see whether my general point of view can be supported. For convenience, I will refer to the studies more or less in the order in which they were discussed earlier.

Cohen and Sandberg (1977), we noted, found that the correlation between IQ and memory span performance, when one controlled for rehearsal, interference, chunking, and other effects, was limited to that part of the task in which the subject repeats the *last few stimuli*. Even though there was evidence (not noted by these authors) of reliable individual difference variance in other aspects of the task, that variance was not associated with IQ. High IQ children were, however, more accurate than low IQ children in repeating the last few stimuli of a supra-span digit memory task, regardless of the modality and the rate of presentation. This was particularly true when the individuals had had a prior opportunity to practice a span task requiring complete recall. These results were in considerable conflict with those of prior studies, which had located the IQ/STM correlation mainly in rehearsal effects. Assuming that the Cohen and Sandberg results are reliable, what can we infer about processes? We have an individual difference variable that is in some way related to whatever IQ is, and perhaps the results tell us something about IQ, but they do not directly tell us about processes. Cohen and Sandberg (1977) themselves argue for what they call an "availability expla-nation":

> In a sequence of known length, inclusion in the rehearsal buffer would be least likely for the final items, so that individual differences in decay rate would exert their greatest influence on the most recent items. The same argument can be made for the final items in the running memory sequences, since they are also unlikely to be maintained in the buffer. (p. 552)

The "availability explanation," then, refers to an assumption of a "decay rate" for recency items, which, according to the theory the authors have adapted from Atkinson and Shiffrin (1968), are "either nonbuffer items from STS [short-term store] or preattentional items from SR [sensory register]" (p. 537). Presumably, further study would be required to decide whether the decay rate applies to the former or the latter, or to both. In any case, we are offered only speculation about what *processes* are involved in the found IQ/STM correlation; the only solid finding is that one aspect of some trait called IQ is the efficiency of repeating the last few digits of a supraspan series. I suppose this is progress, however, all things considered.

The series of alleged findings by Hock and his associates (e.g., Hock, 1973; Hock et al., 1976; Hock & Ross, 1975) might seem a little more promising in allowing inferences about processes, even though their statistical methodologies and results appear open to question. In a variety of tasks, these authors claim to find a contrast between what they call "structural" processing and "analytic" processing. That is, in the same–different comparison of visual displays of vari-ous kinds (dot patterns, pictures and scenes, degraded alphabet letters, etc.), some people are thought to make point-by-point or "analytic" comparisons, while others make comparisons based on a Gestalt perception of the total stimulus, the latter being called "structural" comparisons. I will not attempt to describe here the exact kinds of experimental data that are offered to support these inferences; I will say only that they are highly speculative, based on certain intuitions about how certain stimulus variables might have an effect on behavior. For example, certain few subjects in Hock's (1973) experiment seemed to have longer RTs when the stimuli were asymmetric or rotated; it was inferred that they were perceiving the stimuli "structurally" and thus the asymmetry and rotation interfered with their perceptions. The remaining subjects' RTs were relatively unaffected by rotation or asymmetry; it was *inferred* that they were making point-by-point comparisons of the stimuli (whether rotated or asymmetric or not), thus doing "analytic" comparisons. Nevertheless, an alternative interpretation of the results is that *all* subjects were making point-by-point comparisons, but that some subjects were less able to find the loci of these comparisons when the stimuli were rotated. Perhaps, for example, these subjects would be found to be low on the Spatial Orientation factor isolated in many psychometric investigations. Hock and his associates made no attempt to identify an independent variable to illuminate their results.

I say that these results are promising, but this is not because of anything that Hock and associates have done with their experiments and data. "Structural" and "analytic" processes sound like distinctly different mental operations. Let us suppose that they are. If one could arrange a situation where a subject could be successful only if he made a "structural" comparison, and another situation where a subject could be successful only by making an "analytic" comparison, *and* if some independent way could be found of predicting subjects' performances in the two situations, we might have a case for the reality of the postulated processes.

Let us now examine the theories of Jarman and Das (1977) concerning "simultaneous" and "successive" syntheses. Their results concerning differential use of such processes in groups at different IQ levels are almost completely unconvincing because of limitations in their methodology. Leaving this aside, however, let us look at the reanalysis of their results that I have made by pooling data from the three IQ strata (Table 1). If we consider these results from the standpoint of classical factor-analytic interpretations, it appears that we have a general factor that enters all the tests, plus two group factors, *A* and *B*. Factor *A* looks like a standard, ordinary Space factor; that is, it has high loadings only on tasks in which the subject has to perceive, remember, or otherwise manipulate visual spatial designs involving geometric figures. The Figure Copying and Memory for Designs tests contain this feature, as does also the Raven Progressive Matrices (whatever else it may involve). Whatever process is involved in such a factor can only be described, somewhat tautologically, as "dealing with spatial designs." Apparently a characteristic trait of individuals is their ability to deal with spatial designs, and little more can be said about this because there are not enough variations among the tests to permit further analytic interpretations. We can say, however, that this trait does not extend to *any* visual display, because it does not extend, for example, to the Visual Short-Term Memory task that requires the subject to remember the digits that have been displayed on a five-section grid (essentially a visual digit-span test). It is a pure inference that what is involved here is a "simultaneous synthesis," i.e., apprehending parts of a display simultaneously. To establish that simultaneous synthesis is a process would require the demonstration that it operates in a variety of settings, not restricted to the tasks involving visual patterns and designs that were used in this study. Even then, use of individual differences methodology in such a demonstration would permit only the inference that people differ in their characteristic use of this process when it is appropriate, and thus we would end up with a statement that refers more to a trait than it does to a process.

Similar remarks can be made about the other group factor, B, in the reanalyzed Jarman and Das data. This factor looks like a memory factor that arises when the serial order of the stimuli is important. It is only an inference that some special "successive synthesis" operation is involved.

In my methodological critique, I next considered the study by Underwood, Boruch, and Malmi (1977), which I thought was admirable. From an information-processing standpoint, however, the study was a failure; what these investigators came out with was a series of traits, not processes. That is, it seems that there is some sort of "associative memory" trait whereby some people are better than others at paired-associate and free-recall tasks, although there may be an additional trait that determines which of these two types of tasks one does better at (at least, this is what my reanalysis suggests). This associative memory trait, I believe, is pretty much the same as the associative memory factor (Ma) that has been identified in psychometric researches that are too numerous to list here. (See Ekstrom, 1973, for a recent review.) Also, the memory span factor identified in the Underwood et al. study looks to be the same as the Ms or Memory Span factor identified previously. The fact that Ma and Ms are largely independent would suggest, however, that memory span ability does not operate in free-recall tasks. On its face, this conclusion sounds rather counterintuitive—couldn't one do a free-recall memory task as a *succession* of memory span tasks? But the results say not; if memory span operations are attempted in a long free-recall task, they do not work, perhaps because they interfere with each other. I am not enough of a specialist in memory theory to penetrate deeply into this question. At any rate, the identification of traits of associative and memory span abilities tells us very little about the processes involved; it tells us only that different processes operate in different task settings, and this information might conceivably help in assigning individuals to different task settings.

Underwood et al. made a valiant attempt, however, to design their study in such a way as to reveal the operation of what they call "memory attributes" (imagery, associative, acoustic, temporal, affective, and frequency). They failed to find factors corresponding to these attributes, and I refer the reader to their report for their apparently quite reasonable explanations for this failure. But I would also urge consideration of the possibility that their study was not adequately designed to produce factors for imagery and the other attributes. Consider the imagery attribute, for example. Unless I am mistaken, they had too few measures in which a concrete/abstract attribute would have operated distinctively, too few, that is, for an adequate factor-analytic design. (Remember

Thurstone's recommendation that there be at least three variables to represent a postulated factor in as pure a form as possible.) An alternative design that might have been considered is the multitrait–multimethod design originated by Campbell and Fiske (1959; see also recent refinements proposed by Ray & Heeler, 1975). This design would have required a more systematic crossing of traits with attributes (the attributes being considered analogous to "methods").

Suppose, however, Underwood et al. had been successful in identifying an "imagery" factor, derived, presumably, from sets of variables that would contrast learning of concrete stimuli with learning of abstract stimuli in different kinds of learning tasks. Essentially, such a factor would represent a trait—the extent to which a person "uses" imagery (or some similar process) in a learning task in which opportunity to use that process was offered. The description of the trait would *refer* to a process, but it is not at all clear whether that process had been correctly identified. One could conceive a number of processes that might account for differences in the way people handle concrete words vs. abstract words in a learning task. For example, concrete words might be handled more easily than abstract words by attaching attributes to them, and people might differ in their readiness or predisposition to do so. (Experimentalists often attempt to control such variance by equating words in "associative value," but in an individual differences context such control might actually be counterproductive.)

Now consider the factor interpretations made by Hunt et al. (1975). Factor I was loaded with a variety of psychometric test scores and also some parameters from the "Sunday + Tuesday" mental arithmetic task. They called it "rapid reasoning," since "it is characterized by tasks which involve transformation of information in short term memory, typically in a sequence of steps" (p. 222). They contrasted Factor I with Factor II, which "had its highest loadings on the clerical speed tests, upon scores for naming colors less scores for naming asterisk colors in the Stroop task, and the name identity minus physical identity scores in the Posner et al. paradigm," tasks that were "characterized by a requirement that overlearned codes be accessed, but not by the (Factor I) requirement that the codes thus accessed be transformed in any way" (pp. 222–223). Although these interpretations are plausible, they are at the same time problematical. Undoubtedly the psychometric tests on Factor I involve reliance on the presence of codes in long-term memory (meanings of words in the verbal tests, for example). A more sharply focused series of experimental settings would be required to demonstrate that the factor involves transformations of codes in STM. The interpretation of Factor II as speed in accessing *untransformed* codes in STM could be defended only if it could be shown that it is irrelevant whether codes in LTM, or transformed codes in STM, are involved. In the case of both Factors I and II, the factors are defined by the individual trait findings, and the inferences about processes rely on theories about information-processing operations that would need to be confirmed in procedures that would not rely on individual differences. Perhaps Hunt and his colleagues would argue that these theories have indeed been confirmed in various investigations that do not rely on individual differences. My only point is that from the factor analysis results alone we do not have a confirmation of those theories; we have only certain plausible descriptions of individual difference traits whose appearance is elicited from certain types of tasks.

Similar remarks can be made about the interpretation of Factors III, IV, and V in the Hunt et al. (1975) study and I shall not pursue this line of discussion further. Let me dispel any possible tensions about my remarks by saying that I consider the Hunt, Lunneborg, & Lewis study very valuable. Aside from the methodological and theoretical limitations to which it is subject, it is an important venture into a relatively new field of scientific endeavor, and it should inform us all about research needs and possibilities in this field.

Studies by Sternberg (1977) and Frederiksen (1978a, 1978b) move us into an almost totally new methodology, that of what Sternberg calls "componential analysis." This methodology appears to offer a greater possibility of isolating processes than traditional factor-analytic methodology, and should be examined closely.

Briefly, Sternberg's methodology involves arranging experimental situations that systematically vary the subject's opportunities to engage in different information-processing tasks. The verbal analogies task that Sternberg has chosen to study is particularly well suited for use of this methodology. Thus, if the verbal analogies task is symbolized as the presentation of a series of stimuli that have relations A : B :: C : [D], where [D] represents a number of alternative stimuli, only some of which exhibit "true" analogies, Sternberg can present the stimuli in different temporal sequences such that the processing times that a subject requires at different stages of the solution can be determined. For example, one can present only the stimuli A and B, allowing subjects to process those stimuli (determining a possible relationship) before the presentation of the C and D stimuli. These processing times can then be contrasted with those required if three stimuli, A, B, and C, are presented simultaneously, and the parameters of the processes can be determined on the basis of several alternative models of these processes. Essentially the procedure is a very sophisticated application of the Donders subtraction method.

Sternberg has presented results that suggest that this method can illuminate the description and explanation of the individual differences found on standard psychometric tests, in particular, the verbal analogies test that often appears in mental abilities batteries. I have some problems with his methodology, in particular, the very small number of subjects (for example, $N = 16$ in the "People Piece" experiment) and the shakiness of multiple regression methods employed with such a small number of subjects. Nevertheless, the results are of high interest and are suggestive, and if one limits oneself to the results intrinsic to the experiments, the fits to models are impressive.

Frederiksen's (1978a, 1978b) methodology is highly similar, except that he has been concerned with component processes in reading. Reading does not easily lend itself to the type of sequential stage presentation that is possible in the case of Sternberg's verbal analogies task; instead, it was necessary for Frederiksen to present a number of different tasks that represent, according to a theoretical analysis of the task of reading (in particular, word identification and recognition), the several phases of this process. For example, it is assumed that there is a stage of Perceptual Encoding, with two subphases, Grapheme Encoding (access of letter codes) and Encoding Multiletter Units. The processing times for these phases are measured from two tasks, a Letter Matching task (analogous to the Posner task) and a Bigram Identification Task. Further stages are Decoding, with two subphases, Phonemic Translation, and Articulatory Programming (since an oral response is required), and final Lexical Access stage; measures of these processes are taken from word and pseudoword naming tasks. A maximum likelihood factor analysis of eleven measures exhibited good fit to the five hypothesized sources of variance; these five sources of variance were found to be somewhat correlated, but it is of great interest that, for $N = 20$, these five factors yielded high multiple correlations with scores on standardized reading tests that involved sentence comprehension processes that were not at all tapped by the experimental tasks, which went no further than requiring word identification. The multiple regression weights, producing multiple correlations ranging from .53 (for the Gray Oral Reading Test) to 1.00 (!, for the Total Score on the Nelson-Denny Reading Test), seemed to indicate that the multiletter encoding and the articulatory programming measures were the major predictors. These results can be interpreted as suggesting that good readers use strategies of phonemic decoding, while poor readers recognize words more on the basis of whole-word appearance. They need to be cross-validated, however, with larger sample sizes.

It appears to me that in both the Sternberg and Frederiksen studies, a good case can be made for the confident identification of psychological processes. The theorized stages are operationalized by arranging the experimental tasks in such a way as to permit a subject to perform only on the basis of a definable set of processes. For example, in the Sternberg task the presentation of only the A stimulus permits only an encoding operation; the later presentation of the B and C stimuli permits performance of operations that Sternberg describes as inference and mapping, but not application, which is possible only when the D stimulus is supplied. In Frederiksen's work it is clear that no lexical access operation is normally possible if the stimuli are only single letters.

Nevertheless, in both Sternberg's and Frederiksen's work the identification of stages is almost crucially dependent upon the presence of individual differences that are specific to those stages. This is quite explicit in Frederiksen's work, where the confirmation of the stage analysis is based on a maximum likelihood factor analysis of a correlation matrix of individual difference variables. In Sternberg's work a stage could in principle be identified by associating it with additive constants in which individual differences are negligible, but that seldom happened in Sternberg's data, if at all. *We have here, then, the same kind of parallelism between traits and processes that we have observed in other types of methodologies.*

Now, perhaps this is the way things are—the way the world is. That is, perhaps processes are clearly identifiable *only* through their association with individual differences, and perhaps it is inevitable that there should be individual differences associated with any given psychological process. (Surely the converse of this is not true.) But if this is really the case, it presents a discouraging prospect for any efforts to modify individual differences, or even to utilize individual differences in instruction or training in innovative ways. It would appear that we would have to fall back on the old routines of task analysis, and selection of individuals for training or assignment in terms of their known characteristics in relation to our task analyses. The prospects for meaningful attribute–treatment interactions in learning processes would also appear to be dim.

I do not think the picture is really as dark as it would appear to be, or as I have presented it. I have deliberately presented it in a rather bleak form in order to stimulate thinking. There are a number of considerations that might alleviate the situation.

For one thing, I have painted an undeservedly harsh picture of the potentialities of psychometric and information-processing research for the study of psychological processes. Actually, much of this research lends itself more readily to solid inferences about processes than I have led the reader to think. Processes have a distinct relation to the requirements and characteristics of a particular task; just as in the Sternberg and Frederiksen studies, the tasks studied in both the psychometric and the information-processing literatures have characteristic requirements and constraints that enable one to make fairly confident inferences concerning the processes that can and cannot occur in performing those tasks. For example, in the several tasks loaded on Factor A of my reanalyzed factor analysis of the Jarman and Das (1977) data (Table 1), it is obvious that some kind of apprehension and matching of spatial forms must occur for a subject to be successful in performing the task. At the same time it is obvious that use of long-term memory for retrieving historical dates, say, is irrelevant and useless in performing these spatial tasks. Even if individual differences are inextricably linked with processes, individual difference methodologies should enable us to narrow down the kinds of processes associated with particular tasks, and to investigate the generality of those processes over different tasks. This requires only a systematic effort to vary tasks in such a way that the relevant individual difference traits and the processes associated with them are adequately defined in terms of task characteristics. (This is what factor analysts, in fact, have said all along; unfortunately there are few examples of a systematic series of factorial investigations, other than Guilford's (1967;

Guilford & Hoepfner, 1971), perhaps, that demonstrate the utility of this investigative strategy.)

Second, it is possible in principle to distinguish processes that are *required* by a task from processes that are *optional*. This distinction is seldom observed in psychometric individual difference research, and it appears with low frequency also in the information-processing research that I have surveyed. In psychometric research, the significant loading of a variable on a process-related factor tells us only that *on the average,* subjects tend to use the process that is associated with the factor, rather than some other process that might be effective in performing the task, if indeed there are several alternative optional processes. Earlier, I cited Thurstone's observation that factor analysis cannot tell us which of several alternative processes might be used by a subject in performing a task. In information-processing research, there are few investigations of alternative processes in performing tasks, although one example that comes to mind is Groen and Parkman's (1972) demonstration of alternative processes (counting vs. use of addition facts) in children's solution of arithmetic problems. It may be useful to call *optional* processes "strategies," restricting use of the term *process* for those that are required by the task. It was with this distinction in mind that I (Carroll, 1976) analyzed the tasks represented by the French, Ekstrom, and Price (1963) *Kit of Reference Tests for Cognitive Factors* in terms of *operations* (processes required by the task) and *strategies,* although I may have failed to observe the distinction with sufficient rigor.

It also occurs to me to mention that in the study just referred to, I was careful to distinguish between contents of the memory stores that are operated on and the operations and strategies that perform the processing. In varying tasks to observe the functioning of processes and strategies, it will be important to control or otherwise take account of differential contents of memory stores that may be involved in tasks. Many of the factors isolated in traditional psychometric research seem to be associated with particular content constellations, i.e., with the presence or absence of, or with the quantity and type of, information that is processed. Information-processing research can similarly fall into the trap of failing to distinguish between processes and the content of the information that is processed.

As an illustration of a promising methodology that has thus far been little used in individual difference research in an information-processing mode, I may refer to a study by Frederiksen (1969). This study has apparently received little attention among information-processing theorists, although it has been hailed by Messick (1972, p. 368) as a "milestone study in [the] multivariate experimental probing of complex learning processes." Frederiksen studied college students' learning of a 60-word list, under three experimental conditions: (a) a standard serial anticipation task, (b) a "clustering" task in which the words were artificially presented in clusters of five, and (c) a free-recall task in which the 60 words were presented, as it were, all at once. There was a separate group of 40 cases assigned to each experimental condition. The response data consisted of the scores on each of the 18 trials that were given to each group; these learning curve data were, however, transformed into five components that explained nearly all the variance of the scores according to a principal-component technique for such data devised by Tucker (1966), a technique that has also been used by Leicht (1972) in the analysis of free-recall data. Immediately after the learning task, Frederiksen administered to his subjects a questionnaire on the strategies they thought they employed in performing the learning; these data were also reduced to a series of five components, representing typical strategies such as "Organization by Grouping," "Active Sequential Organization," and "Modification of Strategies." Frederiksen also administered his subjects a series of psychometric tests that yielded scores on seven of the factors represented in the French et al. (1963) *Kit of Reference Tests for Cognitive Factors*. Thus, Frederiksen had three sets of data: the psychometric tests, the strategy scores, and the learning component scores. Using mainly canonical correlation analysis, Frederiksen determined relationships between these sets of data in each of the experimental groups pairwise, i.e., between the ability tests and the learning components, between the ability tests and the strategy components, and between the strategy components and the learning components. Although there were some significant relationships, they showed no very clear pattern overall. Different experimental conditions elicited markedly different strategies, but the effects of the strategies showed up only weakly and inconsistently in the learning components. In the main, the only ability factor that showed reasonably consistent and substantial relationships with learning component data was the associative memory factor Ma; but then, it might be said that such a relation could only be expected, since the memory tasks in the test and in the learning trials had major similarities.

This study by Frederiksen has its frustrating aspects. The sample sizes (40 in each group) were relatively small, and it is difficult to interpret the meaning of the learning curve components. In fact, Frederiksen suggested that "the amount of information about human learning obtainable from the behavior of learning curves may be limited, and that precise prediction of learning performance curves may not be the most important function of a learning theory" (p. 68)—a sentiment echoed by Leicht (1972), among others.

Strangely, Frederiksen apparently never thought to put together his ability factor data and his strategy component data to establish predictors of the learning component data. It occurred to me to do this, using the data reported in his monograph. I hoped to find linear combinations of ability factor scores and strategy component scores such that the combination would predict a learning component score significantly better than the use of either alone. I investigated the five ability scores (Cs, Fa, Fe, Ma, and V) and the two strategy components (3, Active Sequential Organization, and 4, Order Preserving Mnemonics) that seemed to show the stronger and more consistent predictive relations with learning components, and put these in multiple regressions for predicting each of the five learning components, in each of the three experimental groups. In all, there were fifteen multiple regressions. As one may see, this was purely a fishing expedition. But one can enjoy a fishing expedition even if it is unproductive, as this one was. About the closest I came to catching the kind of fish I wanted (one where an ability factor and a strategy component would each have a significant regression weight) was in the case of the Free-Recall group, where Strategy 4, Order Preserving Mnemonics, had a clearly significant weight ($t(32) = 3.17, p < .01$), but factor Fa, Associative Fluency, had a weight that only approached significance ($t(32) = 1.98, p < .10$) in the prediction of Learning Component III. If this finding is regarded as having significance, it would mean that people with high Associative Fluency do particularly well in a certain phase of free-recall learning if they adopt a strategy of using "order preserving mnemonics," such as trying to make sentences from the words presented, rather than merely attending to their sounds. Actually, in this group, there was a negative correlation ($r = -.34$) between Fa and the use of this strategy.

Although my fishing expedition was unsuccessful, it illustrates, as does the Frederiksen study as a whole, the potential use of a methodology whereby information about both abilities and strategies might be collected to predict or account for differences in task performance. Possibly one condition that mitigated against obtaining significant results in my fishing expedition was the use of a purely linear model; I was of course limited to such a model by the data available to me in Frederiksen's publication. Some sort of nonlinear model that would simultaneously predict the probabilities of using alternative strategies on the basis of ability scores and predict performance data on the basis of strategy selection and ability scores would seem to be desirable.

CONCLUSION

After this critical examination of a range of studies that employ correlational methodologies in the study of individual differences in information processing, these methodologies, especially factor analysis and its relatives, can be judged still viable and effective procedures. If studies are designed to exploit the full potentialities of these methodologies, and if the methodologies are properly applied, it seems possible to arrive at reasonable and probably confirmable conclusions concerning the identification and description of a variety of cognitive operations. Thus far, however, many errors have been made in applying these methodologies. Even when they have been correctly applied, their potentialities have not been fully exploited due to poor or inadequate study design.

Results thus far have suggested the existence of a series of cognitive processes that show correspondences to individual difference traits, but the stability and the generality of these traits have not been firmly established. There has been little attention to the possibility that individuals can use alternative, optional processes or strategies in test performance, and to the possibility that these processes or strategies are amenable to manipulation through variation of task characteristics, instruction, practice, or other maneuvers.

Although the state of the art in individual difference research in an information-processing mode can be thought of as little more than embryonic, this type of research appears to have a promising future if the recommendations made in this review can be followed, and if logistic considerations are not insuperable.

REFERENCES

Atkinson, R. C., & Shiffrin, R. M. Human memory: A proposed system and its component processes. In K. W. Spence & J. T. Spence (Eds.), *Advances in the psychology of learning and motivation: Research and theory,* Vol. 2. New York: Academic Press, 1968. Pp. 89–195.

Campbell, D. T., & Fiske, D. W. Convergent and discriminant validation by the multitrait-multimethod matrix. *Psychological Bulletin,* 1959, **56**, 81–105.

Carroll, J. B. The nature of the data, or how to choose a correlation coefficient. *Psychometrika,* 1961, **26**, 347–372.

Carroll, J. B. Psychometric tests as cognitive tasks: A new "Structure of Intellect." In L. B. Resnick (Ed.), *The nature of intelligence.* Hillsdale, N. J.: Lawrence Erlbaum Associates, 1976. Pp. 27–56.

Cliff, N., & Krus, D. J. Interpretation of canonical analysis: Rotated vs. unrotated solutions. *Psychometrika,* 1976, **41**, 35–42.

Cohen, R. L., & Sandberg, T. Relation between intelligence and short-term memory. *Cognitive Psychology,* 1977, **9**, 534–554.

Ekstrom, R. B. Cognitive factors: Some recent literature. Princeton, N. J.: Educational Testing Service, PR-73-30, July 1973. (Technical Report No. 2, Research sponsored by the Office of Naval Research under Contract N00014-71-C-0117, NR 150 329.)

Favero, J., Dombrower, J., Michael, W. B., & Richards, L. Interrelationships among 76 individually-administered tests intended to represent 76 different Structure-of-Intellect abilities and a standardized general intelligence test in a sample of 34 nine-year-old children. *Educational and Psychological Measurement,* 1975, **35**, 993–1004.

Frederiksen, C. H. Abilities, transfer, and information retrieval in verbal learning. *Multivariate Behavioral Research Monographs* No. 69-2, 1969.

Frederiksen, J. R. A chronometric study of component skills in reading. Cambridge, MA: Bolt Beranek and Newman, Inc., January 1978. (Report No. 3757, Technical Report No. 2, ONR Contract N00014-76-C-0461, NR 154 386.) (a)

Frederiksen, J. R. Assessment of perceptual decoding and lexical skills and their relation to reading proficiency. In A. M. Lesgold, J. W. Pellegrino, S. Fokkema, & R. Glaser (Eds.), *Cognitive psychology and instruction.* New York: Plenum Press, 1978. (b)

French, J. W., Ekstrom, R. B., & Price, L. A. *Kit of reference tests for cognitive factors.* Princeton, N. J.: Educational Testing Service, 1963.

Groen, G. J., & Parkman, J. M. A chronometric analysis of simple addition. *Psychological Review,* 1972, **79**, 329–343.

Guilford, J. P. *The nature of human intelligence.* New York: McGraw-Hill, 1967.

Guilford, J. P., & Hoepfner, R. *The analysis of intelligence.* New York: McGraw-Hill, 1971.

Harman, H. H., Ekstrom, R. B., & French, J. W. *Kit of factor reference cognitive tests.* Princeton, N. J.: Educational Testing Service, 1976.

Hock, H. S. The effects of stimulus structure and familiarity on same–different comparison. *Perception & Psychophysics,* 1973, **14**, 413–420.

Hock, H. S., Gordon, G. P., & Corcoran, S. K. Alternative processes in the identification of familiar pictures. *Memory & Cognition,* 1976, **4**, 265–271.

Hock, H. S., & Ross, K. The effect of familiarity on rotational transformation. *Perception & Psychophysics,* 1975, **18**, 15–20.

Hotelling, H. Analysis of a complex of statistical variables into principal components. *Journal of Educational Psychology,* 1933, **24**, 417–441, 498–520.

Hundal, P. S., & Horn, J. L. On the relationship between short-term learning and fluid and crystallized intelligence. *Applied Psychological Measurement,* 1977, **1**, 11–21.

Hunt, E., Frost, N., & Lunneborg, C. Individual differences in cognition. In G. Bower (Ed.), *The psychology of learning and motivation: Advances in research and theory.* Vol. 7. New York: Academic Press, 1973.

Hunt, E., Lunneborg, C., & Lewis, J. What does it mean to be high verbal? *Cognitive Psychology,* 1975, **7**, 194–227.

Jarman, R. F., & Das, J. P. Simultaneous and successive syntheses and intelligence. *Intelligence,* 1977, **1**, 151–169.

Jennrich, R. I., & Sampson, P. F. Rotation for simple loadings. *Psychometrika,* 1966, **31**, 313–323.

Jöreskog, K. G. Some contributions to maximum likelihood factor analysis. *Psychometrika,* 1967, **32**, 443–482.

Jöreskog, K. G. A general method for analysis of covariance structures. *Biometrika,* 1970, **57**, 239–251.

Leicht, K. L. Methods for inferring process similarity in different learning tasks. In C. P. Duncan, L. Seechrest, & A. W. Melton (Eds.), *Human memory: Festschrift in honor of Benton J. Underwood.* New York: Appleton-Century-Crofts, 1972. Pp. 111–131.

Lunneborg, C. E. Choice reaction time: What role in ability measurement? *Applied Psychological Measurement,* 1977, **1**, 309–330.

Messick, S. Beyond structure: In search of functional methods of psychological process. *Psychometrika,* 1972, **37**, 357–375.

Ray, M. L., & Heeler, R. M. Analysis techniques for exploratory use of the multitrait–multimethod matrix. *Educational and Psychological Measurement,* 1975, **35**, 255–265.

Sargent, S. S. How shall we study individual differences? *Psychological Review,* 1942, **49**, 170–182.

Schmid, J., & Leiman, J. M. The development of hierarchical factor solutions. *Psychometrika,* 1957, **22**, 53–61.

Sternberg, R. J. *Intelligence, information processing, and analogical reasoning: The componential analysis of human abilities.* Hillsdale, N. J.: Lawrence Erlbaum Associates, 1977.

Thurstone, L. L. Current issues in factor analysis. *Psychological Bulletin,* 1940, **37**, 189–236.

Thurstone, L. L. *Multiple factor analysis.* Chicago: University of Chicago Press, 1947.

Tucker, L. R. A semianalytical method of factorial rotation to simple structure. *Psychometrika,* 1944, **9**, 43–68.

Tucker, L. R. An interbattery method of factor analysis. *Psychometrika,* 1958, **23**, 111–136.

Tucker, L. R. Learning theory and multivariate experiment: Illustration by determination of generalized learning curves. In R. B. Cattell (Ed.), *Handbook of multivariate experimental psychology.* Chicago: Rand McNally, 1966. Pp. 476–501.

Underwood, B. J., Boruch, R. F., & Malmi, R. A. The composition of episodic memory. Evanston, Ill.: Psychology Dept., Northwestern Univ., May 1977. (Technical Report, ONR Contract N00014-76-C-0270, NR 154-371.)

Wainer, H. Speed vs. reaction time as a measure of cognitive performance. *Memory & Cognition,* 1977, **5**, 278–280.

Wood, D. A., & Erskine, J. A. Strategies in canonical correlation with application to behavioral data. *Educational and Psychological Measurement,* 1976, **36**, 861–878.

2

Intelligence Research at the Interface Between Differential and Cognitive Psychology: Prospects and Proposals

ROBERT J. STERNBERG

Yale University

There seems to be widespread agreement among theoreticians and methodologists alike that new approaches to studying intelligence should somehow combine the differential and cognitive (information-processing) approaches that have been used in the past, and that the combination should somehow enable the investigator to isolate components of intelligence that are elementary (at some level of analysis). Researchers disagree, however, as to how the differential and cognitive approaches should be combined, and consequently, in how elementary components of intelligence should be isolated and in what they are. How does an investigator choose from among the multiple paths available for theory and research? In this article, I propose some guidelines that may help investigators make informed choices. The article is divided into three major parts. In the first, I propose guidelines for choosing from among various methodologies for studying intelligence, and then describe briefly at least some of the methods that meet (or come close to meeting) these guidelines. In the second part, I propose guidelines for the specification of subtheories (and eventually, full-fledged theories) of intelligence, and illustrate how these guidelines can be met. Finally, I describe the direction in which I believe our subtheories and methods should lead us.

Just five years ago, during the spring term of my first year in graduate school, the famous instructor of my course on Human Abilities painted a dim picture of the then current state of intelligence research. Lee Cronbach seemed to view it as his duty to inform us that research on intelligence was not in fashion. My own impression was that Cronbach was being charitable: Research on intelligence seemed to have gone the way of Nehru suits and long dresses.

My history of involvement with the field of intelligence had been less than promising: By any reasonable standard, it seemed to be one of avoidance learning. My first formal exposure to the field was in seventh grade, in a science project on the "development of the mental test." I became excited

Preparation of this article was supported by Contract N0001478C0025 from the Office of Naval Research. Requests for reprints should be sent to Robert J. Sternberg, Department of Psychology, Yale University, Box 11A Yale Station, New Haven, Connecticut 06520.

about what was to me a new and challenging discipline—the study of intelligence and its testing. My science teacher, the late William H. Adams, was most encouraging; but my ideas about experimentation, including the administration of the Stanford–Binet to my classmates, won less than hearty approval from the head psychologist of the school system, who, having gotten wind of what I was doing, promised to burn the Terman–Merrill (1937) book if I ever brought it into school again. During secondary school, I pursued my interest independently, hoping that things would pick up upon my entrance to college. They did not. When I entered Yale in 1963, there was only one psychologist with a commitment to the study of intelligence and individual differences, and he was about to retire. And later, during my first year of graduate school, I was faced with what seemed like an inescapable conclusion—that the whole field had retired.

But Lee Cronbach mentioned near the end of his course that new ideas regarding intelligence and its study were just beginning to emerge, and that Lauren Resnick was organizing a conference to bring some of these ideas (and their sources) together. At about this time, I was beginning to form some ideas of my own (see Sternberg, 1977b), ideas very much in the spirit of those to be published in the proceedings of the Resnick conference (see Resnick, 1976, and especially Carroll, 1976). The whole field had not retired; it had merely resigned temporarily until a better job could be done. And although Nehru suits never did make it back (at least not yet), long dresses, like research on intelligence, are back in fashion again.

In 1978, a diversity of new subtheories of and methods for studying intelligence confront the prospective investigator. There seems to be widespread concurrence among theoreticians and methodologists alike that new approaches to studying intelligence should somehow combine the differential and cognitive (information-processing) approaches that have been used in the past, and that the combination should somehow enable the investigator to isolate components of intelligence that are elementary (at some level of analysis).

Researchers disagree, however, as to how the differential and cognitive approaches should be combined, and consequently, in how elementary components of intelligence should be isolated and in what they are. How does an investigator choose from among the multiple paths available for theory and research? In this article, I will propose some guidelines that may help investigators make informed choices. The article will be divided into four major parts. In the first, I will propose guidelines for choosing from among various methodologies for studying intelligence. In the second, I will describe briefly at least some of the methods that meet (or come close to meeting) these guidelines. In the third part, I will propose guidelines for the specification of subtheories (and eventually, full-fledged theories) of intelligence, and illustrate how these guidelines can be met. Finally, I will describe the direction in which I believe our subtheories and methods should lead us.

GUIDELINES FOR METHODS FOR STUDYING INTELLIGENCE

In proposing methodological guidelines, I realize I risk repeating what many readers may have learned in courses on statistics and research methods. If that be the case, the repetition seems justified, because a review of much of the recent literature on intelligence reveals that in a great majority of cases, many of these guidelines are not being followed. I am therefore prepared to run the risk of being repetitious.

Internal Validation

It was stated earlier that methodologists seem to agree that a major goal of contemporary intelligence research should be to isolate components of intelligence that are elementary at some level of analysis. Internal validation consists of the attempt to demonstrate that the components isolated in a particular analysis are consistent with the latency or error data on the basis of which the existence of the components is claimed to be supported.

Theory Testing. Almost everyone now studying intelligence agrees that one's method for studying intelligence should be theory-based. But theories seem to be serving at least two very different functions in contemporary research on intelligence. On the one hand, a theory can be proposed and assumed to be correct. In this case, the theory may provide a guide for the research, but the theory is not actually tested, or subjected to potential falsification. The theory's connection to the research may be barely visible at all. On the other hand, a theory can be proposed and hypothesized to be correct. In this case, the theory both provides a guide for the research and is tested, thereby subjecting it to potential falsification. I propose that the latter approach to theory utilization is the preferred one. Our collective experience of nearly a century of differential research on intelligence is the best guide as to why. The major obstacle to progress in differential research on intelligence may well have been the nonfalsifiability of the theories that were proposed. New theories were born, but old theories never died, and often did not even fade away. Theorists had no way of controlling the resulting population explosion, and the result seems to have been mass suffocation, if not of the theories, then of interest in them. The root of the problem seems to have been the inadequacy of the factor-analytic method to which many differential theorists were wedded as a means of falsifying theories. (Reasons for its inadequacy in this respect are discussed in Sternberg, 1977b, Chap.2.) If intelligence research is to thrive, we need methodologies that enable us to recognize and replace outworn theories. Several criteria for recognizing such theories are described below.

Comparison of Proposed Theory to True Theory. One criterion for rejecting a theory is inadequacy of the theory relative to the true theory. Obviously, we do not know what the true theory is, or else we would rush to propose it. But we usually do know what the true theory predicts, for example, a perfect correlation between a dependent variable and one or more independent variables (after correction of all variables for attenuation). In order to assess the proposed theory, one must know (a) the proportion of variance in the data accounted for, (b) whether the variance accounted for is statistically significant, and (c) whether the variance unaccounted for is statistically significant. (Ways of testing these are described in Sternberg, 1978c.) All three of these criteria can be applied in analysis-of-variance designs as well as in regression designs, using ω^2 instead of r^2 or R^2 (see Hays, 1973). It is also desirable to have some absolute measure of deviation from fit, such as root-mean-square deviation (RMSD) of observed from predicted values. I am assuming here, as is almost always the case, that one's goal is to maximize the strength of the relation between two or more variables. If, for one reason or another, one's goal is to attain a moderately strong relation between two variables, then one is obliged to indicate the range of values that would falsify the theory being tested.

In comparing one's theory to the true theory, it is important to keep in mind the often-learned but often-forgotten fact that one can never prove that one's own theory is identical to the true theory, but merely that for a given set of data, the predictions of the two theories cannot be distinguished. There may be some third theory that is also indistinguishable in its predictions from true theory.

Comparison of Proposed Theory to Plausible Alternative Theories. In practice, the success of a theory relative to the true theory is often independent of the success of the theory in competing against alternative plausible performance theories. This point was made rather dramatically in the published sequence of research reports on the sentence–picture comparison task. Clark and Chase (1972) found that their theory of the task accounted for extremely high proportions of variance in their latency data (often over 99%), and that the theory generally could not be rejected relative to the true theory. But Carpenter and Just (1975) later showed that quite a different theory could account for the data equally well, and also fail to be rejected relative to the true theory. It is thus important to compare one's theory not only to the true theory, but to a set of plausible alternative performance theories as well. A proposed theory accounting for a given proportion of variance in the data might be viewed favorably or unfavorably depending upon how well alternative theories do in accounting for the data. Indeed, even if a proposed theory is rejected relative to the true theory, it may nevertheless be accepted as the best working approximation to the true theory if there is no better plausible alternative.

Generality of Proposed Theory. In order for a theory to be of any interest, it must have some generality. It is insufficient, therefore, to propose or merely test a theory for a given task with a given content in a given experimental paradigm. Interest in the theory will be enhanced to the degree it is shown to be general across paradigms, contents, and tasks, and so the investigator should feel obliged to demonstrate generality.

External Validation

How do we know that the components of information processing that we have isolated from a particular task are components of "intelligence," or have anything to do with intelligence at all? This question must be taken seriously, since it is possible to fulfill all requirements for internal validation of a theory, and yet have a theory that has little or nothing to do with intelligence. We are beginning to see an amassing of evidence that suggests that a relatively small collection of information-processing components can account for a variety of cognitive task performances, such as visual scanning, memory scanning, stimulus matching, and the like (Chiang & Atkinson, 1976; Rose, 1974). But does level of performance on these components relate to level of performance on the Binet-type (or other) tasks generally believed to require "intelligence?" Available evidence suggests low to moderate levels of relation at best (see, for example, Hunt, Frost, & Lunneborg, 1973; Hunt, Lunneborg, & Lewis, 1975). These relations are investigated by external validation, through which one shows generalization or lack of generalization of patterns of individual differences from tasks that are hypothesized to measure intelligence to tasks that are widely believed to measure intelligence.

Convergent Validation. First, one must demonstrate convergent validity—that the components of interest do correlate with components or tasks that are generally accepted as measures of intelligence. Internal validation may well have shown that the isolated components are likely to be true components of the task or tasks under consideration. But if convergent validity is not, or cannot be, demonstrated, the scientific public has no reason to believe that the components that were isolated have any external validity as measures of intelligence.

Discriminant Validation. Second, one must demonstrate discriminant validity—that the components of interest do not correlate with components or tasks that are not of interest but are possible sources of confounding. Convergent validation may well have shown that the isolated components are correlated with intelligence, or some aspect of it. But if discriminant validity is not, or cannot be, demonstrated, the scientific public has no reason to believe that the correlation of the components that have been isolated with measures of intelligence is not due to confounding with some other uninteresting construct.

Conclusions

Some basic guidelines for research on intelligence have been proposed. These guidelines seem to be minimal ones, at least in the sense that they are the kinds of guidelines experimentalists learn about early in their careers, often in research methods or statistics courses. Yet, a review of recent published research on intelligence reveals that only a small fraction of this research follows even most of these guidelines. The most serious consequence of failure to follow the guidelines is the commission of Type II errors, which have traditionally plagued research on intelligence: We are lured into believing that a phenomenon or relationship exists when it does not. Other researchers are then enticed by these false leads, resulting in increasing amounts of wasted time. We are already beginning to see in the literature reports of failures to replicate relatively recent findings that generated some publicity, and reports that phenomena that do indeed replicate are not what they seemed to be. We can be thankful, at least, that the replications are being done. But we could reduce initial false starts by following some simple guidelines for our research.

PROMISING METHODOLOGIES

In writing a monograph discussing available approaches to research on intelligence (Sternberg, 1977b), I was chagrined by the lack of viable options for researchers to follow. Established differential and information-processing methodologies seemed inadequate, and although I believed the methodology I was proposing (componential analysis) was adequate, a single methodology would leave researchers with little choice. Since then, however, there have been other methodological developments that I view as promising, and that seem to offer the researcher a wider choice to suit his or her research style and predilections. I will briefly describe four promising methodologies here, each of which is an outgrowth of what I believe was an unsatisfactory methodology. The four methodologies I have selected are almost certainly not an exhaustive list of promising sets of techniques. I have chosen them because (a) the sets of techniques have been well specified and shown to work in at least one instance, (b) they have the potential for meeting the guidelines described above, and (c) they meet certain criticisms of their predecessors that I outlined in my earlier work (Sternberg, 1977b) and repeat here.

An Outgrowth of the Differential Approach to Intelligence:
Confirmatory Maximum–Likelihood Factor Analysis and
Analysis of Covariance Structures

I have previously criticized factor-analytic methodology on four grounds (Sternberg, 1977b):

1. *Lack of control over mathematical realization of psychological theory.* The mathematical theory is defined by the machinery of factor analysis rather than by the investigator. An investigator can go into such an analysis without any theory at all, and come out of the analysis with something resembling a theory. (The reasons for the *lack* of resemblance are described in the earlier work.)

2. *Solution indeterminacy: the rotation dilemma.* Since the axes obtained in a factor analysis are subject to arbitrary rotation, an infinite number of possible sets of rotated factors may be obtained, each of which has different psychological implications.

3. *Failure to discover or explicate process.* Factor analysis has generally been used to explicate the *inter*item structure of multiple tests, rather than the *intra*item structure of single tests. But processes occur in the solution of single items, and these single items must therefore be studied in order to elucidate the processes.

4. *Interindividual nature of analysis.* The components of intelligence are intraindividual (they exist within subjects), whereas factor analysis is generally interindividual (it analyzes patterns of individual differences across subjects). Since individual differences are meaningless in the context of single individuals, it is not clear how factor analysis enables us to discover components of processing inside single individuals.

At the time, I noted that confirmatory maximum-likelihood factor analysis (Jöreskog, 1969a; Jöreskog & Lawley, 1968) seemed to provide a possible way out of some of these dilemmas. Confirmatory maximum-likelihood factor analysis extracts factors with predefined characteristics, and then provides the means to determine whether the variance unaccounted for by the factors is statistically significant. The predefined characteristics of the model can be entries in the factor pattern matrix (giving loadings of variables on factors), in the factor intercorrelation matrix (giving intercorrelations between all pairs of factors), or in the matrix of unique variances (giving variances of unique, i.e., not common, factors). Parameters of the model can be prespecified either by assigning them specific values (usually 0 or 1), or by setting them equal to each other, in which case they are free to vary within the constraints of equality.

Frederiksen (1977) has used a variant of confirmatory maximum-likelihood factor analysis, analysis of covariance structures (Jöreskog, 1970), to isolate component skills in reading, and appears to have done so with some success. He proposed a model with five of what he called "component factors": grapheme encoding, encoding of multiletter units, phonemic translation, automaticity of articulation, and depth of processing in word recognition. He hypothesized that if his model is correct, certain basic processes as measured by contrasts for standard laboratory cognitive tasks should load on some factors but not on others. He tested the model using covariance data from 11 response-time measures, chosen to represent the various stages of processing. He was unable to reject the proposed model (p = .2), although he was able to reject three alternative models ($p < .05$). The proposed model accounted for nearly all of the variance in the subjects' general reading ability, as measured by standardized tests of reading comprehension.

The methodology used by Frederiksen permits adherence to all of the guidelines specified earlier, and indeed, Frederiksen followed all but one. He (a) tested a prior theory, by (b) comparing it to the true theory (against which it could not be rejected), and (c) comparing it to alternative theories of the task in question (which did not fare as well). He also (d) demonstrated some generality by having multiple tasks to measure each factor. Convergent validation was accomplished by relating components of the model to scores on standardized reading tests, although discriminant validation was ignored.

The methodology also seems to obviate at least two of the four limitations of factor analysis described above—control over the mathematical theory and solution indeterminacy. In confirmatory maximum-likelihood methods, the mathematical theory is specified in advance, so that the first limitation is overcome. The solution is unique if a total of at least f^2 elements (where f equals the number of factors) in the pattern and factor intercorrelation matrices are specified in advance. (Frederiksen did specify enough parameters in advance to insure uniqueness.) Thus, the second limitation is also overcome.

The third limitation, inability of factorial methods to discover or explicate process, can be addressed (as it is by Frederiksen's clever combination of differential and information-processing methodologies), but I have not seen evidence that it can be overcome. Rather than merely using composite tasks as variables in his factor analysis, Frederiksen used carefully constructed contrasts for the tasks, contrasts that were hypothesized to reflect elementary information processes. Frederiksen was thus able, at least to some extent, to "get inside" the tasks. However, factor analysis remains a structural model, and the factors of Frederiksen's model seem less like elementary component processes than they seem like global stages that contain multiple component processes. In this sense, they are best viewed as reference abilities, "constellations of components (latent traits) that in combination form stable patterns of individual differences across tasks" (Sternberg, 1977b, p. 78). In my own componential framework, factors are mathematical representations of reference abilities, and I believe this framework applies to maximum-likelihood as well as standard factors. The factors simply cannot be equated with basic component processes, which in Frederiksen's research are measured by subtractive contrasts. Maximum-likelihood factor analysis, then, can serve as a useful way of testing models of the structure and interrelations of reference abilities. It does not test whether the isolated components are actually the components of reading. This can be done only by isolating hypothetical components of reading, and testing whether they can account for differential latencies or difficulties resulting from manipulation of independent variables in a reading task.

The fourth limitation of factor analysis (the interindividual nature of the analysis) is also addressed, but not overcome, by the confirmatory maximum-likelihood methods. Frederiksen addresses this problem by analyzing aspects of intraitem structure, rather than merely using composite tasks as the variables in the analysis. But the analysis is based upon individual differences among subjects. A possible solution to the problem might be found in the use of confirmatory maximum-likelihood methods in the context of a three-mode factor analysis (Jöreskog, 1969b), where both individuals and variables could be factored simultaneously. But the success of such a method remains to be demonstrated, so that at least for the time being, the limitation seems to stand.

Used in conjunction with information-processing techniques, confirmatory maximum-likelihood factor analysis (including analysis of covariance structures) seems to offer a promising approach toward understanding intelligence. To date, the methodology has been little tried in research on intelligence, but I believe that those with a psychometric bent will find this methodology a worthwhile one to explore.

Outgrowths of the Information-Processing or Cognitive Approach to Intelligence

During the 1970s, a large number of investigators have taken an information-processing or cognitive approach toward understanding intelligence. The goal in this research is to discover the representations, processes, and strategies subjects use in solving problems widely acknowledged to require "intelligence" for their solution. The information-processing approach has spawned three subapproaches, which may be conveniently organized under the headings of the subtraction method, the additive-factor method, and computer simulation.

An Outgrowth of the Subtraction Method: Componential Analysis. In the subtraction method, one measures the duration of a mental event by comparing the amount of time a subject takes to solve a task requiring that mental event, to the amount of time a subject takes to solve a task that differs from the first task only in the deletion of that event. I have previously criticized subtraction methodology on five grounds (Sternberg, 1977b):

1. *Parameters are often confounded.* Single parameters estimate latencies for multiple component processes, each of which is of interest in its own right, and should therefore be disentangled from the other processes.

2. *Alternative models are often indistinguishable.* Alternative models are rendered indistinguishable when the component processes that could distinguish them are estimated as confounded parameters.

3. *Parameter estimates are based upon too few degrees of freedom for residual.* Large numbers of parameters are estimated on the basis of small numbers of data points, increasing greatly the probability of capitalization upon chance in model fitting.

4. *Ordering of parameters is not mathematically specified.* Although the information-processing model to be tested specifies the ordering of component processes, the model is tested in a way that places too few or no constraints on the order in which the processes actually occur.

5. *Results of external validation may be distorted.* Correlational patterns of parameters with external measures can be distorted if component processes are estimated as confounded parameters, but the underlying component processes are not themselves highly correlated across subjects. In this case, the estimated parameter is not a unitary source of individual differences.

Two more common criticisms of the subtraction method are that its use requires a sophisticated prior theory, and that its use requires the assumption of pure insertion—that in deleting a component process from a task, one is deleting this process and only this process, and that one is not changing the task in any other way. I discuss elsewhere why I believe these criticisms to be less than compelling in modern applications of the subtraction method (Sternberg, 1977b, pp. 57–60).

I have proposed a methodology, componential analysis (Sternberg, 1977b, 1978a), for studying intelligence, that I believe obviates or at least mitigates the force of the five criticisms presented above. The methodology has been applied to the solution of analogies (Sternberg, 1977a, b; Sternberg & Rifkin, 1979; Sternberg & Nigro, 1978), transitive inference problems (Sternberg, in press-a, in press-b), and categorical and conditional syllogisms (Guyote & Sternberg, 1978; Sternberg & Turner, 1978) with encouraging results. It is currently being applied to many other kinds of problems as well.

Componential analysis provides a set of procedures to assist in the identification and testing of the (a) component processes, (b) combination rule for different component processes, (c) combination rule for multiple executions of the same component process, (d) latencies and difficulties of component processes, and (e) relations among the component processes and between these processes and higher-order reference abilities. In some applications, (f) representation of information is assumed; in others, it is tested. A central feature of componential analysis is the breakdown of a composite task into a series of subtasks, each of which requires successively less information processing. This breakdown of the task can be accomplished in a number of different ways (Sternberg, 1978b). I will briefly describe here two ways in which one task, the linear syllogism, was decomposed.

A linear syllogism (also called a three-term series problem) is a kind of transitive inference problem in which a subject is presented with two premises, each describing a relation between two items. One of the items overlaps between premises. The subject's task is to use this overlap to determine a relation between the two items not occurring in the same premise. An example of such a problem is "Joe is taller than Sam. Sam is taller than Ben. Who is tallest?" I have used two different procedures to decompose this task.

In one procedure, the method of precueing, trials were divided into two parts. In the first part, the subject received precueing with part of the item; in the second part, the subject received the whole item. The subject was instructed to use the precueing to do as much information processing as possible, although the subject was not actually told how to process the information. Two precueing conditions were used. In the first, the subject received a blank field in the first part of the trial, followed by the full item in the second part of the trial. In the second, the subject received the two premises in the first part of the trial, followed by the full item in the second part of the trial. A third precueing condition, consisting of only the first premise in the first part of the trial, might also have been used (although it was not because it seemed unnecessary for my experimental purposes).

In the second procedure, the method of partial tasks, subjects received either full three-term series problems or two-term series problems such as "Joe is taller than Sam. Who is tallest?" Solution of the two-term series problems was hypothesized to require a subset of the processes required to solve the three-term series problem, and latencies for the two types of items were modeled jointly.

Three theories of transitive inference—a linguistic theory, a spatial theory, and a mixture theory—were pitted against each other in a series of four experiments (Sternberg, 1977c), and the theory that won the competition was also pitted against the true theory. The mean value of R^2 for the best theory, the mixture theory, was .19 points higher than the mean value for the second best theory, the linguistic theory; the mixture theory, however, could be rejected against the true theory ($p < .05$) in three of the four experiments. Parameters of the mixture theory were correlated with each other, and with scores from tests of verbal reasoning and spatial visualization, in order to ascertain which processes showed linguistic patterns of individual differences and which showed spatial patterns.

Componential analysis permits adherence to the guidelines proposed earlier in this article. In the example application, a theory was proposed (the mixture theory), and tested against both the true theory (it was usually rejected) and against the major alternative theories (it was always better). Generality of the proposed theory was demonstrated by showing its superiority across adjectives, sessions, and a variety of experimental conditions. Convergent and discriminant validity were demonstrated by showing its superiority across adjectives, sessions, and a variety of experimental conditions. Convergent and discriminant validity were demonstrated by showing that components hypothesized to be linguistic correlated with linguistic but not spatial ability tests, and that components hypothesized to be spatial correlated with spatial but not linguistic ability tests.

Componential analysis also addresses and reduces the force of the limitations of subtraction methodology described above. We will consider each limitation in turn.

First, parameters that would be confounded in standard application of the subtraction method are separated by the use of task decomposition. Not all component processes are separated, however. In some cases, processes that could be separated are simply of no theoretical interest in themselves, and are left confounded in order to avert a gain in the number of parameters with no corresponding theoretical gain. In other cases, component processes cannot be (or at least have not been) separated, even with the use of componential task decomposition. Task decomposition, therefore, can reduce the number of confounded parameters but it cannot always eliminate all such parameters. Second, the increase in the number of distinguishable parameters can permit testing of alternative models that might otherwise be confounded. Third, by jointly modeling the dependent variable for the various conditions of precueing (or partial tasks), one substantially increases the number of points to be modeled, and hence the number of degrees of freedom for residual, thereby guarding against spurious good fit. Fourth, breakdown of a task requires the investigator to specify in which subtask(s) each component process occurs, thereby constraining the ordering of parameters in the model as tested, as well as in the model as conceptualized. If the investigator does not know what processes occur when, the empirical fit of the model will be reduced. Fifth, the separation of parameters that would otherwise be confounded helps guard against distortion of results in external validation. A rather dramatic example of such an outcome occurred in my research on analogies (Sternberg, 1977b), where two parameters that were separated through the use of precueing were actually negatively correlated with each other.

In summary, componential analysis seems to offer the benefits of subtraction methodology at the same time that it assuages (but does not always eliminate) its weaknesses. Like Frederiksen's use of analysis of covariance structures, it combines differential and cognitive approaches to intelligence in a way that offers more insight into intelligence than does either approach taken singly.

An Outgrowth of the Additive-Factor Method: Cognitive Dependency Analysis. In the additive-factor method (S. Sternberg, 1969), it is assumed that (a) when an experimental manipulation affects the latency with which an information-processing task is completed, it does so by changing the durations of one or more constituent stages of processing; (b) if two different experimental factors affect two different stages, their effects on solution latency will be additive; (c) if two different experimental factors affect a stage in common, their effects on solution latency will be interactive (that is, they will mutually modify each other's effects) (Pachella, 1974, p. 52). The additive-factor method is employed by studying an information-processing task in the context of a multifactor experimental design, where the experimental factors are chosen so as to lengthen the durations of particular stages. Inferences regarding the stage composition of the task are then made by examining patterns of additivity and interaction between factors (see Sternberg, 1977b, pp. 41–44).

I have previously criticized additive-factor methodology on four grounds (Sternberg, 1977b):

1. *The method does not reveal stage duration.* It can reveal the amount by which a particular experimental manipulation lengthens the duration of a particular stage, but it cannot reveal the duration of the stage itself.

2. *The method provides no direct indication of stage order.* As in the subtraction method, one can make plausible conjectures, but these conjectures are not actually tested.

3. *The method provides no direct indication of the substantive interpretation of any stage.* The nature of the stage is inferred on the basis of the kind of experimental manipulation that lengthens the duration of the stage. But to the extent that a given experimental manipulation (or set of manipulations) could lengthen various types of stages, the nature of the stage remains a matter of conjecture.

4. *The fundamental assumption regarding the means of identifying separate stages is questionable.* It is quite conceivable that two factors might affect a single stage additively, or that they might affect multiple stages and interact.

Some of these criticisms are addressed (although none are fully answered) under special circumstances (temporal overlap of stages) by a generalization of the additive-factor method proposed by Schweickert (1977), although Schweickert's method is complex and not yet clearly applicable to research on intelligence. I know of no generalization of the additive-factor method that answers any of the criticisms in a definitive way. Calfee (1976), however, has proposed a generalization of the additive-factor method that combines aspects of the differential and cognitive approaches in a way that seems greatly to increase the power of the method as a tool for investigating intelligence.

Calfee's generalization makes two major contributions. First, it generalizes the additive-factor method to the multivariate case, allowing for the possibility that multiple measures of particular processes may be employed in a multifactorial experiment. Second, it distinguishes among six different sources of dependency of cognitive processes that seem, in at least some instances, to be confused in contemporary research on intelligence (and other constructs). These sources of dependence were initially investigated in the context of an experiment on motor ability that unfortunately was not designed as a test of the methodology, and which did not, in fact, provide a particularly good test of it. Children in kindergarten and first grade were asked to draw connecting paths from drawings of rabbits to drawings of carrots. Each item consisted of a picture of a rabbit, a straight path, and a drawing of a carrot. The paths were bounded by lines that were either relatively close together or relatively far apart. Problems were administered either in a neutral set (stressing neither accuracy nor speed) or in an accuracy set (stressing accuracy over speed). The two basic independent factors of interest were path difficulty (easy, wide path vs. difficult, narrow path) and instructional set (neutral vs. accuracy). The two basic dependent variables were errors and latencies for drawing. An error was scored if the child either touched or went outside the boundary lines of the path. The two hypothetical stages of interest were labeled accuracy of movement and rate of movement.

Calfee (1976) hypothesized that task difficulty should affect the accuracy of movement stage but not the rate of movement stage, and that this effect should show itself in drawing errors but not in drawing latencies. He also hypothesized that instructional set should affect the rate of movement stage but not the accuracy of movement stage, and that this effect should show itself in drawing latencies but not in drawing errors. The effect of each independent variable was hypothesized, therefore, to be upon one stage but not the other, and the validity of the hypotheses could be tested by determining whether each independent variable affected only the dependent variable linked to the corresponding stage.

Calfee investigated six sources of independence in cognitive processing (see Calfee, 1976, p. 35):

1. *Process independence averaged over subjects.* The question addressed here is whether any between-process source of variance is so large, on the average, that the hypothesis of process independence is untenable. This is the source of independence typically investigated in additive-factor analyses. Calfee proposes testing main effects of the factors against interactions of these main effects with subjects. (A residual error term such as replications would be better, since the interaction puts individual differences in strength of effect into the error term.) In the example, process independence would be supported by a significant effect of either (a) task difficulty on drawing errors, or (b) instructional set on solution latency. Process independence would be counterindicated by a significant effect of either (a) task difficulty on solution latency or (b) instructional set on drawing errors.

2. *Process independence for individual differences.* The question addressed here is whether any between-process subject-factor interactions are so

large that the hypothesis of process independence is untenable. Here, one tests subject by treatment interactions against a residual error term. Again, significance of certain effects is consistent with process independence, but significance of other effects is inconsistent with it. In the example, process independence would be counterindicated by a significant interaction of either (a) subjects with task difficulty for solution latency or (b) subjects with instructional set for drawing errors.

3. *Intraprocess parameter independence.* The question addressed here is whether parameters representing effects of within-process factors are correlated or not. It is possible to obtain for each subject and to intercorrelate parameter estimates computed as contrasts for the effect of each factor. These parameter estimates represent the additional difficulty or latency attributable to the experimental manipulation of each factor. In the example, only one factor is hypothesized to affect each stage of processing, so it is not possible to test intraprocess parameter independence. Were there at least two factors hypothesized to affect each stage of processing, however, process independence would be indicated by nonsignificant correlations between the two (or more) factors affecting each stage. Suppose, for example, that an additional Factor X were hypothesized only to affect rate movement (and to manifest this effect through solution latency), and an additional Factor Y were hypothesized only to affect accuracy of movement (and to manifest this effect through drawing errors). Then intraprocess parameter independence would be supported by nonsignificant correlations between the contrasts for (a) instructional set and Factor X, and (b) task difficulty and Factor Y.

4. *Interprocess parameter independence.* The question addressed here is whether parameters representing effects of between-process factors are correlated or not. In the example, one would test whether the contrast for instructional set (hypothesized to affect rate of movement) is significantly correlated with the contrast for task difficulty (hypothesized to affect accuracy of movement). Interprocess parameter independence would be supported by a nonsignificant correlation.

5. *General parameter independence.* Calfee refers to total (composite) scores as general parameters (and the contrast scores as specific parameters). The question addressed here is whether total scores for the different measures are correlated or not. In the example, one would correlate solution latency with drawing errors. General parameter independence would be supported by a nonsignificant correlation.

6. *General-specific parameter independence.* The question addressed here is whether general parameters (total scores) are significantly correlated with specific parameters (contrast scores). In the example, one would correlate the solution latency and drawing error measures with the contrasts for instructional set and task difficulty. Obviously, the general and specific parameters hypothesized to affect a given stage will exhibit some degree of

artifactual correlation, since they are computed on the basis of the same dependent variable for the same factor. Process independence across factors, however, would be supported by nonsignificant correlations.

Calfee presents a wealth of data regarding the outcomes of the experiment. For our purposes, the main ones of interest are that process independence was rejected for sources 1, 2, 5 (at the kindergarten level), and 6. It was supported for source 4.

The demonstration experiment followed some, but not all, of the guidelines proposed earlier. Calfee did propose a prior theory, which he tested through an analysis of sources of cognitive dependency. Note that the form of the theory, and what is being tested, differ in this example from each of the two previous examples (which, in turn, differed from each other). Here, one is testing a hypothesis regarding the plausibility of a stage model by analysis of the various sources of dependency. Calfee also tested his theory against the true theory—that theory which would predict the patterns of dependence and independence shown in the data. His theory was rejected. Calfee did not compare alternative plausible theories of information processing, although he might easily have done so by proposing alternative patterns of dependence and independence that would form equally plausible, or almost as plausible, theories. Generality of the theory was not demonstrated. Although Calfee proposed and performed extensive analyses of individual differences, they were all internal. Tests of intraprocess and interprocess parameter independence might be seen as providing weak tests of convergent and discriminant validity, if one takes the position that intraprocess parameters should be highly intercorrelated (showing convergent validity) and interprocess parameters should be uncorrelated (showing discriminant validity). This position has no clear justification, however. It would be a small step to incorporate external measures of appropriate abilities into the experimental design, and to test convergent and discriminant validity by correlating specific parameters with these measures.

As mentioned earlier, neither cognitive dependency analysis nor any other generalization of the additive-factor method satisfactorily deals with the limitations of the method that I have noted. With provisions made for external validation, however, cognitive dependency analysis, although barely tested, seems to be a promising methodology. It provides a unique and well integrated combination of information-processing notions of process independence (the last four kinds listed), and further distinguishes among kinds of process independence within each of these general categories. I believe the methodology is well worth further pursuit, perhaps in some kind of combination with componential analysis.

An Application of Computer Simulation.   In computer simulation, one seeks to create or test models that mimic human behavior on the computer.

Ideally, patterns of data generated by "computer subjects" will mimic those of human subjects. I have previously criticized computer models on three grounds (Sternberg, 1977b):

1. *Computer theories are inaccessible to the scientific public.* The theories seem by their nature to be particularly inaccessible, both physically, and for most psychologists, conceptually. Verbal descriptions often fail to make clear just what the empirical claims of the theories are. The inaccessibility of the theories may thwart the public nature of the scientific enterprise.

2. *Computer theories lack parsimony.* Whereas parsimony for its own sake is of questionable value, computer theories are often so complex and interactive that it is difficult to separate the psychological claims made for such theories from the mechanical bookkeeping details that are needed to build a working program but that have no psychological relevance.

3. *Computer theories do not generally provide process parameter estimates.* If one wants to find out the latency or difficulty of a particular component process, this information may be difficult to obtain because of the large number of interactive variables operating in most computer programs.

In my earlier discussion, I did not clearly distinguish between two uses of computer simulation that I am now convinced ought carefully to be distinguished. The first is the use of computer simulation as theory; the second is the use of computer simulation as a means of testing theory. I believe the criticisms I leveled against computer simulation as theory apply equally well today as they did when I first leveled them. But as a means of testing theory, computer simulation is as important and useful as any other means, since it provides a way of testing theories that while well specified in information-processing terms are of a complexity that does not permit ready derivation of straightforward mathematical predictions. I will discuss in this section what I consider to be an excellent example of computer simulation used as a means to test a subtheory of intelligence, in this case, problem solving in the solution of a class of what are sometimes called MOVE problems. Although the authors did not combine differential and information-processing approaches to intelligence in their work, such a combination could be effected and increase the power of what is already a most impressive analysis.

Jeffries, Polson, Razran, and Atwood (1977) have proposed a theory that accounts for both legal and illegal moves in the solution of several variants of both water–jug problems and missionaries and cannibals problems (see also Atwood & Polson, 1976). In water–jug problems, subjects are presented with three jugs of varying capacity for holding water. Initially, the largest jug is full and the two smaller jugs are empty. The subject's task is to determine a series of moves (that is, pouring operations) that will evenly divide the water between the largest and middle-sized jugs. In missionaries and cannibals problems (also known as water-crossing problems), three missionaries and three cannibals wish to cross from one bank of a river to the other. A boat is available for this purpose, but it will hold only two travellers at a time. The subject's task is to determine a series of moves (that is, traveling combinations of missionaries and cannibals) that will transport the individuals across the river, under the constraint that the number of cannibals on either side of the river can never exceed the number of missionaries, since if cannibals outnumber missionaries, the cannibals will eat the missionaries. Both the water–jug and missionaries and cannibals problems can be varied in details while retaining the same basic problem structure.

Polson and his colleagues had subjects solve several variants of both types of problems. They proposed a detailed theory of how subjects solve the problems, which assumes that subjects integrate information from two sources—evaluation processes (by which the problem solver examines the desirability of a move and its resulting state) and memory processes (by which the subject retrieves information about previous entries into a given problem state). The actual move-selection process is divided into three stages: consideration of acceptable moves, finding of a move leading to a new state, and an attempt to select an optimal move. A move can be found in any stage, leading to self-termination in the sequence of stages. Six information-processing parameters are specified, four of whose values are hypothesized to be common across variations of each task, and two of whose values are hypothesized to be specific to each task variant. Interestingly, the common parameters proved to have remarkably similar values when estimated separately for the two types of problems, suggesting that these parameters are remarkably stable across at least two basic types of MOVE problems.

Jeffries et al. (1977) and Atwood and Polson (1976) used computer simulation to estimate parameters and test their theory. The difference between mean numbers of predicted and observed moves was not significant in any experiment. In all comparisons, the theory appears to have given an excellent account of the data.

In their research, the authors followed most of the guidelines proposed earlier in this article. They started with a well-specified theory of problem solving. They then tested the theory against the data, and found that it could not be rejected (for group means, although it could be rejected for other statistics). They did not perform quantitative comparisons of their theory against any others, largely because theories proposed previously were not specified in the kind of detail that would have permitted such tests. They did perform qualitative comparisons with other theories, however, and these comparisons supported their own theory. The authors demonstrated the generality of the proposed theory by showing its applicability to two types of MOVE problems, and to variants of each problem type. Unfortunately, the authors did not compare parameter estimates for individuals to scores on any external measures. Such comparisons would have been most informative, however, as a means of determining which parameters of the theory capture those aspects of problem solving that contribute to general intelligence, and which capture aspects of problem solving that may be specific to MOVE or similar problems and not of much interest beyond such tasks. Comparisons of this kind could be readily carried out.

Computer simulation, as used by Polson and his colleagues, is immune to the specific criticisms of computer theories listed above, because computer simulation is used as a means of testing a theory rather than as a means of realizing a theory. Whereas a computer theory becomes inaccessible to the scientific public if it is literally embedded inside a computer, the present theory is not so embedded, and the authors provide sufficient information in their article for others to test and extend (or refute) the theory. It is clear from the presentation just what psychological claims are being made. The theory is parsimonious in its use of just six parameters to model performance on a complex task. Assumptions regarding the psychological origins of these parameters are plausible and not unreasonably complex. Finally, process-parameter estimates are provided, indeed, are calculated by computer.

Polson and his colleagues are by no means the first to use computer simulation as a means of testing a theory. I found their work to be particularly elegant, however, in a substantive domain (problem solving) and methodological domain (computer simulation) each of which historically has often lent itself to work lacking in elegance and certain kinds of simplicity. With the incorporation of differential techniques of external validation, the methodology employed could provide a fruitful way of studying intelligence.

Conclusions

The question for methodologists to address today seems not to be whether differential and information-processing approaches to intelligence should be combined, but rather how they should be combined. The four methodologies described above seem like promising starts in this direction, although in some cases I have taken the liberty of suggesting ways in which further integration (or in the case of Polson and his colleagues' research, any integration) might be obtained. Differential methodology by itself is inadequate: It fails to elucidate the processes and strategies that constitute a large part of what we mean by intelligence. Information-processing methodology by itself is inadequate: It does not provide a means for systematically studying correlates of individual differences in performance, and is particularly susceptible to overvaluation of processing components that are task-specific. The virtues of each methodology are the flaws of the other, so that a skillful synthesis of the two methodologies can offer considerable promise indeed.

GUIDELINES FOR SUBTHEORIES OF
INTELLIGENCE

Differential and cognitive psychologists have followed rather different strategies in theorizing about intelligence. Differential psychologists attempted to synthesize full-fledged theories of intelligence even from the earliest stages of research. Cognitive psychologists generally started with smaller subtheories of performance in particular tasks, or occasionally, classes of tasks (although there have been exceptions, such as Anderson, 1976). The direction in contemporary research integrating the differential and cognitive approaches seems to be toward subtheories of intelligence that are moderate in scope. These subtheories of intelligence take the form of theories of aspects of intelligence (such as reading, reasoning, spatial visualization, and the like) or of large chunks of each of these sets of behaviors. I will briefly describe in this section some guidelines for what ought minimally to be included in such theories.

Specification of Representation of Information

As its name implies, information-processing psychology has stressed detailed specification of the processes people exhibit in various kinds of behavior. Processes must act upon some kind of representation, however, and one cannot well understand information processing without understanding the representation(s) upon which the processes act. Nowhere has this been more clear than in the debate regarding the representations and processes used in solving transitive inference problems, where claims regarding representation and process have been interdependent without the relations between them being made clear (see Sternberg, in press-a, in press-b).

Information may be represented in different ways for different tasks, or for the use of different strategies in solving the same task, or for different stages of processing within a given strategy applied to a single task. Thus, there may be no point to debates regarding whether information is represented in a way that is discrete or continuous, imaginal or linguistic, like a network or set-theoretic. The distinctions are meaningful only in the context of particular processes applied to particular tasks solved by particular strategies.

Identification of Component Processes

Just as processes cannot be understood fully without understanding of the representation(s) upon which the processes act, so is the concept of representation incomprehensible without a specification of the processes acting upon the representation. Indeed, we have no experimental access to the form a representation might take except through the study of processes that act upon that representation. In a subtheory of intelligence, therefore, the theorist should identify a set of component processes that is sufficient to account for the domain of behavior under investigation.

Specification of Strategies for Combining Component Processes

In specifying one or more strategies by which subjects may combine component processes, the theorist must indicate both the order and mode of component execution. The specification of order must include a description of all branching points and feedback loops in the chain of command. The specification of mode must indicate whether processes are serial or parallel, exhaustive or self-terminating, and independent or dependent. These specifications, in turn, must be made both for combination of different component processes and for combination of multiple executions of the same component process.

Strategy for Combining Different Component Processes. Consider three different component processes, x, y, and z, used in the solution of some type of problem. The processes may be executed in any of 3! different orders. Moreover, the processes may be executed serially (for example, x, then y, then z), in parallel (x, y, and z occur simultaneously), or in some combination (for example, x and y occur simultaneously, followed by z). The processes may also be executed exhaustively (x, y, and z always performed) or with self-termination (for example, x and y always performed, but z performed only if x and y fail to yield a solution). Finally, execution of the processes may be independent (the occurrence of x is uncorrelated across item types with the occurrence of y, which is in turn uncorrelated across item types with the occurrence of z), dependent (x, y, and z always co-occur, so that their occurrences are perfectly correlated across item types), or partially dependent (x, y, and z tend to co-occur or not to co-occur across item types). Processes that are fully dependent will be confounded in parameter estimation procedures, since they cannot be disentangled.

Strategy for Combining Multiple Executions of the Same Component Process. Consider three repetitions of the same component process, x_1, x_2, and x_3 that occur during solution of some type of problem. The same distinctions that were discussed above for different component processes can be applied also to multiple executions of a single process. The same examples apply, except for the substitution of x_1, x_2, and x_3 for x, y, and z, respectively.

*Provision for Estimation of Component Latencies and
Difficulties*

A theory should be capable of specifying the latency and difficulty of each
component process, although such specification need not be made in
advance: Parameters corresponding to process latencies and difficulties will
usually be estimated from one's data. In some kinds of methodologies, such as
those deriving from the additive-factor method, it will be possible only to
specify the amount by which each experimental factor lengthens the latency
or increases the difficulty of each process, again by estimation of (contrast)
parameters from the data.

*Specification of Relations of Component Processes to Each
Other Across Subjects*

A theory should indicate which processes will demonstrate correlations
with each other across subjects in latency and difficulty. For example, if
processes x and y both operate upon a linguistic representation, and z
operates upon a spatial representation, or if processes x and y are both
encoding operations, and z is a feature-comparison operation, then one might
expect x and y to be correlated with each other but not with z. Note that this
aspect of the theory indicates dependence versus independence of processes
across subjects, whereas an aspect of the theory discussed above under the
heading of "strategy" indicated dependence versus independence of processes
across item types.

*Specification of Relations of Component Processes to
External Reference Abilities*

A theory should specify external reference abilities with which each
component process should and should not be correlated across subjects. For
example, if a process x involves selective encoding of letters presented in
strings, its latency should probably be correlated with scores on standardized
measures of perceptual speed, but not with (or only poorly with) scores on
standardized measures of letter-series extrapolation.

Conclusions

Six guidelines, including one subdivided one (for specification of strategy
or strategies), were proposed for adequate specification of a subtheory of
intelligence. Obviously, this is by no means an exhaustive list of guidelines for
"good" theories, but this seems like a reasonable minimal set. The reasons for
following these guidelines are much the same as those for following the

methodological guidelines proposed earlier (in particular, the minimization of the probability of Type II errors in research). If a theory can be shown to provide the required predictions, and to be successful in at least most of these predictions, then it seems like a good foundation upon which to build in further research. To the extent that a theory fails to make or makes incorrectly the required predictions, it seems less likely to provide a solid foundation.

A Brief Illustration of the Guidelines Applied to Research on Intelligence

I would have liked to have included here a section entitled "Promising Theories" that paralleled the earlier section entitled "Promising Method-ologies." The conspicuous absence of such a section is perhaps a reflection of two factors. First, research combining the differential and cognitive approaches to intelligence is of relatively recent origin, and so there has not been much time for cognitive-differential theories that inspire overwhelming confidence to develop. Second, and paradoxically in some respects, the success of extant methodologies can be gauged in part by the rate of turnover in theories. Differential methodology, for example, was ultimately unsuccess-ful in large part because it could spawn theories but not bury them.

Under the present circumstances, I will have to be content to present briefly an illustration of the proposed guidelines for theories. The illustration, my mixture theory of transitive inference mentioned earlier in the article, is described in detail elsewhere (Sternberg, in press-b). The theory has the desirable characteristic of being superior to other existing information-processing theories in making the predictions about data required by the guidelines; it has the undesirable characteristic of being wrong, that is, of being rejected in most comparisons against the true theory.

The theory, it will be recalled, applies to transitive inference problems such as "Joe is taller than Sam. Sam is taller than Ben. Who is tallest?" According to the theory, information about relations between terms is represented both in terms of linguistic deep structures and in terms of spatial arrays. Thus, "Joe is taller than Sam" would be represented, ultimately, both as (Joe is tall+; Sam is tall) and as $^{Joe}_{Sam}$. The theory specifies ten component processes that can be used in solving transitive inference problems, and is presented in two forms, as an information-processing flow chart and as a linear mathematical model. The flow chart specifies the strategy subjects are theorized to use in combining both different processes and multiple executions of the same processes. The linear model permits estimation of the durations and difficulties of some (but not all) of the processes subjects are theorized to use in solving the problems. According to the theory, component processes fall into two major classes, those that operate upon the linguistic representation and those that operate upon the spatial representation. Thus, it predicts that processes acting upon the linguistic representation will be intercorrelated across subjects; that processes acting upon the spatial representation will be intercorrelated across subjects; but that processes acting upon different representations will be intercorrelated only minimally, or not at all. Furthermore, it predicts that processes acting upon the linguistic representation will be correlated across subjects with tests of linguistic abilities but not of spatial abilities, and that processes acting upon the spatial representation will be correlated across subjects with tests of spatial abilities, but not of linguistic abilities. In general, the various predictions of the theory are borne out. Although the theory does not account for all of the reliable variance in the latency data, it does account for almost all of it. Error rates on transitive inference problems are low, so that the same kind of detailed model testing cannot be applied to the error data as can be applied to the latency data.

THE FUTURE OF RESEARCH ON INTELLIGENCE

My vision of the future of research on intelligence is component-centered. I believe our two major tasks will be to identify the components that constitute part of what we consider "intelligent behavior," and to discover relations between these components and other constructs.

Identification of the Components of Intelligence

Like Carroll (1976) and Simon (1976a), I foresee our compiling a relatively small catalogue of information-processing components that in various combinations account for performance on tasks requiring intelligence (see Sternberg, 1978d, for a description of my current partial catalogue). The catalogue will be a difficult one to compile. First, we wish it to include all those components, but only those components, that are psychologically interesting in the sense that they are general to a nontrivial class of tasks. There may well be a multitude of component processes that are specific to single tasks and minor variants of them. Such components will add bulk that is of little value to any general theory of intelligence. Second, we wish to include in our catalogue only those components that are nonredundant. In order to guard the uniqueness of each entry, we must take considerable care in our research to distinguish different components, on the one hand, from aliases of the same components, on the other. Our techniques for assessing the identity of processes across tasks are still being developed, and this development will prove increasingly more important as we generalize our theory to larger and larger classes of behavior. Third, we must seek a level for these elementary processes that strikes the proper balance between molecular and molar units of behavior. The level we choose to call "elementary" is arbitrary. Components, like factors, can probably be split almost indefinitely.

We need to find the point at which we start attaining diminishing returns, and avoid splitting processes beyond that point.

Relations of Components to Other Components

We will want to know the interrelations among components, both across tasks or item types within tasks, and across subjects. Indeed, we will need such information as a prerequisite for understanding the relations between components and other constructs, such as factors. General and large group factors arise, for example, when component processes that tend to cooccur across large classes of tasks are highly intercorrelated across subjects.

Relations of Components to Tasks

We will want in our catalogue a detailed index that specifies which components occur in the accomplishment of which tasks, meaning that we need a carefully constructed taxonomy of tasks. Interestingly, one of the first to appreciate this fully was Guilford (1967; Guilford & Hoepfner, 1971). On the one hand, Guilford's research has been highly susceptible to the pitfalls of differential methodology (see Sternberg, 1977b, pp. 31–32; Undheim & Horn, 1977). On the other hand, Guilford realized better than any other differential psychologist, and better than many information-processing psychologists, that a theory of tasks is prerequisite for a theory of intelligence. Carroll (1976) appropriately subtitled his article "A new 'structure of intellect,'" since it was certainly Guilford in his structure-of intellect model who began the careful faceted classification and cross-classification of tasks that is continuing today.

Relations of Components to Factors

We will also want in our catalogue a second detailed index, one that specifies which components constitute which factors (see Carroll, 1976). Any new theory of intelligence will have to subsume the factorial theories of the differentialists. I believe this can be done, because the factorial theories, at least in many cases, can be viewed as different perspectives on a single theory rather than as different theories. Much of the difference in perspectives derived from disagreements regarding the preferred rotation of factorial axes (see Sternberg, 1977b, pp. 24–25, 31–32). Thus, one might repeatedly see a single factorial space appearing under many different guises. I doubt there is any one rotation that is always preferred: The preferred rotation is a matter of convenience for a particular purpose. Through reference-ability modeling— the use of multiple regression to predict factor scores from component scores—the choice of factorial axes ceases to be a matter of much importance.

The true components can account for the obtained factors, regardless of which rotation is used.

Relations of Components to Strategies

Like Estes (1976), I doubt that intelligence can be equated with a set of component processes. Part of intelligent behavior is the selection and execution of strategies that optimize task performance. It is for this reason that a theory of intelligence must take care to specify in detail the strategy or strategies subjects use in solving various classes of problems. Whereas I have found individual differences in strategies to be minor in the reasoning tasks I have studied (Guyote & Sternberg, 1977; Sternberg, 1977a, in press-b; Sternberg & Rifkin, 1979), others have found them to be of major importance; for example, Simon (1976b) in his work on problem solving.

Relations of Components to Intelligence

Finally, we come to the most important relation of all, that of components to intelligence. Would an understanding of all of the above lead us to an understanding of intelligence? I would like to think so, but I feel obliged to interject a note of caution. In my own research, I have rather consistently found that the best predictor of scores on reference ability tests measuring significant aspects of intelligence is the residual or constant component, the component that is estimated as the intercept of a linear regression model after all of the slopes have been accounted for (see Sternberg, 1977a, b, for examples). Similar findings have been reported by others (Egan, 1977; Hunt, Lunneborg, & Lewis, 1975; Lunneborg, 1977). On the one hand, we can feel pleased to be rediscovering Spearman's g in information-processing terms. On the other hand, it is a sobering thought to realize that it is precisely this g that is unexplained by our models: We may not know just what it is any better than Spearman (1923) did a half-century ago. So, as we enter the second half-century following the publication of Spearman's landmark book, perhaps the first published work to adumbrate our current syntheses of differential and cognitive approaches to intelligence, we find our greatest challenge to be the same one that faced Spearman: to understand the nature of g.

REFERENCES

Anderson, J. R. *Language, memory, and thought.* Hillsdale, N.J.: Erlbaum, 1976.

Atwood, M. E., & Polson, P. G. A process model for water-jug problems. *Cognitive Psychology,* 1976, *8,* 191–216.

Calfee, R. C. Sources of dependency in cognitive processes. In D. Klahr (Ed.), *Cognition and instruction.* Hillsdale, N.J.: Lawrence Erlbaum, Assoc., 1976.

Carpenter, P. A., & Just, M. A. Sentence comprehension: A psycholinguistic processing model of verification. *Psychological Review,* 1975, *82,* 45–73.

Carroll, J. B. Psychometric tests as cognitive tasks: A new "structure of intellect." In L. B. Resnick (Ed.), *The nature of intelligence.* Hillsdale, N.J.: Erlbaum, 1976.

Chiang, A., & Atkinson, R. C. Individual differences and interrelationships among a select set of cognitive skills. *Memory and Cognition,* 1976, *4,* 661–672.

Clark, H. H., & Chase, W. On the process of comparing sentences against pictures. *Cognitive Psychology,* 1972, *3,* 472–517.

Egan, D. E. Characterizing spatial ability: Different mental processes reflected in accuracy and latency scores. Unpublished manuscript, 1977.

Estes, W. K. Intelligence and cognitive psychology. In L. Resnick (Ed.), *The nature of intelligence.* Hillsdale, N.J.: Lawrence Erlbaum Assoc., 1976.

Frederiksen, J. R. A chronometric study of component skills in reading. Unpublished manuscript, 1977.

Guilford, J. P. *The nature of human intelligence.* New York: McGraw-Hill, 1967.

Guilford, J. P., & Hoepfner, R. *The analysis of intelligence.* New York: McGraw-Hill, 1971.

Guyote, M. J., & Sternberg, R. J. A transitive-chain theory of syllogistic reasoning. NR 150–412 ONR Technical Reports No. 5. New Haven: Department of Psychology, Yale University, 1978.

Hays, W. L. *Statistics for the social sciences* (2nd ed.). New York: Holt, Rinehart, & Winston, 1973.

Hunt, E. B., Frost, N., & Lunneborg, C. L. Individual differences in cognition: A new approach to intelligence. In G. Bower (Ed.), *Advances in learning and motivation* (Vol. 7). New York: Academic Press, 1973.

Hunt, E., Lunneborg, C., & Lewis, J. What does it mean to be high verbal? *Cognitive Psychology,* 1975, *7,* 194–227.

Jeffries, R., Polson, P. G., Razran, L., & Atwood, M. E. A process model for missionaries-cannibals and other river-crossing problems. *Cognitive Psychology,* 1977, *9,* 412–440.

Jöreskog, K. G. A general approach to confirmatory maximum likelihood factor analysis. *Psychometrika,* 1969, *34,* 183–202. (a)

Jöreskog, K. G. Factoring the multitest-multioccasion correlation matrix. *Research Bulletin.* Princeton: Educational Testing Service, 1969. (b)

Jöreskog, K. G. A general method for analysis of covariance structures. *Biometrika,* 1970, *57,* 239–251.

Jöreskog, K. G., & Lawley, D. N. New methods in maximum likelihood factor analysis. *British Journal of Mathematical and Statistical Psychology,* 1968, *21,* 85–96.

Lunneborg, C. Choice reaction time: What role in ability measurement? *Applied Psychological Measurement,* 1977, *1,* 309–330.

Pachella, R. G. The interpretation of reaction time in information processing research. In B. Kantowitz (Ed.), *Human information processing: Tutorials in performance and cognition.* Hillsdale, N.J.: Erlbaum, 1974.

Resnick, L. B. (Ed.). *The nature of intelligence.* Hillsdale, N.J.: Erlbaum, 1976.

Rose, A. M. *Human information processing: An assessment and research battery.* Human Performance Center, University of Michigan Technical report, No. 46, January, 1974.

Schweickert, R. *A generalization of the additive factor method.* Michigan Mathematical Psychology Program Technical Report MMPP 77-2, March, 1977.

Simon, H. A. Identifying basic abilities underlying intelligent performance of complex tasks. In L. Resnick (Ed.), *The nature of intelligence.* Hillsdale, N.J.: Lawrence Erlbaum Assoc., 1976. (a)

Simon, H. A. Carl Hovland Memorial Lecture No. 1. Yale University, December, 1976. (b)

Spearman, C. *The nature of "intelligence" and the principles of cognition.* London: Macmillan, 1923.

Sternberg, R. J. Component processes in analogical reasoning. *Psychological Review*, 1977, *84*, 353–378. (a)

Sternberg, R. J. *Intelligence, information processing, and analogical reasoning: The componential analysis of human abilities.* Hillsdale, N.J.: Erlbaum, 1977. (b)

Sternberg, R. J. Componential investigations of human intelligence. In A. Lesgold, J. Pellegrino, S. Fokkema, & R. Glaser (Eds.), *Cognitive psychology and instruction.* New York: Plenum, 1978. (a)

Sternberg, R. J. Isolating the components of intelligence. *Intelligence,* 1978, *2*, 117–128. (b)

Sternberg, R. J. Toward a unified componential theory of human reasoning. NR150-412 ONR Technical Report No. 4. New Haven: Department of Psychology, Yale University, 1978. (c)

Sternberg, R. J. A proposed resolution of curious conflicts in the literature on linear syllogism. In R. Nickerson (Ed.), *Attention and performance VIII.* Hillsdale, N.J.: Lawrence Erlbaum Assoc., in press-a.

Sternberg, R. J. Representation and process in linear syllogistic reasoning. *Journal of Experimental Psychology: General,* in press-b.

Sternberg, R. J., & Nigro, G. The development of verbal relations in analogical reasoning. Unpublished manuscript, 1978.

Sternberg, R. J., & Rifkin, B. The development of analogical reasoning processes. *Journal of Experimental Child Psychology,* 1979, *27*, 195–232.

Sternberg, R. J., & Turner, M. Components of syllogistic reasoning. NR150-412 ONR Technical Report No. 6. New Haven: Department of Psychology, Yale University, 1978.

Sternberg, S. The discovery of processing stages: Extensions of Donders' method. *Acta Psychologica,* 1969, *30,* 276–315.

Terman, L. M., & Merrill, M. *Measuring intelligence.* Cambridge, Mass.: Riverside Press, 1937.

Undheim, J. O., & Horn, J. L. Critical evaluation of Guilford's structure-of-intellect theory. *Intelligence,* 1977, *1*, 65–81.

3

Cognitive Correlates and Components in the Analysis of Individual Differences

JAMES W. PELLEGRINO AND ROBERT GLASER
University of Pittsburgh

I. INTRODUCTION

There is a growing discontinuity between past and current thinking about the way in which individual differences should be viewed and assessed for the purposes of education. This conceptual break is mandated by social and scientific advances that now make it necessary and possible to understand the concepts of intelligence and aptitude in ways different from the past. The tradition of mental testing has been uniquely oriented toward the selection of individuals for instructional programs based upon the prediction of intellectual achievement. In contrast, present viewpoints emphasize that the significant use of measures of intelligence and aptitude is not primarily for the purposes of prediction, but for indicating how intellectual performance can be improved. This desired goal might be achieved if individual differences could be interpreted in terms of processes that enhance or retard cognitive performance. Conditions of education might then be implemented that adapt to these individual characteristics or directly or indirectly teach prerequisite cognitive performances that facilitate learning and development. Such practical benefits are the distant goals of the theory and laboratory investigations described in this paper. At the moment, it is possible to offer only a progress report. The work that we describe has been carried out during the last eight years in the attempt to characterize individual differences in terms of the hypothetical structures and processes emanating from the

Preparation of this paper was supported by funds provided by the Learning Research and Development Center, University of Pittsburgh, which is supported in part by the National Institute of Education, U.S. Department of Health, Education, and Welfare. The authors would like to express their appreciation to Jeffrey Bisanz for his helpful comments on an earlier version of this manuscript that was presented at the American Educational Research Association meetings, 1977.

theoretical and empirical study of human cognition and cognitive development.

The purpose of this paper is to provide a temporary framework that describes the work that has been conducted. This framework emphasizes a contrast between two different approaches to the experimental analysis of individual differences. We will consider the research tactics, empirical findings and theoretical outcomes of each approach. Both approaches are currently popular, but careful analysis leads us to the conclusion that one way of proceeding incorporates the other, avoids the explanatory inadequacy of correlational methods, and has the theoretical power to model individual differences on various dimensions of cognitive functioning.

In the field as it now exists, the two general approaches that can be identified will be called the *cognitive correlates* approach and the *cognitive components* approach. The cognitive correlates approach seeks to specify the information processing abilities that are differentially related to high and low levels of aptitude. Tests of aptitude or intelligence are used to identify subgroups that are compared on laboratory tasks that have cognitive processing characteristics defined by prior experimental investigation. The cognitive components approach is task analytic and attempts to directly identify the information processing components of performance on tasks that have been generally used to assess mental abilities. Performance on standardized tests of aptitude and intelligence becomes the object of theoretical and empirical analysis, and the goal is to develop models of task performance and apply such models to individual differences analysis.

The two approaches are tied to prevalent theories of human cognition, and both attempt to understand the mental activities that contribute to individual differences as measured by psychometric instruments. In the cognitive correlates approach, the questions being asked are of the form "What does it mean to be high verbal?" and the answers are sought in the attempt to link the experimental tasks and paradigms used in the investigation of cognition with psychometric test score classification. For the task analytic approach, the questions being asked are of the form "What do intelligence tests test?" and the answers are sought through rational and empirical analyses of the information processing demands of the specific tasks that comprise these tests. Having derived models for task performance, it is then possible to investigate sources of individual differences that contribute to the assessment of mental abilities and to test item characteristics.

Our discussion is organized in terms of these two approaches. Within the correlational approach, we examine research on the correlates of verbal aptitude and general intelligence measures. Within the task analytical approach, we concentrate on the analysis of the performance components of tasks commonly found on both individual and group standarized tests—in particular, memory span, spatial visualization, and inductive reasoning tasks.

II. THE COGNITIVE CORRELATES APPROACH

An Overview of Experimental Findings

The cognitive correlates approach is best typified by the work of Earl Hunt and his colleagues (Hunt, Frost, & Lunneborg, 1973; Hunt, Lunneborg, & Lewis, 1975; Hunt & Lansman, 1975; Hunt, 1976, 1978). This research has been set in the context of a general model of memory that depicts the flow of information through a series of sensory buffers into a short-term memory, and then through an intermediate-term memory into a long-term memory. An executive system controls the flow of information and has access to the various levels of memory storage (Hunt, 1971, 1973). With this model as a frame of reference, Hunt has asked a series of questions about the differences between high and low verbal ability groups that relate to structures, processes, and parameters of the information processing system.

The intent of this work has been to show that verbal intelligence as measured by conventional means is related to key variables studied in a modern theory of cognition, particularly the parameters of models that describe the transformation of information in short- and long-term memory. An extensive series of experiments has suggested that university students who score high on a verbal ability college entrance examination show, in contrast to lower scoring individuals, faster performance on tasks that require accessing information in long-term memory and manipulating information in short-term memory. Specifically, this performance included: (a) the ability to make a rapid conversion from a physical representation of a letter to a higher level code as indicated in the Posner, Boies, Eichelman, and Taylor (1969) letter matching paradigm; (b) the ability to retain the order of information in short-term memory, such as indicated by the Peterson and Peterson (1959) immediate serial recall task; and (c) the ability to manipulate rapidly data in STM, as indicated by the Sternberg (1966, 1969) scanning task. In general, Hunt and his co-workers conclude that verbal intelligence tests *directly* tap a person's knowledge of language, such as the meaning of words, syntactic rules, and semantic relations between concepts denoted by words, and that these tests also *indirectly* assess the information processing capacities that are fundamental elements in experimental studies of memory.

Although the results obtained by Hunt and his colleagues provide strong suggestions of basic information processing differences between high and low verbal ability groups, subsequent research has not presented so simple and consistent a picture. A study by Chiang and Atkinson (1976) failed to find any significant relationship between short-term memory processing speed and verbal SAT scores for a combined group of male and female college students. A relationship only appeared when the males and females were examined separately. The data for males replicated the Hunt et al. results, while the data for the females showed the opposite relationship—women with high SAT scores showed slower processing rates. These data make it difficult to draw a general conclusion about verbal ability and information processing speed in short-term memory. (See Snow [1978] for a more detailed discussion of these data.)

Additional constraints on the generality of the initial findings also appear as a function of cognitive development. Keating and Bobbitt (1977) administered the Posner et al. letter identification tasks and the Sternberg memory scanning task to children at three age levels—9, 13, and 17. Each group consisted of half males and half females of either average or above average mental ability as defined by scores on the Raven Progressive Matrices test. Proficiency as a function of age was indicated for the Posner et al. task; neither task was differentially related to the sex variable; and both tasks were performed faster by the high ability groups. However, Keating and Bobbitt particularly emphasize a nearly significant age-by-ability interaction for the slope parameter of the Sternberg task. High ability groups appeared to be functioning at the near adult level as early as 9 years old, whereas the average ability groups achieved that level only by age 17. These data suggest that the relationship between intelligence score and cognitive processing variables may change as a function of developmental level and this interaction must be considered when investigating ability differences in cognitive processes.

Task characteristics further complicate the interpretation of the finding that high verbal ability students are faster in accessing name codes in long-term memory. Recent research conducted by Bisanz and Resnick (1978; Resnick, Danner, & Bisanz, 1977) points out some potential limits of this relationship (see also Hogaboam & Pellegrino, 1978). Instead of the letter stimuli used by Hunt, picture stimuli were employed in a similar matching task. These picture stimuli did not show any systematic change in long-term memory access speed across developmental level or with intelligence test score. The source of the discrepancy between these findings with pictures and the Hunt et al. result with letters may lie in the differences between processing verbal and nonverbal material (perhaps related to verbal and nonverbal factors of intelligence). Support for this hypothesized processing difference comes from a second experiment carried out on the same individuals, but examining processing speed for verbal material (Bisanz & Resnick, 1978). The results showed a relationship between letter identification speed and differences in age and verbal intelligence scores. The pattern of results obtained in the foregoing studies suggests a processing difference between verbal and nonverbal material. Symbolic input in the form of letters shows both developmental and ability level differences in the speed of accessing name codes in long-term memory, while pictorial input fails to show any such differences. Hence, it might be concluded that individual differences in verbal aptitude and general verbal intelligence reflect the ability to process rapidly abstract symbolic input—specifically, to manipulate the verbal and numerical symbol systems that may underlie differences in the academic performances that depend quite heavily on these symbol systems. The results pertaining to pictorial or nonverbal input remain less clear.

Differences between verbal and nonverbal processing may also enter into explanations of individual differences in preferred cognitive strategies for performing a task. Hunt (1978) reports a number of studies on the Clark and Chase (1972) picture-sentence verification paradigm. In an initial study (Hunt, et al., 1975), it was found that high verbal college students were less affected by increases in task complexity than lower verbal students, suggesting that the sentence verification task was an important cognitive correlate that could be used in the analysis of verbal aptitude. Upon further investigation, however, the situation turned out to be more complicated.

Several models for the sentence verification task have been proposed—the most detailed one being the "constituent comparison model" by Carpenter and Just (1975). In essence, this model assumes that knowledge representations in the form of verbal propositions are derived from the pictorial image and the sentence and then compared on a constituent-by-constituent basis. Each sequence of constituent comparisons is called a scan, and different tasks of varying complexity require a different number of scans. Similar to the reasoning involved in the Sternberg search task, it is assumed that each scan takes a constant time so that an individual's scan speed can be estimated by the slope parameter of the function relating reaction time across conditions of task complexity. This slope parameter was used in a study by MacLeod, Hunt, and Mathews (in press) as a cognitive correlate for analyzing individual differences in test scores. For group data, the slope parameter correlated –.31 with the Nelsen–Denny test of reading comprehension and –.33 with the WPCT verbal composite score indicating faster scan times for individuals with higher test scores.

When the fit of the Carpenter and Just model to individual data was examined, however, it was found that out of 70 subjects, 43 were "well described" by the Carpenter and Just model and 16 were "ill described" by it. In contrast to the verbal processing model of Carpenter and Just, the latter group was better fit by a model that assumed a visual processing strategy in solving the picture-sentence verification task. When the verbal and spatial ability scores of the two groups were examined, verbal ability scores were more highly correlated with the verification reaction times than were spatial ability scores in the verbal-model group, while the reverse was true for the visual-model group. The conclusion drawn from this investigation clearly points to a difficulty in applying the cognitive correlates approach to the analysis of individual differences. As Hunt (1978) writes:

On the other hand, before sentence comprehension can be treated as a test of information processing, we must be sure that the subjects are indeed treating the task as a verbal one. This observation raises an important point. Process measurements are defined relative to a particular model. If information-processing theories are to be applied to the analysis of individual differences, we must know which models apply to which individuals. (p. 124)

Multiple Dimensions of Analyses

Consideration of other dimensions of performance is demanded by the fact that simple processing speed is only one of several cognitive components of complex tasks. Many memory and problem solving tasks depend on the use of higher level executive strategies that facilitate the appropriate sequencing of basic processing activities and the activation and manipulation of memory codes. The speed, efficiency, or automaticity of these operations may contribute substantially to individual differences in performance, particularly since increases in task complexity involve increased demands upon limited memory space and processing resources. In handling complexity, the speed of performing certain operations as well as the coordination of these activities can combine to affect performance substantially. Thus, it becomes important to raise questions about individual differences in the functioning of the "executive routines" that have achieved a central status in most cognitive theories. The importance of the executive routines is further highlighted by the literature on the nature of memory development. One of the things that seems to change most with age is the spontaneous implementation of mnemonic strategies, a change ascribed to the development of more task appropriate and flexible executive routines. While the efficiency of a process may improve with age or development, major changes also seem to take place in the executive control over the use of these cognitive strategies.

The analysis of processing speed, content knowledge, and executive strategies of high and low aptitude groups suggests a rather extensive program of research with many questions and few currently available answers in the context of the cognitive correlates approach. The tasks that are chosen for study in future research should be determined both by current cognitive theory and by the analysis of psychometric test items. The results of the cognitive correlates approach can only become meaningful when they can be mapped back onto the tests that have been used to identify subgroups of individuals. If high and low aptitude groups are found to differ on a variety of basic cognitive processes, the further requirement is to demonstrate how these processes are directly or indirectly tapped by the tasks found on psychometric tests. Such a mapping process requires the direct analysis of components of performance on psychometric tasks.

In a recent article, Hunt (1978) has supported the foregoing view of the complex of factors apparently required to account for individual differences in cognition. He suggests three different sources: knowledge, information-free mechanistic processes, and general strategies. The effect of knowledge has been minimized or held constant in the work on cognitive correlates of aptitude. The mechanics of information processing are divided by Hunt into two components—automatic and controlled attention-demanding processes. Hunt suggests that the automatic processes appear to be stable individual traits, particularly over the wide range represented by brain-damaged and retardate groups through high verbal ability adults and outstanding mnemonists. The controlled processes are more labile and thus are not effective long-term predictors of cognitive performance. General strategies include such cognitive performances as rehearsal strategies and the metacognitive activities involved in problem solving.

Our own view of what will contribute to a major proportion of the variance in cognitive abilities in the population of individuals generally involved in the normal course of schooling stems from what is known about the development of the basic processes of memory. These processes improve as a child develops, asymptote with maturity, and show a high degree of automaticity. It is our hypothesis that individual differences after maturity will not be manifested primarily by these automatic processes, but more by the executive processes to which we have previously alluded. Individual differences in these executive processes interact with differences in content knowledge that includes task specific strategies.

Finally, in assessing the utility of the cognitive correlates approach, one must focus upon the goal of the enterprise. It is pointed out (Hunt, 1978) that research on the analysis of aptitude can complement and may contribute to psychometric endeavors such as the prediction of intellectual performance in specific situations. However, to our way of thinking, the cognitive correlates approach will not influence the design of new testing practices so long as the new tests are designed to play the same roles as the tests now in use. Even if the goals of intelligence testing were reoriented so that they did not emphasize prediction and classification, but focused on the assessment of cognitive competence thereby providing a basis for improving intellectual performance, the cognitive correlates approach, as so far pursued, would be doing only part of the task required. The more complete task is to understand the nature of the human behavior that has been labeled intelligence and aptitude and to use this understanding to optimize the human performances associated with them. An initial step toward this goal is to attempt to understand the performance assessed on tasks that have been used to measure intelligence and aptitude in order to explain their correlations with criterion performances used to establish test validity. This requires the analysis of test tasks and criterion performances that reflect individual differences in both the content of knowledge and the processes by which this knowledge is remembered, organized, and utilized.

The cognitive correlates approach discussed in this section appears to have been only a starting tactic that has been useful to the extent that it has uncovered the complexities involved in individual differences analyses. The cognitive correlate studies, however, are incomplete in that they lead to an overemphasis on the "mechanics of thought" and return us to the position of Galton who attempted to measure simple sensory capacities and related psychological processes. These measures proved to be of little practical utility, and Binet found it necessary on the basis of strictly empirical findings to move on to more complex and content specific tasks. For further progress, it now seems necessary to avoid a neo-Galtonian approach and instead pursue a direct analysis of the cognitive components of performance in tasks that have been used to assess mental abilities. It is toward this sort of direct analysis that we now turn.

III. THE COGNITIVE COMPONENTS APPROACH

Additional argument for a direct analysis of the cognitive components of performance on aptitude and intelligence tests has been provided by Estes (1974):

> Rather than looking to learning or physiological theory for some correlate of intelligence, I should like to focus attention on intellectual activity itself. By bringing the concepts and methods of other disciplines to bear on the analysis of intellectual behavior we may come to understand how the conditions responsible for the development of its constituent processes and the manner of their organization lead to variations in effectiveness of intellectual functioning. If this approach has appeal in principle, we need next to consider just what behaviors to analyze in order to be sure that the activity we are dealing with is closely related to that involved in the measurement of intelligence. The simplest and most direct approach, it seems, is to begin with the specific behaviors involved in responding to items on intelligence tests. (pp. 742–743)

Current analyses of the cognitive components of test performance range from broad analyses of many tests to more specific and detailed models for performance on a single item type. The methods for analysis similarly range from intuitive analyses through computer simulation, protocol analysis, and mathematical modeling with many combinations of these various methods. Carroll (1976) has attempted a rational analysis of the cognitive components of individual differences as measured by 74 tests constituting 24 factors in the French, Ekstrom, and Price (1963) Kit of Reference Tests for Cognitive Factors. The theoretical framework in which these tests were analyzed was the same memory model adopted by Hunt. Carroll developed a uniform system for classifying the characteristics of the tasks represented by the items of each test. The classificatory scheme included the types of stimuli presented, the kinds of overt responses that were required, the sequencing of subtasks within the task, and the cognitive operations and strategies that Carroll, conceiving himself as a subject, would employ in performing the test tasks. He considered the cognitive operations and strategies that would probably be employed in a central executive processor and the types of memory that would probably be involved in storage, search, and retrieval operations. Carroll then used his classification scheme as a basis for specifying the potential sources of individual differences for each of the 24 cognitive factors.

Illustrative examples of Carroll's analysis include the factors of memory span, spatial orientation, and induction. Tasks related to these psychometric factors have been theoretically and empirically investigated, as will be discussed shortly. Carroll concluded that memory span involves the storage and retrieval of information in short-term memory, with capacity limitation as the primary individual difference variable, although strategies of chunking or grouping that extend capacity may be helpful to some individuals. With respect to spatial orientation, Carroll hypothesized that tasks representing this factor involve processes of mental rotation within short-term visual memory. Individual differences in such tasks may depend on the capacity of short-term memory, and the rate at which the process of mental rotation can be performed. For the factor of induction, he argued that this involves

> searching for relevant hypothesis in...LTM....Success would depend primarily on whether the contents of this store are adequate to yield solution to the problem. Some subjects, however, might adopt the possibly helpful strategy of performing serial operations with STM contents to construct new hypotheses. (p. 50)

Carroll's analysis of the cognitive components of individual differences is global and speculative, as he himself admits, but it illustrates the possible application of cognitive theory in order to generate hypotheses about psychologically meaningful process differences between individuals. This is a preliminary step and what must follow are empirical tests. For this purpose, the hypotheses must become more refined; the precision that is required can come about through attempts to construct and validate performance models for specific tasks. Such modeling has been attempted within both computer simulation and experimental psychological frameworks. In the discussion that follows, we outline theoretical and empirical studies of performance on tasks representing the three psychometric factors mentioned above. We proceed from simple to more complex tasks. The elements contributing to this ordering of tasks represent (a) the degree of involvement of multiple elementary processes, strategic processes, executive functions, and factual knowledge as potential sources of individual differences; and (b) the extent to which a particular psychometric factor is represented by multiple task forms and/or content stimuli. These two sets of factors dictate an organization in which we consider: memory span, measured by simple digit span tasks; spatial visualization, measured by two-dimensional and three-dimensional rotation tasks; and inductive reasoning, measured by series completion and analogy tasks.

STUDIES OF MEMORY SPAN

An obvious test associated with immediate memory capability is the simple memory span task that appears on individual intelligence tests such as the Stanford–Binet and Wechsler tests. The prototypical example of this task is the digit span task which requires an individual to serially recall an ordered list of simple digits. Large individual and developmental differences can be obtained in this task, and the predominant interpretation of such differences has been that they reflect basic differences in short-term memory capacity and/or in the use of mnemonic strategies such as rehearsal or chunking. Such an interpretation has considerable appeal since it readily maps onto information processing models of the human memory system, particularly onto the distinction in such models between structural aspects of the system and control processes or executive routines (e.g., Atkinson & Shiffrin, 1968).

A number of investigators have recently raised questions about the appropriate interpretation of individual differences in such span tasks, particularly in terms of the capacity of short-term or working memory (e.g., Chi, 1976, 1977; Estes, 1974; Huttenlocher & Burke, 1976; Lyon, 1975). In a discussion of the digit span task, Estes (1974) pointed out a number of potential sources of individual differences. For example, young or mentally retarded children might fail the task because of insufficient familiarity with the sequence of ordinal numbers, or because of inexperience in using number sequences to order materials. Individuals also might differ in their tendency to use grouping strategies and in the skills of selective inhibition necessary for appropriate ordering of output.

Such sources of influence upon performance seem to be strongly implicated when one observes age differences in memory span performance as assessed in a variety of span or serial retention tasks with digits and other materials. In a review of age differences in memory span, Chi (1976) argued that there is no clear evidence to support the conclusion that the capacity of short-term memory changes with age. Part of this argument is based upon the fact that situations showing developmental changes in memory span confound capacity estimates with familiarity of content material and with the probable use of mnemonic strategies such as rehearsal, recoding, and grouping. In a subsequent series of experiments (Chi, 1977), she concluded that:

> The level of recall in adults' performance is greatly influenced by the number of processing strategies made available to them. Furthermore, it takes children longer to encode a stimulus to a level that is accessible to processing strategies. This retardation in the speed

of information processing may result from limitations in their semantic and recognition networks. All these factors collectively contribute to the commonly observed age difference in memory span. (p. 20)

A similar conclusion has been tentatively suggested by Lyon (1975, 1977) with respect to individual differences in digit span performance for a college age sample. In addressing the question of why individuals differ in digit span size, Lyon (1975) conducted a series of experiments in which the use of strategies such as the probability of rehearsal and the use of grouping were controlled. The result was that neither of these factors substantially reduced the variation in individual differences in performance, despite the fact that absolute levels of performance changed as a function of the experimental conditions. In an additional experiment, Lyon showed that digit span performance had no substantial relationship to the rate of reading information out of short-term memory. Currently, Lyon is pursuing the possiblity that adult individual differences in digit span may be partially due to the speed with which stimuli can be identified. Such a possibility is consistent with the developmental data of Chi (1977) and the previously discussed data of Hunt et al. (1973) showing that high verbal college students may be faster at accessing codes in long-term memory.

The experimental analysis of memory span performance within an information processing framework is helping to delimit the potential sources of individual differences within this seemingly simple task. This work has also served to point out the complexities and the myriad possibilities involved in the search for cognitive components of individual differences. The question being asked is: To what extent is digit span performance a function of structural changes that may be related to developmental level and degree of retardation, and to what extent is it a function of developing abilities in mnemonic processing strategies? To date, an interpretation solely in terms of processing strategies appears to be ruled out by studies that have trained individuals to use rehearsal and grouping strategies, and failed as yet to influence significantly developmental and individual differences in performance (e.g., Butterfield, Wambold, & Belmont, 1973; Huttenlocher & Burke, 1976).

At a general level, the analysis of memory span performance reflects the multiple dimensions of analysis problem referred to earlier. Difficulties arise when multiple and interactive levels of processing can determine task performance. To date, experiments designed to understand differences in memory span have independently manipulated factors operating at only one level. This tactic implicitly assumes independent and additive contributions of the various processes and strategies that may be involved, and these assumptions may not be warranted. Related to this problem, and perhaps the cause of it, is the absence of detailed and adequately validated models of task performance. Progress in understanding individual differences in aptitude task performance is precluded in the absence of adequate performance models that can provide the context for individual differences analyses. Adequate models go beyond the informal level of designating possible components of performance. They provide detailed specifications of the intellectual functions required by a task such as declarative and procedural knowledge, memory demands, and processing strategies. Initial attempts at formulating and applying such models are considered in the context of spatial aptitude and inductive reasoning tasks.

STUDIES OF SPATIAL TRANSFORMATION

Spatial ability is frequently assessed by speeded tests in which an individual must decide about the identity of two-dimensional or three-dimensional figures by mentally rotating and comparing one or more of the figures in a comparison set. Psychometric and experimental variations of this task primarily involve manipulations of the type of figures to be rotated and compared, e.g., asymmetric alphanumeric characters, simple and complex two-dimensional shapes, and three-dimensional block configurations as shown in Figure 1. An extensive analysis of performance in this type of "mental rotation" task has been carried out by Shepard and his colleagues (e.g., Cooper & Shepard, 1973; Metzler & Shepard, 1974; Shepard, 1975). The typical finding in such studies is that the time to decide that two stimuli are identical is a linear function of the number of degrees of angular disparity between target and standard, as shown in Figure 1. The linearity of the function is presumed to result from an internal process of mental rotation of a visual stimulus representation. This process is an analog of the process of actual physical rotation. The time to complete such a mental or physical rotation depends upon the distance or degrees of rotation.

Two-Dimensional Rotation

Attempts to construct information processing models that represent performance in this type of task indicate that there may be important differences in the processing of simple two-dimensional vs. three-dimensional stimuli. The differences in the processes required for each of these two forms of the task are subtle and their existence is overshadowed by the fact that performance is always a linear function of the angular disparity between stimuli being compared. In the case of processing two-dimensional stimuli such as alphanumeric characters, it is assumed that there is an initial encoding process followed by rotation and comparison processes with subsequent decision and response processes. The linear function obtained for group and individual subject data has an intercept parameter that presumably reflects

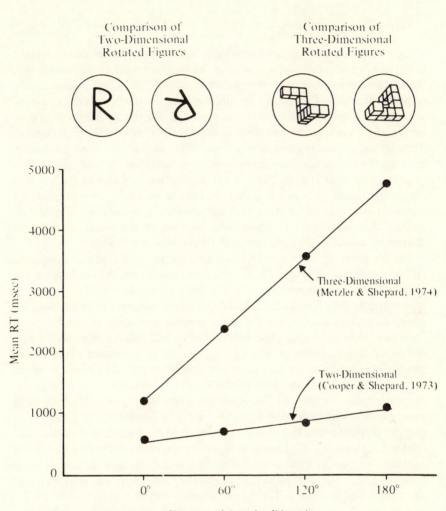

FIG. 1 Example stimuli and results from studies examining the speed of mental rotation of two- and three-dimensional stimuli.

the base speed of the encoding and decision-response processes. The slope parameter is interpreted as representing the speed of the rotation process. Individual differences may exist in either or both of these parameters, but there have been few systematic attempts to explore the precise locus of individual differences in this task. It is likely, however, that individual differences are localized within such speed parameters, and data provided by Egan (1978) indicate differences in the intercept parameter associated with coding and decision-response processes.

73

Three-Dimensional Rotation

Aspects of task performance with three-dimensional stimuli can be related
to the same processing model applied to the data for two-dimensional stimuli.
Given the assumption that the intercept reflects encoding and decision-
response processes, then intercept differences across the two types of stimuli,
as shown in Figure 1, are readily interpreted as increments in encoding time
for the more complex three-dimensional stimuli. Problems begin to appear
when consideration is given to the large differences in the slope parameter
between the two- and three-dimensional stimulus types. The differences that
exist indicate that the process of mental rotation is different for the two
classes of stimuli. It is possible that the time to rotate an internal stimulus
representation is some function of the dimensional properties of the stimulus,
and/or that additional processes are involved in the rotation task that
contribute to the slope parameter for three-dimensional stimuli.

The latter interpretation is supported by the work of Just and Carpenter
(1976; Carpenter & Just, 1978). They examined eye movements in the
performance of the mental rotation task with three-dimensional block stimuli
of the type used by Shepard and Metzler. The eye movement and latency data
allowed them to decompose the total process into a set of subprocesses,
including an initial search process in which an individual attempts to locate
corresponding elements of the two figures to be compared. This search
process was followed by transformation and comparison processes which
included rotation of one part of the figures followed by a confirmation
process applied to the remaining parts of the two figures. Each of these
processes showed general monotonic increases in time as a function of
angular disparity, and thus each contributed to the overall slope value. The
Just and Carpenter (1976) analysis of performance thus indicates a number of
potential sources of individual differences, and these include not only the
speed of executing each process, but also the organization or sequencing of
the total set of processes. This work makes available a performance model
and an analytic scheme, but no systematic studies of individual differences
have yet been conducted.

Related Tasks

The spatial visualization requirements of the tasks described above are
illustrative of the processing demands of tasks commonly used to measure
spatial aptitude. Other related tasks include block design and assembly and
mental paper folding. These tasks vary in the extent to which they involve
small to large sets of basic processes that can be organized into generally
applicable routines for task execution with few performance options as
opposed to complex interactive strategies with varying options available in

the composition, execution, and sequencing of component processes. Some of these tasks such as paper folding have been subjected to chronometric (e.g., Shepard & Feng, 1972) and eye movement analyses (e.g., Snow, 1978), but there is currently insufficient data to pinpoint the sources of individual differences.

Analyses of spatial tasks similar to those just discussed have been carried out by Cooper (1978). This work seems to indicate that individual differences in spatial processing are also associated with various strategies of information processing such that different models of task performance fit different individuals. Thus, currently available data imply that individual differences exist not only in process speed, but also in the strategy for task execution as well as the nature of the internal representation or code established by an individual (e.g., Egan, 1978).

STUDIES OF INDUCTIVE REASONING

Series Extrapolation

There are two common types of test items that belong to the subclass of tasks generally identified with the factor of inductive reasoning—a factor that Thurstone and Thurstone (1941) suggested might be identified with Spearman's g. These are series completion items and analogy items as shown in Figure 2. Series completion items are found at several age levels on many standardized aptitude tests. Items of this kind may be represented as letter series, number series, picture series, or abstract geometric form series. In all cases, the task structure is the same, such that the elements comprising the series are ordered according to some specific interitem relationships and the individual's task is to extract the basic relationships and generate the next item(s) in the series. Simon and Kotovsky (1963; Kotovsky & Simon, 1973) have carried out a detailed protocol analysis and computer simulation of performance on letter series problems of the type used by Thurstone and Thurstone in their factorial studies of intelligence.

An important aspect of the Simon and Kotovsky analysis is the separation of two contributing aspects of performance, namely, content or declarative knowledge and processes or procedural knowledge. Content refers to the basic knowledge that must be available in long-term memory, and process refers to the specific operations or strategies that utilize this knowledge base. Successful performance implies that the necessary information or semantic knowledge is both available and accessible to an individual, and that the component processes that manipulate this information are also available and successfully executed. Deficient performance can result from inadequacies in one or both of these aspects. Thus, it is important to recognize a distinction

ITEM FORM	ITEM DESCRIPTION
Letter Series Extrapolation	
axbxcxd _ _ _ _	period length two; next and identity relations; one memory placekeeper required
qzhrrahqsb _ _ _ _	period length four; next, next, identity, and backwards next relations; three memory placekeepers required
Geometric Analogy	
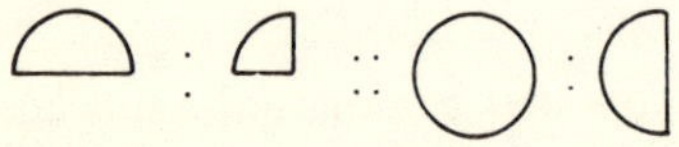	one element (semicircle), one transformation (halving)
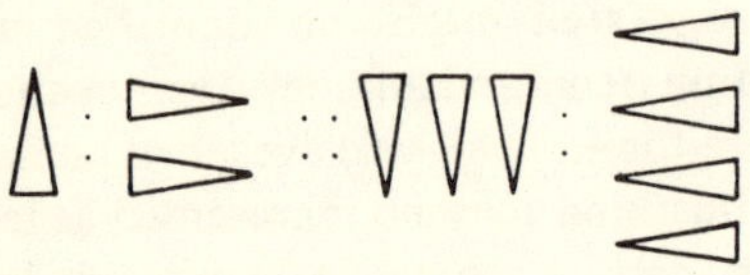	one element (triangle), two transformations (90° clockwise rotation, addition of same element)
Verbal Analogy	
Arm : Elbow :: Leg :	part - whole & function; high semantic constraint
Profit : Selling :: Fame :	effect - cause; low semantic constraint
Iron : Steel :: Sand :	conversion; low semantic constraint

FIG. 2 Examples of the different item forms used to assess inductive reasoning. Item descriptions are in terms of the relational content or features that must be processed and held in memory.

between semantic or declarative knowledge and operations or procedural knowledge.

The semantic knowledge base required for letter series items is limited to information about the alphabet and three basic relations among individual letters. These three relations are identify (identical letters), next (the next letter), and backwards next or reverse alphabetical ordering. Thus, since the letter series task requires only knowing the alphabet and does not require an extensive declarative knowledge component, it would not be expected that the knowledge base would be an individual difference factor. Given that the appropriate letter knowledge is available, the completion of any letter series problem then requires: (a) determining the interletter relations within the problem; (b) using this information to extract period length, i.e., the regularity with which a relation or break in a relation occurs within the problem; (c) generation of a pattern description or rule that involves assembling information about both the relations and the periodic structure of the problem; and (d) extrapolation or continuation of the series based upon the pattern description that is held in memory. Individual differences in performance on specific letter series problems can result from differences in the performance of any or all of these component processes.

Available data on problem difficulty in adults, adolescents, and children suggest that differences may exist as a function of the kind of interletter relation involved—identity generally is an easier relationship than next which is easier than backwards next. Individual differences may also exist as a function of increases in period length and rule complexity. In various types of test items, the type of relation, the periodic structure, and the working memory requirements associated with each problem are highly correlated with the item difficulty (see Kotovsky & Simon, 1973, Table 4). The role of such factors in contributing to item difficulty can be seen by comparing the two series problems in Figure 2.

The Simon and Kotovsky simulation provides a good fit to adult performance and hence provides a partial validation of the model. In our own laboratory, we have been concerned with yet another way in which such models can be validated and perhaps eventually applied. Our reasoning is as follows: If the processes embodied in a simulation model are similar to those used by humans, then the processes identified may be trainable for individuals whose performance represents a low or intermediate level of task competency. Such training should facilitate performance in both a quantitative and qualitative manner. Indeed, in a study conducted by Holzman, Glaser, and Pellegrino (1976), we were able to show substantial gains in performance for children from grades 1 to 6 after training on only the initial two component processes specified by the model—the two being the detection of interletter relations and the discovery of periodicity. As a result of brief training, children at each of the age levels acquired an information management strategy that frequently allowed them to reach perfect solutions even on difficult problems.

Certainly, many questions remain to be answered with respect to the question of individual differences in series completion performance and the extent to which performance can be improved by specific process training. The type of analyses that we have described, however, suggests how one might begin to examine psychometric test performance toward the goal of diagnosing the sources of cognitive process deficiencies with subsequent attempts to develop appropriate cognitive strengths.

In the course of this type of analysis, it is constantly necessary to question the generality of the processes being postulated. After all, we have only looked at one representative type of inductive reasoning task. It is, therefore, important to ask what relevance the processes of relation detection, discovery of periodicity, pattern description generation, and extrapolation may have outside the domain of letter series problems or series problems in general. It is possible that these processes apply to the large group of test tasks including analogy problems and matrix problems, all of which load on the same psychometric factor called induction or inductive reasoning. Recently, Greeno (1978) has argued for such generality:

> The psychological process of solving any analogy or series extrapolation problem involves identifying relations among components and fitting the relations together in a pattern. These processes of apprehending relations and constructing an integrated representation are the main processes involved in understanding. (p. 243)

Obviously, a substantial amount of work must be done to provide empirical support for such an argument. If it is the case that we are dealing with general processes that apply across a wide range of content domains and task forms, then influencing cognitive competence in a wide range of situations will be a viable possibility. That we can even begin to raise the question of such a possibility will, in large part, stem from task analytic work that identifies common processes over a variety of inductive reasoning tasks.

Analogy Solution

Of the many tasks that are assumed to assess inductive reasoning on psychometric tests, the analogy problem is the most pervasive. Analogy items have constituted a significant portion of intelligence test items over the course of the entire testing movement. Burt introduced the task in 1911. Thurstone, Otis, and Thorndike all included analogy items on tests published in 1919, at which time Thorndike introduced the nonverbal, geometric analogy. Examples of the centrality of this type of reasoning with respect to the concept and measurement of intelligence can be found in the writings of individuals such as Spearman and Raven. The experimental analysis of the component cognitive processes involved in analogical reasoning has only recently become a major area of investigation.

A significant attempt to develop and verify process models for performance on a variety of analogical reasoning tasks has been provided by Sternberg (1977). He has proposed a componential theory of analogical reasoning that specifies several processes that may apply across all analogical reasoning tasks. The component processes include: (a) encoding the individual terms of the analogy; (b) inferring the relationship between the first two terms; (c) mapping the relationship between the first and third terms; (d) applying the results of the inference and mapping processes to the third term to generate an ideal fourth term which is then used to evaluate the several alternative answers presented; (e) an optional justification process which is used to select among alternative answers, none of which precisely matches the ideal answer; and (f) a response process which indicates the choice of an answer.

Sternberg distinguishes between models which include all or some of these processes. In order to test a variety of possible models, Sternberg estimated parameters associated with each of the hypothesized component processes and then tested the models in several experiments dealing with verbal, pictorial, and geometric materials. His analyses supported a model which included all of the component processes. Of particular interest is Sternberg's attempt to relate latency measures for the various component processes to general reasoning scores derived from a standardized test battery. He obtained multiple correlations between .68 and .87 for these latency estimates and general reasoning scores. However, processing speed for the separate components was not uniformly positively related to general reasoning ability. Individuals with high general reasoning scores were slower on certain component processes.

The foregoing brief statement cannot adequately reflect the theoretical and empirical detail of Sternberg's work. He sees his efforts as the beginning of a larger attempt at understanding what is meant by general intelligence and the sources of individual differences in intellectual ability. His initial emphasis has been placed upon developing general models of analogy solution and upon specifying individual differences in terms of latency parameters for the various processes. However, a more fine-grained analysis of individual performance on processes such as encoding, inference, mapping, and application is required if we are to understand individual differences in these cognitive operations. This is particularly the case if we assume that individual differences exist not only in process latency but also in the successful execution of a process. As Sternberg writes:

Although the models specify in some detail the alternative ways in which attribute information can be combined to arrive at a solution for analogy problems, the models do not specify what the possible attributes are for different types of analogies, nor do they specify how subjects discover these attributes in the first place. (Sternberg, 1977, p. 6)

This comment reemphasizes the importance of the distinction between content and process we referred to earlier. Questions about process address that aspect of analogy solution that may be common to all forms of the task including verbal, numerical, and geometric. Such questions focus upon the sequence of steps in the total process as is the case in Sternberg's research. In contrast, the content question is concerned with determining the types of information that are encoded, inferred, mapped, and applied and the general strategies that are employed in various content domains. Thus, the content question addresses that aspect of verbal, numerical, and geometric analogies that makes them different, i.e., the knowledge that must be tapped to determine the relations involved in each domain. Nuances of word meanings and types of semantic relations must be considered in verbal analogies, whereas mathematical operations and spatial transformations are of importance in numerical and geometric analogies, respectively. How these different types of information are abstracted and further processed and integrated into problem solving strategies may be very different in the various forms of the task and may account for differences in various specific factors of intelligence.

Geometric Analogies

An example of the investigation of the content and process factors contributing to analogy solution is a study conducted by Mulholland, Pellegrino, and Glaser (1977) on geometric analogies. Psychometric tests were examined to determine the possible features contributing to item difficulty. This analysis indicated that item difficulty reflected increases in two features: the number of constituent elements used to construct the analogy terms and increases in the number of transformations that were performed on the constitutent elements. The elements used to construct the item terms could be largely classified as easily perceived geometric figures and item difficulty did not seem to depend upon constituent recognizability. The basic transformations that were employed included removing or adding elements; rotating, reflecting, and displacing elements; size changes and variations in shading. This analysis, together with the results of previous studies (Evans, 1968), indicates that there are two basic types of declarative or content knowledge necessary for solving most geometric analogy problems— knowledge of the constituent elements used to construct the individual terms and knowledge of the transformations that relate the pairs of terms. This declarative knowledge base, as in the letter series case, is not very extensive. The real effort in solution appears to involve the procedural knowledge and cognitive processes that are required to decompose complex figures into constituent elements and to identify, order, and test the transformations performed on the separate elements.

Mulholland, Pellegrino, and Glaser (1977) systematically constructed geometric analogies varying in the number of elements present and the number of transformations applied to the elements. The results of the study showed that individuals' latencies for solving the' analogies differed as a function of item structure in a highly systematic and reliable manner. Individuals appeared to decompose the patterns in a serial manner by isolating the constituent elements one by one. They also appeared to perform the transformations that relate the patterns in a serial manner. The number of required transformations contributed more to item difficulty and latency than the number of elements involved. Each of these operations took time, and the more processing operations required, the longer the time to solve the item. Thus, the second geometric analogy in Figure 2 would have a longer solution latency and a higher error probability because of its multiple transformations. Latency and errors showed nonlinear increases for complex items where multiple transformations had to be retained in memory and updated as each successive operation was executed.

Thus, the variations in item structure that were studied suggested hypotheses about sources of difficulty in this psychometric task. In particular, each operation performed in decomposing and transforming the terms of the analogy takes up space in memory, and the increasing memory load required by more complex items contributes to error and to increased solution time. Errors were greatest when multiple transformations of single elements were required, and this suggests that in items of this type, the special cognitive demand is retaining the intermediate products of transformation in memory. In summary, then, a detailed task analysis of geometric analogy test items begins to suggest how the specific manipulations of item content can contribute to difficulties in performance for different individuals.

Verbal Analogies

Perhaps the most compelling example of the need to consider both content and process aspects of performance is in the case of verbal analogy items. Global analyses of such test items reveal that the majority of verbal analogies can be classified by a relatively limited set of basic types of semantic relations. Included among these are the relations of class membership, location, function, property, conversion, part-whole,and order in time. The speed and ease of solving any particular analogy can depend upon the type of relationships represented, and upon the underlying knowledge of concepts and the various types of relationships among concepts in semantic memory. An example of the importance of such factors can be found in Sternberg's work where, although latency measures showed systematic trends, none of the models was able to adequately account for error rates on verbal analogies. He argued that errors were primarily a function of gaps in the content knowledge required for solution. Hence, if our goal is to determine the total set of factors contributing to individual differences, it is necessary to examine the contribution of both content and process factors.

The results of several studies (Pellegrino & Glaser, in press) indicate that performance in verbal analogy tests is consistent with general models of semantic processing. For example, the acceptance or rejection of any given alternative is a function of the congruence between the semantic features that define the A is to B and C is to D rules. While this is the case for all items, the time and likelihood of accepting the "best" alternative for an item varies considerably across items. This variability is partially accounted for by the type of relationship involved and the degree of constraint on the set of possible answers for an item as indicated by item differences of the type shown in Figure 2. The constraint factor refers to the likelihood that the A, B, and C terms elicit one or more answers. Thus, the first analogy in Figure 2 elicits only one response, but the other two verbal analogies elicit several candidate answers.

Our data also suggest that skilled individuals (as defined by high aptitude test scores) specify more precisely the set of semantic features representing the interrelationships among the individual terms of the item, and that this difference in the quality of encoding gives rise to different latency and error patterns. Protocol analyses of individual subjects to investigate this issue further have highlighted a number of performance characteristics that differentiate between items of high and low difficulty. Items that are relatively easy lend themselves to a solution process in which the relationship is readily specifiable, and a potential completion term for the item is easily generated. Thus, the process of solution follows a generate and test model in which the processing of the alternatives involves a simple search for the hypothesized answer—this can be called a working-forward strategy. In contrast, difficult items are ones in which the relationship is not well specified and there is difficulty in generating a potential answer. In this case, solution is partially or completely guided by the set of answer alternatives, and the relationship is defined by working backward from these alternatives. Thus, items appear to vary on a continuum from a generate and test process for easy items where there is little change in the level of feature analysis, through to a process for difficult items that is almost totally driven by the alternative set with constant redefinition of the possible relevant features of the problem.

In general, the difficulty associated with the solution of any verbal analogy is a function of the fuzziness of the individual concepts, and this determines whether precise rules can be formulated. A working-forward strategy only is possible for relatively easy and unambiguous items, whereas for many difficult items, solution involves partially or completely working backward from the set of choices. The variability in the path to solution as a function of task ambiguity appears to be a particularly relevant aspect of performance and individual differences in this task.

Summary of Inductive Reasoning

The experimental analysis of the cognitive components of individual differences in analogical reasoning has begun to provide us with some insights on the nature of the skills tapped by this prevalent type of test task, and a beginning is being made in understanding item difficulty factors that influence test scores. The experimental task analysis work also emphasizes the commonality in the general processes required for analogy solution and series completion performance, specifically the ability to extract relations among elements of a problem and assemble those relations into a rule governing the entire problem. An important factor that seems to be implicated in all inductive reasoning tasks is the necessity to maintain and update in working memory the accumulated results of ongoing analyses. The capacity and efficiency of working memory can interact with individual differences in the other processes affecting performance on inductive reasoning tasks. As was strongly indicated by the cognitive correlate studies of verbal ability, this implicates memory capability as an important process component of performance of psychometric tasks, and indeed, memory often constitutes a separately measured factor on intelligence tests as noted earlier.

There appear to be two major factors that contribute to task difficulty in the task forms used to measure inductive reasoning on aptitude and intelligence tests; these include: (a) the complexity of the rule to be inferred, and (b) the representational variability or initial ambiguity in the possible rules that may be inferred. These factors of *rule complexity* and *representational variability* provide a scheme within which to consider sources of individual differences. Rule complexity refers to the number of operators that must be represented in working memory and complex rules often lead to difficulties in assembling and maintaining in memory a complete description of element-operator combinations. Such descriptions may exceed memory capacity and only partial representations of the rule to be induced and applied may be established. Data relating to the representational variability factor (as manifested in verbal analogies) indicate that skill differences in an undergraduate sample are associated with: (a) processes of establishing a reasonably well-defined problem representation, (b) the subsequent utilization of that representation as a basis for selecting among alternatives, and (c) modifying the representation as necessary. The time spent establishing an initial representation (or representations) may differ as a function of skill level, but latency differences may be less important than the particular representation(s) achieved. Indeed, there is evidence in our data and Sternberg's (1977) that high aptitude individuals, who presumably have more elaborate semantic memory structures, may encode more item features and take more time in this aspect of processing, but with subsequent facilitation in the speed and accuracy of selection among alternatives.

IV. SUMMARY AND CONCLUSIONS

This progress report of work attempting to apply current theories of human cognition to the analysis of individual differences in intelligence and aptitude suggests general dimensions along which these differences are manifested. It is tempting to argue that two major dimensions are, in fact, the operating and structural characteristics of the human information processing system. The operating characteristics of the system include the speed and efficiency with which information is processed and managed. Individual differences exist in the speed with which stored memory representations and codes are accessed. It is also likely that differences result not only from the speed of basic processes, but the executive control or management in the selection and sequencing of these processes. The analysis of high and low aptitude groups shows differences in speed, and analyses of item performance on psychometric tasks implicate the efficiency of executive control. The structural properties of the information processing system are also implicated in the task analytic studies of test item performance. These structural properties include storage capacity, the way knowledge in memory is organized, and the different types of semantic, procedural, and strategic knowledge available. These are potential sources of individual differences that interact with the operating characteristics of the system and are related to developmental level, educational history, and general experience.

Reality, in the form of experimental data and successful models of performance, however, points out that dichotomies such as operating versus structural characteristics, or put another way, process versus content, are heuristically useful, but are oversimplifications. The relative contributions of process and content knowledge become difficult to distinguish in actual performance situations. In memory span performance, knowledge structure influences speed of encoding and together, these two components influence the selection and execution of mnemonic strategies. In inductive reasoning performance, the process of inferring relations and constructing rules depend on the individual's knowledge of relational concepts and the ability to retain in memory the results of preliminary analyses leading to solution. An adequate explanation of individual differences must ultimately come to grips with these interactive aspects of process and content.

With respect to the intelligence and aptitude testing enterprise, the attempt to conceptualize individual differences in intellectual ability in terms of general theories of human cognition and cognitive development can free us from the limitations inherent in the traditional techniques and restricted generality of psychometric assessment. As we begin to understand measures of intelligence in terms of theories not primarily derived from the intercorrelations of performance on the tests themselves, our base of knowledge becomes more broadly applicable. The components of intellectual performance, as they occur on test instruments, in environments for learning, and in everyday life, can be related on increasingly more precise operational dimensions. Consider the possible relevance and generality of processes that have been identified in the small set of studies of inductive reasoning tasks. The rule induction processes involved in analogical reasoning and series completion appear to be similar to many forms of problem solving and concept formation. The essence of this similarity is the ability to search for relations among elements resulting in new interconnections between concepts stored in memory. Consistent with this contention, it has been argued that one of the learner's essential roles in classroom learning is to recognize the structural form or pattern of the facts conveyed by instruction and to detect relations between this newly communicated material and the material already existing in a semantic network in memory (Norman, Gentner, & Stevens, 1976).

When we are able to specify intellectual abilities in terms of psychological processes, we have information that enables us to do more than predict performance on a criterion task. We have information that provides a basis for doing something about performance—either by engaging in specific process training designed to improve performance or by changing the learning situation to make the attainment of criterion performance more likely. An increasing number of studies are being carried out to determine the direct instructability of specific processes that underlie intelligence and aptitude. Much of this work is being done in the context of research on mental retardation (Belmont & Butterfield, 1977; Brown, 1974; Campione & Brown, in press). However, testing the limits of such training on a wider spectrum of abilities has not yet begun. Experimental studies investigating the possibility of changing the learning situation to adapt to individual differences have been largely represented by studies of aptitude-treatment interaction. But aptitudes and treatments have been rarely analyzed in terms of similar underlying performance processes that could relate the two, and this probably accounts for the many negative findings in this area (e.g., Cronbach & Snow, 1977). Success might be expected when we have a more refined process analysis that relates individual capabilities and learning requirements.

The potential benefits that can be derived from an understanding of the cognitive components of individual differences are consistent with the nature and purposes of education. It is no longer possible to consider testing only as a means of determining which individuals are already adapted to or have the potential for adapting to mainstream educational practice. A conceivable alternative goal is to reverse this sequence of adaptation; rather than requiring individuals to adapt to means of instruction, the desired objective is to adapt the conditions of instruction to individuals to maximize their potential for success.

This objective can be realized if learning can be designed to take account of an individual's profile of cognitive skills. If we analyze the performance requirements of various school activities and then analyze the skills that individuals bring to these task environments, we should be able to match the two. Learning could then be assisted in two ways. First, the cognitive skills that individuals bring to schooling could be matched to various instructional environments that utilize these skills. Second, the cognitive skills of an individual could be improved to meet the demands of the instructional environments that are available. Providing for both the development of cognitive skills and accommodating to different cognitive capabilities offers maximum adaptability for enhancing the likelihood of effective education.

Finally, it might be said that for some time now, we have been in the position of supplying psychometric procedures, as applied to the assessment of human cognition, with minor technological assistance when the real need was for major understanding of the psychological processes involved. The work referred to here is only a beginning, but if successfully accomplished, might provide a new basis for guiding the development and improvement of human intellectual performance.

REFERENCES

Atkinson, R. C., & Shiffrin, R. M. Human memory: A proposed system and its control processes. In K. W. Spence & J. T. Spence (Eds.), *The psychology of learning and motivation* (Vol. 2). New York: Academic Press, 1968.

Belmont, J. M., & Butterfield, E. C. The instructional approach to developmental cognitive research. In R. V. Kail, Jr. & J. Hagen (Eds.), *Perspectives on the development of memory and cognition*. Hillsdale, N.J.: Lawrence Erlbaum Associates, 1977.

Bisanz, J. H., & Resnick, L. B. Changes with age in two components of visual search speed. *Journal of Experimental Child Psychology*, 1978, *25*, 129–142.

Brown, A. L. The role of strategic behavior in retardate memory. In N. R. Ellis (Ed.), *International review of research in mental retardation* (Vol. 7). New York: Academic Press, 1974.

Butterfield, E. C., Wambold, C., & Belmont, J. M. On the theory and practice of improving short-term memory. *American Journal of Mental Deficiency*, 1973, *77*, 654–669.

Campione, J. C., & Brown, A. L. Toward a theory of intelligence: Contributions from research with retarded children. *Intelligence*, in press.

Carpenter, P. A., & Just, M. A. Sentence comprehension: A psycholinguistic processing model of verification. *Psychological Review*, 1975, *82*, 45–73.

Carpenter, P. A., & Just, M. A. Eye fixations during mental rotation. In J. Senders, R. Monty, & D. Fisher (Eds.), *Eye movements and psychological processes II.* Hillsdale, N.J.: Lawrence Erlbaum Associates, 1978.

Carroll, J. B. Psychometric tests as cognitive tasks: A new "structure of intellect." In L. B. Resnick (Ed.), *The nature of intelligence.* Hillsdale, N.J.: Lawrence Erlbaum Associates, 1976.

Chi, M. T. H. Short-term memory limitations in children: Capacity or processing deficits? *Memory & Cognition,* 1976, *4,* 559–572.

Chi, M. T. H. Age differences in memory span. *Journal of Experimental Child Psychology,* 1977, *23,* 266–281.

Chiang, A., & Atkinson, R. C. Individual differences and interrelationships among a select set of cognitive skills. *Memory & Cognition,* 1976, *4,* 661–672.

Clark, H. H., & Chase, W. G. On the process of comparing sentences against pictures. *Cognitive Psychology,* 1972, *3,* 472–517.

Cooper, L. A. *Spatial information processing: Strategies for research.* Paper presented at the Office of Naval Research/Navy Personnel Research and Development Center Conference on Aptitude, Learning, and Instruction: Cognitive Process Analyses, San Diego, March, 1978.

Cooper, L. A., & Shepard, R. N. Chronometric studies of the rotation of mental images. In W. G. Chase (Ed.), *Visual information processing.* New York: Academic Press, 1973.

Cronbach, L. J., & Snow, R. E. *Aptitudes and instructional methods: A handbook for research on interactions.* New York: Irvington Publishers, 1977.

Egan, D. E. *Characterizing spatial ability: Different mental processes reflected in accuracy and latency scores.* Unpublished manuscript, 1978.

Estes, W. K. Learning theory and intelligence. *American Psychologist,* 1974, *29,* 740–749.

Evans, T. G. Program for the solution of a class of geometric-analogy intelligence-test questions. In M. Minsky (Ed.), *Semantic information processing.* Cambridge, Mass.: MIT Press, 1968.

French, J. W., Ekstrom, R. B., & Price, L. A. *Kit of reference tests for cognitive factors.* Princeton, N.J.: Educational Testing Service, 1963.

Greeno, J. G. Natures of problem-solving abilities. In W. K. Estes (Ed.), *Handbook of learning and cognitive processes* (Vol. 5). Hillsdale, N.J.: Lawrence Erlbaum Associates, 1978.

Hogaboam, T. W., & Pellegrino, J. W. Hunting for individual differences in cognitive processes: Verbal ability and semantic processing of pictures and words. *Memory & Cognition,* 1978, *6,* 189–193.

Holzman, T. G., Glaser, R., & Pellegrino, J. W. Process training derived from a computer simulation theory. *Memory & Cognition,* 1976, *4,* 349–356.

Hunt, E. What kind of computer is man? *Cognitive Psychology,* 1971, *2,* 57–98.

Hunt, E. The memory we must have. In R. Schank & K. Colby (Eds.), *Computer models of thought and language.* San Francisco: Freeman, 1973.

Hunt, E. Varieties of cognitive power. In L. B. Resnick (Ed.), *The nature of intelligence.* Hillsdale, N.J.: Lawrence Erlbaum Associates, 1976.

Hunt, E. Mechanics of verbal abilities. *Psychological Review,* 1978, *85,* 109–130.

Hunt, E., Frost, N., & Lunneborg, C. Individual differences in cognition: A new approach to intelligence. In G. H. Bower (Ed.), *The psychology of learning and motivation* (Vol. 7). New York: Academic Press, 1973.

Hunt, E., & Lansman, M. Cognitive theory applied to individual differences. In W. K. Estes (Ed.), *Handbook of learning and cognitive processes: Introduction to concepts and issues* (Vol. 1). Hillsdale, N.J.: Lawrence Erlbaum Associates, 1975.

Hunt, E., Lunneborg, C., & Lewis, J. What does it mean to be high verbal? *Cognitive Psychology,* 1975, *7,* 194–227.

Huttenlocher, J., & Burke, D. Why does memory span increase with age? *Cognitive Psychology,* 1976, *8,* 1–31.

Just, M. A., & Carpenter, P. A. Eye fixations and cognitive processes. *Cognitive Psychology,* 1976, *8,* 441–480.

Keating, D. P., & Bobbitt, B. L. Individual and developmental differences in cognitive processing components of mental ability. *Child Development,* 1978, *49,* 155–167.

Kotovsky, K., & Simon, H. A. Empirical tests of a theory of human acquisition of concepts for sequential patterns. *Cognitive Psychology,* 1973, *4,* 399–424.

Lyon, D. R. *Sources of individual differences in digit span.* Unpublished doctoral dissertation, University of Oregon, 1975.

Lyon, D. R. Individual differences in immediate serial recall: A matter of mnemonics? *Cognitive Psychology,* 1977, *9,* 403–411.

MacLeod, C. M., Hunt, E. B., & Mathews, N. N. Individual differences in the verification of sentence-picture relationships. *Journal of Verbal Learning and Verbal Behavior,* in press.

Metzler, J., & Shepard, R. N. Transformational studies of the internal representation of three-dimensional objects. In R. L. Solso (Ed.), *Theories in cognitive psychology: The Loyola Symposium.* Potomac, Md.: Lawrence Erlbaum Associates, 1974.

Mulholland, T. M., Pellegrino, J. W., & Glaser, R. *Components of geometric analogy solution.* Paper presented at the meeting of the Psychonomic Society, Washington, D. C., November 1977.

Norman, D. A., Gentner, D. R., & Stevens, A. L. Comments on learning schemata and memory. In D. Klahr (Ed.), *Cognition and instruction.* Hillsdale, N.J.: Lawrence Erlbaum Associates, 1976.

Pellegrino, J. W., & Glaser, R. Components of inductive reasoning. In R. E. Snow, P.-A. Federico, & W. E. Montague (Eds.), *Aptitude, learning, and instruction: Cognitive process analyses.* Hillsdale, N.J.: Lawrence Erlbaum Associates, in press.

Peterson, L. R., & Peterson, M. J. Short-term retention of individual verbal items. *Journal of Experimental Psychology,* 1959, *58,* 193–198.

Posner, M., Boies, S., Eichelman, W., & Taylor, R. Retention of visual and name codes of single letters. *Journal of Experimental Psychology Monographs,* 1959, *79*(1, Pt. 2).

Resnick, L. B., Danner, F., & Bisanz, J. H. *Psychometric abilities and cognitive development: Processing speed as a component of intelligence.* Paper presented at the meeting of the Psychonomic Society, Washington, D.C., November 1977.

Shepard, R. N. Form, formation, and transformation of internal representations. In R. L. Solso (Ed.), *Information processing and cognition: The Loyola Symposium.* Hillsdale, N.J.: Lawrence Erlbaum Associates, 1975.

Shepard, R. N., & Feng, C. A chronometric study of mental paper folding. *Cognitive Psychology,* 1972, *3,* 228–243.

Simon, H. A., & Kotovsky, K. Human acquisition of concepts for sequential patterns. *Psychological Review,* 1963, *70,* 534–546.

Snow, R. E. Theory and method for research on aptitude processes: A prospectus. *Intelligence,* in press.

Sternberg, R. J. *Intelligence, information processing, and analogical reasoning: The componential analysis of human abilities.* Hillsdale, N.J.: Lawrence Erlbaum Associates, 1977.

Sternberg, S. High-speed scanning in human memory. *Science,* 1966, *153,* 652–654.

Sternberg, S. Memory-scanning: Mental processes revealed by reaction-time experiments. *American Scientist,* 1969, *57,* 421–457.

Thurstone, L. L., & Thurstone, T. C. *Factoral studies of intelligence.* Chicago: University of Chicago Press, 1941.

4

The Sentence-Verification Paradigm: A Case Study of Two Conflicting Approaches to Individual Differences

EARL HUNT AND COLIN M. MACLEOD

University of Washington

The contrasting approaches of differential psychology and cognitive psychology to the same individual differences data are outlined. Using illustrative data from the Clark and Chase (1972) sentence–picture verification task, four loci of conflict between these two disciplines are identified. These areas of conflict center around issues of (1) theory versus measurement, (2) meaningfulness versus reliability, (3) linearity of relationships, and (4) discontinuities in performance. We conclude on the basis of observed incompatabilities that a simple derivation of differential psychology from cognitive psychology is not likely, but separate development of complementary theories may be possible.

Differential psychology deals with the description of relative individual performance. By adopting a pragmatic attitude toward theory development, differential psychologists have constructed an impressive array of useful measurement instruments. There has, however, been relatively little progress in our understanding of the processes by which individuals achieve the scores that they do. Cognitive psychology, on the other hand, deals with the process of human information handling. Quite sophisticated models have been developed for the analysis of performance in limited laboratory situations, said to represent prototypical cognitive acts. While this work has considerably advanced our understanding of the thinking process, it has not had great impact upon applied psychology. Indeed, Cronbach (1957) has decried the existence of the two disciplines of scientific psychology and has urged that they be reunited.

Within the last few years a number of people, including ourselves, have tried to respond to Cronbach's call. These efforts have taken two forms. We and other experimental psychologists have tried to apply the statistical procedures of the psychometrician to data gathered in laboratory situations, while psychometricians have tried to interpret their measures in terms of the theories of cognitive psychology (Carroll, 1976). Intermediate procedures have also been used

This research was supported by the National Institute of Education grant G77-0012 and the National Institute of Mental Health grant MH-21795 to the University of Washington.

(Sternberg, 1977). Such steps toward the reunification of the disciplines can be applauded as attempts to establish the basic unity of scientific psychology. Reunification would also be desirable for the practical reason that it would aid in establishing a scientific justification for gathering data that is often influential in important social and personal decision making.

The reunification movement implicitly assumes that there is a conceptual unity underlying the way that cognitive and differential psychologists approach the study of human thought processes. Any surface discrepancies in their procedures or their conclusions are believed to be due to an unfortunate historical divergence in their procedures for data collection, rather than any basic conceptual incompatability in their thinking about psychological data in general or about cognition in particular. Is it possible that this assumption is wrong? We have begun to suspect that it is. Hunt, MacLeod, and Lansman (1978) raised four issues that seem to indicate deep underlying conceptual differences between the differential and cognitive psychology approaches to thought. In this paper we shall illustrate the issues raised by Hunt et al. through the use of a detailed case study of how a single experimental paradigm from cognitive psychology has been applied to the study of individual differences.

THE PARADIGM

Clark and Chase (1972) introduced the *sentence-verification task* as a procedure for studying comprehension, which is certainly a basic cognitive skill. In this task the subject is to verify or deny that simple sentences are descriptions of simple pictures. The sentences are of the form PLUS IS ABOVE STAR, STAR IS NOT ABOVE PLUS, etc. The pictures are simply pictures of a plus above a star ($^+_*$) or a star above a plus ($^*_+$). There are three versions of the paradigm. In the *sentence-first* procedure, the sentence is shown, read, and then replaced by the picture. The sequence of events is shown in Fig. 1. The dependent variable is the time required for the subject to examine the picture and verify that the sentence does indeed describe it. In the *picture-first* variation of the paradigm, the order of the picture and the sentence is reversed. In the *simultaneous* condition both picture and sentence are presented at the same time. The simultaneous condition is of interest to psychometricians because it can be used in "paper and pencil" testing, whereas the other procedures require individually timed presentations of stimuli and recording of responses. In the paper and pencil version of the simultaneous condition, the number of trials completed in a fixed time may be used to derive an estimate of the time per trial.

Clark and Chase justified the study of sentence verification on the grounds that the coordination of linguistic descriptions and nonlinguistic reality is a basic step in verbal cognition. One can hardly disagree. In addition, the task has several valuable features. From a methodological standpoint, one can focus upon a single dependent variable, reaction time, as a measure of linguistic information

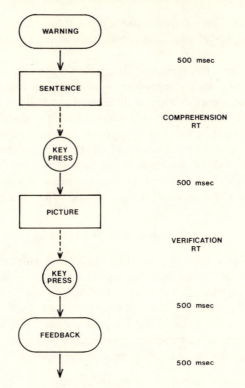

FIG. 1   The sequence of events in the sentence-first version of the sentence–picture verification task.

processing, for errors are seldom made. Moreover, the paradigm is reliable and the phenomenon it taps is robust. Since Clark and Chase's original study, many other investigators have found that reaction time does vary systematically with the linguistic complexity of the sentence (cf. the review in Carpenter & Just, 1975). Consequently, this task can be used to relate psychological complexity, as determined by reaction time, to linguistic complexity, as determined by a linguistic analysis of the sentence structure.

In an earlier related study, Baddeley (1968) found that the time required to verify sentences had a substantial correlation with performance on a much longer verbal aptitude test. We have verified his observation, using procedures more closely approximating the now standard sentence-verification task. We have found correlations ranging from .35 to .70 between sentence verification and verbal aptitude measures, even within the restricted range of talent found in a university student body (Lansman, 1978; Lansman & Hunt, 1978). Such results are of interest in differential psychology because the task is easy to administer and does not require any specialized knowledge beyond the ability to read very simple sentences. Thus, it is a face-valid candidate for culture fair testing of some aspects of verbal cognition for all high school graduates in an English speaking country.

Having completed this optimistic description of the task, let us turn to a less sanguine analysis of the conceptual and methodological issues raised when sentence verification is used as a tool in differential psychology. First, however, we want to stress that the sentence-verification task is only one of several paradigms that we could have chosen to make our points. In fact, we debated our choice of illustration at the outset of preparation of this paper. It is rather arbitrary that the issues we raise shall be demonstrated using sentence verification and verbal aptitude. We believe that the issues are relevant to the development of any experimental paradigm as a tool for any sort of differential psychology.

INCOMPATIBILITY ISSUES

Two of the issues posed by Hunt et al. (1978) deal with the measurement and analysis of data. In our case study we shall deal with these issues first. We shall then deal with two issues that Hunt et al. concluded arose from differences about the concept of cognition and its distribution over individuals. In discussing each issue we shall use the same format for presentation. First, we will present an illustrative problem using the sentence-verification procedure, and then we shall make some comments intended to generalize the example.

Issue 1. Theoretical Specificity of Measurements

By conventional standards of writing and conversation, none of the sentences used in a verification paradigm is difficult. It is hard to say anything very complicated about a picture of a plus above a star. Still, the various types of sentences do vary in their complexity. Figure 2 shows a propositional analysis of four types of sentence–picture combinations. Note that there are two sources of complexity in the comparison; whether or not the sentence is true and whether or not the sentence contains a negation. Only the latter source of variation is a strictly linguistic variable. It is well-known that sentence-verification time increases as the propositional complexity of the task increases. Several models of linguistic information processing have been proposed to account for this relation.

The most detailed linguistic model is the *constituent comparison* model due to Carpenter and Just (1975). Carpenter and Just assumed that the subject derives propositions from both the sentence and the picture, and then compares them to determine whether or not they are logically equivalent. The propositional form of the picture is presumed to be constant, whereas the propositional form of the sentence will vary with its linguistic structure, as shown in Fig. 2. The model is essentially an algorithm for comparing propositional representation in a particular manner, based upon the notion that each comparison requires a scan through the contents of short-term memory. The more complex the picture–sentence

Trial Type	Number of Constituent Comparisons	Sentence	Picture	Sentence Representation	Picture Representation
TRUE AFFIRMATIVE (TA)	K	PLUS IS ABOVE STAR STAR IS BELOW PLUS		[Aff, (PLUS, Top)]	
FALSE AFFIRMATIVE (FA)	K+1	STAR IS ABOVE PLUS PLUS IS BELOW STAR	+ *	[Aff, (STAR, Top)]	(PLUS, Top)
TRUE NEGATIVE (TN)	K+5	STAR IS NOT ABOVE PLUS PLUS IS NOT BELOW STAR		{Neg, [Aff, (STAR, Top)]}	
FALSE NEGATIVE (FN)	K+4	PLUS IS NOT ABOVE STAR STAR IS NOT BELOW PLUS		{Neg, [Aff, (PLUS, Top)]}	

FIG. 2   The sentence–picture stimulus pairs as a function of trial type, hypothetical representation, and number of constituent comparisons.

comparison, the more scans are required. If one accepts this model, it is possible to analyze the relationship between verification reaction times to the four different types of sentence–picture comparison (True Affirmative, False Affirmative, True Negative, False Negative) in order to derive a single parameter said to represent the time required to complete a single scan. Virtually any theory of language and thought would have to regard such a measure as a measure of an elementary process. Hence, measurement of scan time on an individual basis should tell us a great deal about a person's capacity for rapid verbal comprehension. On the other hand, as Carpenter and Just point out, other algorithms for scanning and comparing propositions are possible, and other algorithms would dictate other procedures for parameter estimation given the same data.

To apply sentence-verification data to the study of individual differences, then, one must take one of two approaches. One way to proceed is to regard sentence verification itself as primitive, and to study the correlation between some summary statistic describing sentence verification, such as the mean reaction time over trials, and other measures of psychological traits. This is the approach taken by Baddeley (1968) and Lansman (1978). This approach has the advantage of relying upon well-understood statistical procedures and of not depending upon the truth of any particular theory. It has the disadvantage of being limited to regarding sentence verification as a primitive to be accepted rather than to be described. The analysis of averages discards any information contained in the relations between subsets of the data, in this case, in the differences between individual reaction times as a function of sentence complexity. As we have indicated in discussing the constituent comparison model, it is possible to use this information to infer measures of the efficiency of short-term memory during linguistic comprehension.

MacLeod, Hunt, and Mathews (1978) took the more theoretical approach of using the constituent comparison model to make such an inference. They found a correlation of −.33 between verbal aptitude, as measured by an omnibus scholastic aptitude battery, and the scanning parameter of the Carpenter and Just model. One could use this information to draw the conclusion that there was a relation between "high verbal ability" and speed of information processing in short-term memory, which is an intuitively more interesting conclusion than the simple statement that people with high verbal aptitude are more rapid in sentence comprehension and verification. But this approach has its complementary pitfall. The conclusion is tied to acceptance of a particular theory. The constituent comparison model may be found wanting on the basis of research quite outside the individual differences field. (See, for instance, discussions by Tanenhaus, Carroll, and Bever, 1976; and by Catlin and Jones, 1976.) One is skating on thin ice when conclusions about differential psychology are drawn from correlational studies based upon model-specific parameters.

This is obviously a general problem. Given that one has observed performance on some cognitive task, one's most reliable summary is a statement about average performance. Such a statement sets a lower limit upon the primitiveness of one's conclusions about the task and its correlations with other measures. If one decides to go beyond a discussion of average performance by deriving parameters for a model of task performance, then one becomes committed to that model. If the model requires that more than one parameter be derived from the data, there is the additional technical problem that the same errors of measurement contaminate all parameter estimates. Conceptually, the problem is one of balancing between the value of obtaining a more basic explanation of a phenomenon and the risk of having an explanation that relies more heavily upon unproven assumptions. The idea of making such a tradeoff is certainly not a new one, but the assignment of numbers to the costs and benefits is not a simple task.

Issue 2. Formal Meaningfulness and Statistical Reliability

Suppes and Zinnes (1963) have observed that meaningful scientific statements must be invariant over equivalent ways of measuring one's results. To take a trivial example, the statement that dogs are heavier than cats should be true regardless of whether weight is to be stated in grams or pounds. It is equally important that statements be based upon reliable data. If two out of three physicians are said to prescribe brand X, we are interested in knowing whether the assertion is based on a sample of three or three hundred. Modern cognitive psychology has emphasized the importance of meaningfulness, whereas psychometrics has been concerned with reliability. Although these two goals are both valid, they may be in conflict.

To set the stage for an illustration of such a conflict, we describe part of a recently completed sentence-verification study in which we were interested in the use of a concurrent task as a measure of information-processing load (cf. Kahneman, 1973; Norman & Bobrow, 1975). The study used a sentence-first procedure, with the added feature that a tone was presented during some of the picture presentations. The exact sequence of events is shown in Fig. 3. The subject's task was to turn off the tone as soon as it sounded and then proceed with sentence verification.

As a preliminary to other analyses, we wished to know whether the processing of the tone resulted in interference with sentence–picture processing. Of course, we know that there will be some interference in responding, simply because the time to make a second response will typically be delayed by the making of a first response (Kantowitz, 1974). Is there also interference that is not related to response execution?

Following Anderson (1974), we have conducted a functional analysis of this situation. Let I(total) be the total information load in the situation, let I(comparison) be the information load imposed by the sentence–picture comparison, and

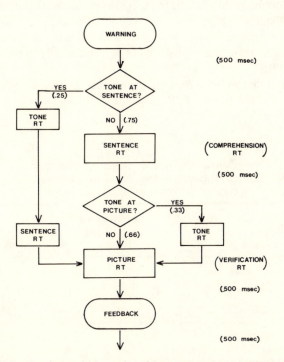

FIG. 3   The sequence of events in the version of the sentence–picture verification task using tones as a secondary task.

let I(tone) be the information load imposed by the tone. "Information load" is the psychological variable that we wish to study. If information loads from the two sources do not interact, then

$$I(\text{total}) = I(\text{comparison}) + I(\text{tone}). \tag{1}$$

Next consider the relationship between reaction time (which, unlike information load, is observable) and the experimental conditions. Applying Anderson's functional analysis technique, we conclude that if reaction time is a linear measure of information load, and if Eq. (1) is true, then there will be no interaction between comparison complexity and the presence or absence of a tone in determining reaction time. Note the conjunction in this statement; the scaling assumption is an inseparable part of the theory.

The top half of Table 1 presents the data, reaction times for the factorial experiment varying comparison complexity and tone present or absent. There is no interaction at all. This conclusion is based upon an analysis of variance of reaction times, which introduces a technical assumption that will become important later. The analysis of variance assumes that the underlying data are normally distributed within each condition of the experiment. However, reaction times are typically not normally distributed. In the particular application of the analysis of variance technique which we made, this was not of concern because, if anything, the result of deviations from the assumptions of normality and equality of variance is to increase the probability of a "statistically significant" F test (Scheffé, 1959).

Now suppose that we wish to study the correlation between information load and some psychological trait, Y. Because the correlation coefficient is invariant

TABLE 1

Mean Verification Reaction Times and Verification Speeds for Trials with and without Tone Probes as a Function of Sentence-Picture Complexity

Tone condition	Sentence complexity			
	TA	FA	TN	FN
Reaction times				
With	931	1034	1254	1239
Without	591	718	858	915
Difference	340	316	396	324
Speeds				
With	1.074	.967	.797	.807
Without	1.692	1.392	1.166	1.093
Difference	.618	.425	.369	.286

over a linear transformation, it is clearly appropriate to consider the correlation between Y and verification reaction time. As Carroll (1978) has correctly pointed out, this raises a question about reliability, because the correlation coefficient is not a robust statistic when its distribution assumptions are relaxed. Indeed, it is unusually sensitive to the presence of outliers, and outliers frequently do occur in reaction time studies. The problem will be much worse if our eventual statement is to be about some derivative of the correlation matrix (e.g., a factor analysis), because the assumption of multivariate normal distributions for the basic variables will have been used quite strongly.

When this sort of problem appears in data analysis psychometricians generally recommend taking some nonlinear transformation of the original measures, in order to produce well-behaved distributions. In this case the obvious transformation to use is speed, the inverse of reaction time. Let us assume that this transformation does produce normally distributed data, so that correlation matrices based on speed can be regarded as reliable. We could then determine the linear components of the speed measure, in terms of some basic underlying traits derived from an analysis of the multivariate experiment.

But what would we have found the linear components of? The bottom half of Table 1 presents the transforms into speeds of those reaction times shown in the upper half of the table. The interaction is now significant, so either the two sources of information load do interact, or the speed measure is not a linear measure of information load, or both. We again suspect the correlation matrix, but this time because we cannot assign meaning to it even though we do not doubt its reliability.

Again we have a case of a specific example of a general problem. Suppose that we wish to study the covariation of two theoretical variables, x and y. By appropriate experimental procedures, we justify two observable measures, X and Y, that can be regarded as linear measures of x and y. That is, we believe that

$$X = a + bx + e_x,$$
$$Y = c + dy + e_y, \tag{2}$$

where e_x and e_y are errors of measurement. The correlation between the observables, $r(XY)$, establishes a lower bound upon the correlation of theoretical interest, $r(xy)$. There is no guarantee that X and Y will be bivariately normally distributed. Indeed, there is no guarantee that e_x and e_y will be normally distributed; whether they will or not depends upon the process model one assumes for generation of the overt measure. Therefore one cannot establish the reliability of $r(XY)$ or any linear transformation of it. On the other hand, one can assign meaning only to these measures.

We do not despair of ever seeing this problem solved. It should be possible to develop techniques to handle our simultaneous concerns for meaningfulness and reliability. Our point is simply that these techniques remain to be developed and widely used.

Issue 3. Nonlinear Relationships

The differential psychology view of cognition is that cognitive performance in any specific situation is due to an individual's position on some underlying trait. Thus, the probability of a person's choosing any of the possible responses to, say, a Raven Matrix test item, can be specified by stating that person's position on the trait that underlies performance on the item in question. The traits underlying specific performances are themselves considered to be derived from a set of basic traits. To continue the example, one might have a theory in which the trait underlying the Raven Matrix test was a linear combination of positions on more basic functions, such as spatial ability and logical reasoning. Letting T_i be the position of person i on the trait underlying the behavior observed, and letting x_i and y_i be that person's position on some basic traits x and y, we have

$$T_i = ax_i + by_i. \tag{3}$$

Equation (3) implies that there is a complete tradeoff between talent on ability x and talent on ability y, and deficiency in one can be compensated for by excess capacity on the other. This is foreign to a number of cognitive psychology models, which specify that some capacity must exist in a sufficient amount to ensure performance, but that once this capacity requirement has been met, excess capacity will exert no further effect on performance. It is also a consequence of Eq. (3) that the same relationship should exist between T and x (or y) throughout the range of T. (In practice, one would have to adjust for a drop in correlations due to restriction in the range of variation, but this is an easily handled technical problem.) A cognitive theory that depended upon the existence of minimum capacities would not make this assumption.

Hunt et al. (1978) refer to the assumption of Eq. (3) as the linearity assumption of differential psychology. We now illustrate its failure within a quite homogeneous and psychologically ubiquitous population—college students. Together with John Palmer, we have just completed a large study on the correlation between reading measures and information-processing measures in the college population. Our sample was carefully constructed to be a stratified sample of reading comprehension ability in the University of Washington student body. One of the tasks we used was sentence verification. Table 2 presents the correlation coefficients between mean sentence-verification reaction time and reading comprehension scores for the entire sample, and then for subjects who were either above or below the median in reading comprehension. If the linearity assumption holds, we would expect the correlations between sentence verification and reading comprehension to shrink slightly and uniformly as we moved from the large sample to the two subsets. Clearly, this is not what happens. One correlation shrinks and the other rises. Whatever the underlying traits for these measures are, the relation between them is different in the subsamples. Any correlation, and certainly any factor analysis, based upon the entire sample

TABLE 2
Correlations of WPC Reading Comprehension Scores
with Mean Picture–Sentence Verification Times for All Subjects
and for Two Subgroups, Good and Poor Readers

Group	Number of subjects	Correlation (r)	Significance (p)
All	91	−.34	<.001
Good readers	45	−.52	<.001
Poor readers	40	−.05	.37

would be misleading. Yet samples of university students are generally criticized for being too homogeneous to represent the real world.

Many, if not most, information-processing theories of cognitive processes regard performance as a nonlinear function of the primitive variables of the model. To the extent that such cognitive theories are correct, psychometric techniques and differential psychology theories that assume linearity are simply not relevant to the analysis of experimental data. This is not a technical problem in data analysis, as the meaningfulness–reliability paradox was. It represents a distinction between the two disciplines of scientific psychology in their concept of mental capacity itself.

Issue 4. Discontinuities in Performance

The nonlinearity issue deals with changes in the relations between variables that occur over the range of a particular behavior being studied. Hunt et al. observe that similar changes in relationships can occur because of qualitative changes in the way that different individuals approach cognitive tasks, or even because the same individual's approach may change from time to time. This effect can be demonstrated by considering the results of two experiments we have conducted in collaboration with Nancy Mathews.

These experiments used the sentence-verification paradigm described in Fig. 1. In the first study (MacLeod et al., 1978), we simply observed the strategies that people used to deal with the task. Two strategies were identified. The first was to read the sentence as it was presented, remember it in whatever form sentences are normally remembered, look at the picture, describe it, and compare the picture description to the sentence representation. We shall refer to this as the linguistic strategy. The second strategy was to read the sentence and, from this information, to form an image of the picture the sentence described. When the picture was presented it was compared directly to the subject's expectation. We shall call this the visual strategy.

We were able to identify subjects who had clear preferences for the one or the other strategy. (Some subjects are also capable of switching.) The best

TABLE 3

Overall and Partial Correlations of Mean Sentence–Picture
Verification Times with WPC Verbal and Spatial Ability Scores for
the Subjects Who Were Well-Fit and Poorly-Fit by the Constituent
Comparison Model

Group	WPC Verbal	WPC Spatial
Well-fit (n = 43)	−.52*	−.32
Poorly-fit (n = 16)	−.33	−.68*
	(Spatial partialed out)	(Verbal partialed out)
Well-fit	−.44*	.07
Poorly-fit	−.05	−.64*

Note: Those correlations marked with an asterisk are significant beyond $p < .01$.

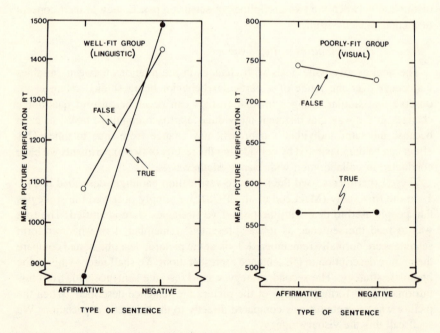

FIG. 4   Mean verification time as a function of the linguistic complexity of the sentence (affirmative vs. negative). The curve parameter is the truth value of the sentence–picture relationship (true vs. false). The left panel represents the Well-Fit group; the right panel represents the Poorly-Fit group.

psychometric predictor of verification reaction time for the subjects using the linguistic strategy was a measure of verbal aptitude, whereas the best psychometric predictor of performance for the visual strategy users was a spatial aptitude measure. The relevant correlations are shown in Table 3. We call attention especially to the partial correlations, as spatial and verbal aptitude are themselves correlated. Furthermore, our conclusions about different relations do not depend upon any assumption about the truth of a particular model of linguistic processing. To appreciate why this is true, consider Fig. 4, where verification reaction times are plotted as a function of group membership, the presence or absence of a linguistic variable (negation), and the presence or absence of a logical variable (truth value of the sentence as a description of the picture). The linguistic variable has an effect only for the users of the linguistic strategy.

A differential psychology theory might handle this data by asserting that choice of strategy is itself a trait that functions as a moderator variable. Strategy choice could then be entered into a linear model of behavior. Such a treatment could handle the MacLeod et al. (1978) results, but would have difficulty with our second experiment. In this study (not yet formally reported) subjects participated in six days of sentence-verification sessions. The first two days were replications of the first experiment, and were used to identify the subject's natural strategy choice. On the third and fourth day the subjects were instructed to use either the linguistic or visual strategies; on the fifth and sixth days they were instructed to change strategies. There was no extended training period; we simply described the strategies to the subjects and asked them to use the appropriate method. This proved remarkably easy to do. Figure 5 shows the data from a subject who initially chose the linguistic strategy, while Fig. 6 shows the corresponding data from a subject who initially preferred the visual strategy. The influence of linguistic complexity evidently appears to depend upon a rather casual choice of strategy.

According to an information-processing theory, performance on a cognitive task is the product of an interaction between knowledge possessed, elementary information-processing capacity, and one's choice of strategy for executing information-processing steps based upon knowledge. Some information-processing capacities may indeed be stable characteristics of an individual, others may be quite labile. The influence of a particular information-processing capacity upon task performance depends crucially upon the strategy used for task execution. Since strategy is a choice, there is no reason to assume that it is a stable characteristic of the individual. However, information-processing theories cannot be used to predict behavior unless task strategy can be specified.

CONCLUDING COMMENTS

The sentence-verification paradigm has been used to illustrate four incompatabilities between the experimental and differential psychology approaches to

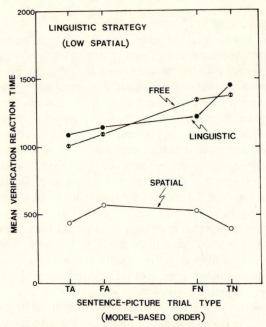

FIG. 5 Mean verification time as a function of sentence complexity for a subject using the linguistic strategy. The curve parameter represents the instructions given for each 2-day period.

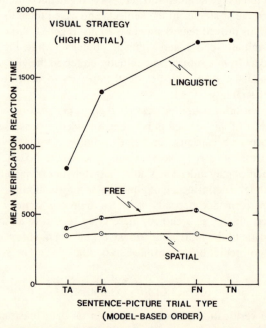

FIG. 6 Mean verification time as a function of sentence complexity for a subject using the visual strategy. The curve parameter represents the instructions given for each 2-day period.

the study of individual differences in cognition. We believe that these incompatabilities are basic ones. The differential psychologist seeks the underlying traits of intelligence. For the cognitive psychologist the concept of intelligence itself simply disappears, to be replaced by the specification of permanent and labile information-processing capacities and a library of available strategies.

Perhaps largely because of these differences in view about thought, the differential and cognitive psychologists have also developed different techniques for data analysis, and these techniques are bound to the theories that generated them. It is also obvious that the availability of particular data analysis procedures has had an effect upon theorizing, and this, too, has increased the incompatability between the disciplines of scientific psychology.

The fact that there are really two disciplines of scientific psychology does not mean that one of them is right and the other is wrong. Differential psychologists have dealt with the description and prediction of relative performance, a legitimate and important goal in both scientific and applied psychology. Certainly the concepts and techniques of differential psychology will continue to be useful in personnel selection procedures in education, government, and industry. They will also provide basic scientific constructs for use in theories aimed at a more global level of mental performance, e.g., in social psychology and anthropology. We also hope to see the development of a cognitive psychology of individual differences. Such a theory should be useful in relating mental performance to more reductionist scientific theories in such fields as physiology and genetics. Surely the variables studied in these sciences have their effect upon information-processing structures and processes rather than upon statistical abstractions such as traits.

In considering where one should use a differential or a cognitive approach, we would be inclined not to make a theoretical versus applied distinction. Instead, we would make a distinction between global versus reductionist views of mental performance, and the prediction of relative or absolute performance. Each of Cronbach's two disciplines seems to have its forte in different fields.

What, then, has happened to the reunification of the disciplines? The term "separate but equal" has been discredited in one field of human affairs. It is not wise to carry an analogy too far. Cultural pluralism may indeed be the appropriate course of action for the psychology of individual differences.

ACKNOWLEDGMENTS

We are grateful for the assistance of Marcy Lansman, Nancy Mathews, John Palmer, Janet Davidson, and Colene McKee.

REFERENCES

Anderson, N. Information integration theory: A brief survey. In D. Krantz, R. Atkinson, R. D. Luce, & P. Suppes (Eds.), *Contemporary developments in mathematical psychology,* Vol. II. San Francisco: Freeman, 1974.

Baddeley, A. D. A 3-minute reasoning test based on grammatical transformation. *Psychonomic Science,* 1968, **10**, 341–342.

Carpenter, P. A., & Just, M. A. Sentence comprehension: A psycholinguistic processing model of verification. *Psychological Review,* 1975, **82**, 45–73.

Carroll, J. B. Psychometric tests as cognitive tasks: A new structure of intellect. In L. B. Resnick (Ed.), *The nature of intelligence.* Hillsdale, N. J.: Lawrence Erlbaum Associates, 1976.

Carroll, J. B. How shall we study individual differences in cognitive abilities? Methodological and theoretical perspectives. *Intelligence,* 1978, **2,** 87–115 (this issue).

Catlin, J., & Jones, N. K. Verifying affirmative and negative sentences. *Psychological Review,* 1976, **83**, 497–501.

Clark, H. H., & Chase, W. G. On the process of comparing sentences against pictures. *Cognitive Psychology,* 1972, **3**, 472–517.

Cronbach, L. The two disciplines of scientific psychology. *American Psychologist,* 1957, **12**, 671–684.

Hunt, E., MacLeod, C. M., & Lansman, M. *On the incompatibility of two views of intelligence.* University of Washington Technical Report, 1978.

Kahneman, D. *Attention and effort.* New York: Academic Press, 1973.

Kantowitz, B. H. Double stimulation. In B. H. Kantowitz (Ed.), *Human information processing.* Hillsdale, N. J.: Lawrence Erlbaum Associates, 1974.

Lansman, M. An attentional approach to individual differences in immediate memory. University of Washington Ph.D. dissertation, 1978.

Lansman, M., & Hunt, E. *Group testing procedures for measuring information processing variables.* University of Washington Technical Report, 1978.

MacLeod, C. M., Hunt, E. B., & Mathews, N. N. Individual differences in the verification of sentence–picture relationships. *Journal of Verbal Learning and Verbal Behavior,* 1978, in press.

Norman, D., & Bobrow, D. On data limited and resource limited processes. *Cognitive Psychology,* 1975, **7**, 44–64.

Scheffé, H. *The analysis of variance.* New York: Wiley, 1959.

Sternberg, R. *Intelligence, information processing, and analogical reasoning.* Hillsdale, N. J.: Lawrence Erlbaum Associates, 1977.

Suppes, P., & Zinnes, J. Basic measurement theory. In R. D. Luce, R. R. Bush, & E. Galanter (Eds.), *Handbook of mathematical psychology.* New York: Wiley, 1963.

Tanenhaus, M. K., Carroll, J. M., & Bever, T. G. Sentence–picture verification models as theories of sentence comprehension: A critique of Carpenter and Just. *Psychological Review,* 1976, **83**, 310–317.

5

Theory and Method for Research on Aptitude Processes

RICHARD E. SNOW

Stanford University

The theoretical and methodological concepts available to, and needed by, research on aptitudes as cognitive processes are discussed. Contemporary views of cognitive processes are examined in relation to individual difference constructs and methods used to examine their reliability and validity. Individual difference constructs are discussed in relation to cognitive process models and research thereon. Studies of short-term memory processes are reviewed to demonstrate the complementary strengths and weaknesses of experimental and correlational methods and concepts. A coordinated approach to the study of aptitude as information processing is suggested.

A vast literature in educational psychology attests to the fact that individual differences in learner aptitudes predict learning outcomes, and a substantial body of literature also now demonstrates that aptitude variables often interact with instructional or training treatment variables in these predictions (Cronbach & Snow, 1977). These aptitude–treatment interactions (ATI) have important implications for the development of instructional theory and research and for instructional improvement. But if practical and theoretical use is to be made of aptitude information in instructional work, then individual differences in aptitude for learning will need to be understood, at a more analytic level, as individual differences in psychological processes.

An earlier report (Snow, 1977) gave a summary of recent instructional ATI studies concerning those aptitude constructs judged most worthy of future research, reviewed two methodological developments relevant to such studies, and then began the task of collating laboratory research on relations between aptitude measures and measures reflecting cognitive processes. It was suggested that a laboratory science of aptitude could be constructed to complement continuing ATI research on instruction by pursuing common

The research reported in this article was sponsored by Personnel and Training Research Programs, Psychological Sciences Division, Office of Naval Research and Advanced Research Projects Agency under Contract No. N00014–75–C–0882. The views and conclusions contained in this document are those of the author, and should not be interpreted as necessarily representing the official policies, either expressed or implied, of the Office of Naval Research, the Advanced Research Projects Agency, or the U.S. Government. This article is an abbreviated version of the article that first appeared in *Intelligence*.

process analyses of individual differences in aptitude and learning. The present report reviews the theoretical and methodological foundation on which such a science might build, and sketches some directions in which a process theory of aptitude might be sought.

ORIENTATION

Background

The idea of a laboratory science for the analysis and interrelation of aptitude tests and learning tasks is not new. The problem of individual differences in learning has been of interest periodically in experimental psychology since its early days. Glaser (1967) has reviewed this history. In one form or another new research in this direction has been suggested by several recent writers (Estes, 1970, 1974; Gagné, 1970; Glaser, 1972, 1976). Glaser and Resnick (1972) gave some examples of experiments serving task-analytic purposes. Some of the instructional ATI experiments are also useful for such purposes, if reinterpreted as suggesting only possible ATI mechanisms rather than probable generalizations to instruction. They combine with laboratory studies arising from experimental psychologists' renewed interest in cognitive processes related to intelligence (see, e.g., Resnick, 1976) and from attempts to alter aptitudes through direct training (e.g., Guinaugh, 1969; Jacobs & Vandeventer, 1971a, b). These form a loose but growing collection of provocative suggestions. Some use experimental manipulations to examine the construct validity of aptitude measures. Some use aptitudes to examine the construct validity of measures of learning processes, and some generate new conceptions of aptitude and learning as a result. But as yet there has been no systematic compilation of this literature or development of a theoretical framework with which to plan further efforts. The last time an experimental psychology textbook paid extensive attention to individual differences in learning was a chapter by McGeogh and Irion (1952), although Underwood (1957) devoted some pages to a discussion of the methodology of experimental research on individual differences. In 1957, Cronbach issued his famous call for unification of correlational and experimental psychology. This was the impetus for the growth of ATI research on instruction through the 1960s. The milestone symposium edited by Gagné (1967) included several views of laboratory research on individual differences in learning, although no substantive connections between that work and ATI research have been attempted. There is still only minor contact between research on aptitude and research on cognition in instruction. (See, for example, Klahr, 1976.)

Periodically over recent years, however, various other writers have proposed one or another general means of combining experimental and correlational psychology (e.g., Hunt & Sullivan, 1974; Owens, 1968; Vale &

Vale, 1969). The general implications of person–situation interactions has become an issue of concern in many quarters of psychology. (Compare, for example, Cronbach, 1975; Mischel, 1973; McGuire, 1973). And currently there are new suggestions for the experimental analysis of individual differences and their use in theories of learning and cognition (e.g., Estes, 1974; E. Hunt, & Lansman, 1975; Underwood, 1975). Thus individual differences in aptitude, in learning, and in related cognitive processes seems now to be a topic on the agenda for basic theory and research, both in the U.S. and abroad (see e.g., Flammer, 1975). The time has finally come for combined, concerted efforts.

The present discussion cannot hope to provide a thorough updating of this field, or a thorough examination of all the relevant theoretical and methodological issues. Nor can it consider in detail all domains of aptitude and learning variables.

Starting Assumptions

Definition of Aptitude.   An aptitude is an individual difference construct, with its associated measures, that bears an hypothesized or demonstrated relation to individual differences in learning in some particular setting. In education, aptitudes are student characteristics that predict response to instruction under a given instructional treatment. In educational research, then, the defining characteristics of aptitude is *relation to learning.* Measures of "intelligence" or "scholastic ability" identify aptitude because they predict achievement in conventional schooling. Through decades of demonstrations of this prediction, "ability" and "aptitude" came to be thought of as synonyms. But any special ability, cognitive style, personality, motivation, or interest variable that shows relation to learning ought also to be considered as identifying aptitude. There is, then, no traditional domain of differential psychology that should be called "aptitudes" *a priori.* By adopting this broader definition, the field is left open to the study of new and old constructs alike and to hypotheses about combinations of constructs from different traditional domains. More detailed discussion of this definition is given by Snow (1977) and Cronbach and Snow (1977).

Within this broad definition, it is nonetheless true that most research on aptitude for learning has concentrated on cognitive ability, and this report focuses here also. The concept of general mental ability will be a first cornerstone for any theory of aptitude. The central hypothesis of this report and the research program it advocates, is that individual differences in performance on ability tests and learning tasks are manifestations of cognitive processes common to each. Despite historical arguments to the contrary, notably by Woodrow (1946), intelligence is still often defined as the ability to learn. This definition persists because it is parsimonious and intuitively appealing, and because it makes psychological sense. There are theoretical reasons to believe that individual differences in ability and learning derive from the same psychological phenomena, whether one takes an environmentalist (e.g., Ferguson, 1954, 1956; J. McV. Hunt, 1961) or hereditarian (e.g., Garrett, 1946; Jensen, 1972) view. And the research often cited in denying the connection is not convincing (Cronbach & Snow, 1977). The two disciplines of differential and experimental psychology, focusing on different aspects of the whole, devised different representation systems and terminology for their points of view—one based on static quantities and vectors in mental space, the other on mechanistic functions and group acquisition curves. Progress will now best be served by relegating this division of labor, and all that it implies, to the historical closet, and by avoiding where possible the limitations of discipline specific terminology.

With this view as an entry point, several basic propositions about alternative approaches to research on aptitude and its incorporation into theories of learning and cognition can now be added.

Idiosyncracies Versus General Laws. Two extreme positions represent opposing and equally counterproductive views about individual differences in aptitude. One holds that there are none of import; learning can be explained sufficiently by general laws applicable to everyone. The other holds that each individual is unique; only idiographic study of the single case can provide understanding. An intermediate position is likely to be most productive. The fact that a variety of individual differences have been successfully measured across persons, and related to a variety of learning outcomes, argues against both extreme positions. General laws can be stated and studied, but included in their study must be an assessment of the boundaries beyond which they cannot be generalized. Idiosyncratic processes can be studied, but included in their study must be some assessment of the possibility of interindividual similarity. We can expect that both approaches would eventually sort individuals into arrays of relatively homogeneous groups of $1 < N < \infty$, one approach by recognizing boundary differences, the other by recognizing similarities.

Typologies Versus Multivariate Measurement. But sorting individuals into labeled categories according to boundary conditions or similarities identified in one type of experiment breeds an archaic form of thinking about individual differences. Typologies were discarded by modern psychologists when it was recognized that many dimensions were needed to characterize an individual. No type category ever contains individuals homogeneous in all relevant respects. Typological distinctions may define hypothesized dimensions worth further study; there may even be occasions where the bimodal character of an individual difference distribution supports some form of categorical thinking. But multivariate continuous parametric measurement has so far proven to be the most efficient and versatile approach to the problem of studying individual differences of all kinds. Until enough is known about individual differences in cognitive processes to rule out curvilinearity and/or to support hypotheses about discontinuities, typological thinking, and the arbitrary cleavage of continuous variables that it promotes, should be avoided in favor of multidimensional conceptualization and multivariate statistical analysis.

Hypothesis Testing Versus Estimation of Relationships.   If individual differences in aptitude and learning variables are viewed as continuous, then it follows that a primary aim is to estimate the form and strength of relationships among them. This view holds as well for the study of relations between experimental variations and individual differences. Significance testing is then of secondary importance—of value as one guide to efficient use of research resources, but hardly the final arbiter of what is substance and what is shadow for the construction of theory.

Complexity.   With this position, it must also be noted that one-to-one correspondences between present aptitude and learning constructs will not likely be found. What is to be sought is some kind of mapping of each set of constructs onto the other. Relationships in this mapping are unlikely to be simple.

Causality.   Particularly to be avoided in such a mapping are assumptions that place aptitude constructs at either more or less "basic" a level of understanding than learning or other process constructs. Individual difference measures, whether based on cognitive test scores or laboratory task parameters, do not automatically reflect "fundamental unities." One kind of measure cannot be routinely taken as providing causal explanation of the other. While it is possible, for example, that some aptitude constructs may come to be explained as complex functions of "more basic" information-processing constructs, it is also possible that other aptitude constructs will be found to reflect rather directly some "more basic" biological features of the individual, which in turn control information processing.

Generalization.   Finally, conceptions of aptitude in learning built from laboratory analyses should not be expected to generalize directly to instructional settings. Laboratory models are analogs which can enrich conceptualizations of aptitude in instruction and can suggest improvements in aptitude measurement there. Ultimately, however, a theory of aptitude will need to be a theory of aptitude in situ.

Categories of Process Differences.   We can define four different forms or sources of individual differences in information processing: parameter differences (*p*-variables); sequence differences (*q*-variables); route differences (*r*-variables); and summation or strategic differences (*s*-variables). The distinctions between *p*-, *q*-, and *r*-variables can be clarified by imagining two flow charts that characterize the performance of two different individuals on some task; *p*-variables would refer to differences between the individuals on particular steps or components (e.g., capacity of STM, time needed for stimulus encoding, etc.); *q*-variables would be shown by the two flow charts taking the same steps but in different sequences (e.g., early vs. late work on some subgoal); *r*-variables would be indicated by the inclusion of qualitatively different steps in the two flow charts (e.g., visual-image rotation, or double checking, used in one chart and not in the other.)

This extension, together with the fact that we are ultimately concerned with individual differences in complex learning and problem solving, suggests the need for the fourth category, *s*-variables, representing individual differences in summative, strategic, or other more molar properties of information-processing models. The category of *s*-variables would include gross differences in the assembly and structure of the program systems used by different subjects (as opposed to *r*-variables representing variations within the same basic program). Taylor (1976) classified memory models as being of four basic types: serial versus parallel processing, and exhaustive versus self-terminating search. Individual differences associated with these kinds of differences in models would be classed as *s*-variables.

But other variables are implied here as well. Laboratory tasks and test items are often repetitive and noncumulative. They require little or no prior knowledge on the part of the learner. One might imagine a learner cycling through a sequence of steps for each item in a test or list to be learned, without showing intercycle interaction. In contrast, learning from instruction is usually cumulative; prior knowledge, skills, and predispositions are intimately involved in present learning, and instruction is usually geared to take advantage of these. Even repetitive laboratory tasks have their cumulative properties, as when an early guess builds confidence, continued practice yields a stable strategy, or persistent errors breed anxiety, defensiveness, or change in strategy. Learning-to-learn, transfer, and retention differences operate across trials and tasks, and may do so also across items and tests. There is evidence that familiarization alters individual differences in learning (Cronbach & Snow, 1977), that learning occurs within tests (Whitcomb & Travers, 1957), that early and late parts of some tests may relate differently to learning task measures (Koran, Snow, & McDonald, 1971), that anxiety is both a predictor and a product of learning task performance (Gaudry & Spielberger, 1971), and that various motivational constructs may moderate the role of ability in learning (Snow, 1977). While simple cognitive models may provide parsimonious starting points, we expect them to be far too simple in their account of individual differences in instructional learning. The category of s-variables keeps this likelihood in focus.

Thus the problem for further research will be to distinguish p, q, r, and s sources of individual differences, and to show how they can be combined and/or further differentiated. Information-processing models of particular tasks or tests will need to show how these kinds of differences work in consort to produce observable differences in performance. Aptitude variables (A), and instructional treatment variables (T), and their interactions will need to be analyzed and understood in these common terms. This will best be accomplished by a combination of correlational research that relates A, p, q, r, and s variables, and experimental research that manipulates T in ways that influence these relationships.

A RESEARCH STRATEGY

How should the research effort now proceed? Can a detailed strategy be adopted that will not only guide further work, but will also show clearly how and where prior studies connect with an overall framework?

Summary of Starting Points

Theoretical Framework. Figure 1 shows the categories of variables that have been identified, and indicates by arrows the direction analysis has taken or can take in the future. Standing predictive relationships between aptitude variables (A) and learning outcomes (O) from instruction have been shown to be moderated by instructional treatment variables (T), with the recognition that ATI often occurs. It is clear that AT combinations can be studied in real instructional settings, and should continue to be, but that this research must be supplemented by analyses conducted in laboratory settings where there is more chance of building theoretical models of psychological processes operating in ATI. The cognitive information-processing approach of modern experimental psychology seems best equipped to guide and inform such analyses. But computer simulations and related work already completed show that individual differences in these aptitude processes probably take a variety of complex forms. A distinction among four major forms or sources of apparent individual differences in processing should help to unravel these aptitude complexes. It appears that individuals can differ in parameters (p) reflecting efficiency and capacity in particular processing steps or components, in how a sequence (q) of processing components is organized, in the inclusion of different components or processing routes (r), and in the overall summation (s) of assembly and adaptation of processing to particular tasks. These forms are indicated as p, q, r, and s variables in Fig. 1.

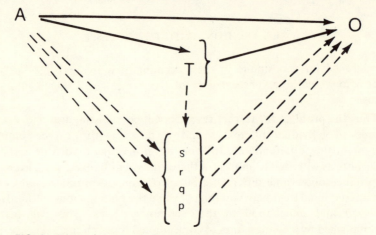

FIG. 1   Schematic representation of standing correlations between aptitude
(A) and outcome (O) variables, A x treatment (T) interactions, and the analysis
of A and T variables into information-processing variables. Brackets indicate
complex interaction.

Methodology.   Research designed to fill in this framework will need to
combine multivariate experimental and correlational methods. This is not to
say that exploratory correlational work will not be useful, or that experiments
must always include multiple individual measures. But adequate theory will
be built and tested primarily on the combined paradigm.

In particular, the requirements of parsimony and construct validation
demand the inclusion of multimethod measurement and a representative set
of reference factors. And generalizability estimates for all measures will be
required, so that key relationships can be disattenuated. More than typical
care is also needed in sample selection and description. College populations
will differ from high school populations, for example, in a variety of reference
factors, whether measured or unmeasured. Attempts to collate findings
across studies will need to pay close attention to such "hidden" individual
differences.

Procedure

Aptitude Selection.   One could conceivably start with any aptitude
construct of interest practically or theoretically. The main issue, of course, is
whether there is good evidence that the aptitude chosen is related in important
ways to learning under given instructional conditions.

The two major aptitude complexes discussed earlier are starting choices
particularly to be recommended. The clearest first choice is G, general mental
ability, and the first level of its differentiation into G_c, G_f, and G_v. An
information-processing analysis would strive to show whether the crystal-
lized-fluid–visualization ability distinction is describable in process terms.
A second choice is a motivational complex: achievement via conformity (A_c),
achievement via independence (A_i), and anxiety (A_x). These aptitudes have

been shown to interact with instructional treatments in their own right, and they appear also to combine with one another and/or with G in higher-order ATI. Information-processing analyses that could characterize how such individual differences functioned in combination with G to influence learning would begin to bridge the age-old but artificial gap between cognitive and affective domains, producing a more coordinated and comprehensive view of aptitude.

Reference Factors. Any process analysis of an aptitude construct needs to include a battery of representative reference factors. The aptitude constructs identified above would be prime candidates for inclusion in any such battery. In addition, some ability constructs available from differential psychology appear more closely identified with processing concepts and so would justify inclusion. These are: short-term memory span, visual memory, perceptual speed, closure speed, and various cognitive style constructs. Measures of these and other ability factors would be chosen from the hierarchical factor model to fit the task at hand.

Exploratory Empirical Analysis. Some empirical studies have begun identifying individual differences in processes related to learning. (Snow, 1977, began a review of these.) Some aptitude measures have already begun to show correlations with measures from information-processing tasks. (One category of these studies is examined in a later section.) We can expect this empirical exploration to continue to generate concepts and relationships bearing on the network depicted in Fig. 1. These deserve thorough review in the analysis of any particular aptitude construct.

Task Analysis. Given a chosen aptitude, one still needs a fruitful method of task analysis. Different approaches to task analysis have been developed for different purposes, and they represent aptitude–learning relations in different ways. Gagné (1970) constructs learning hierarchies to specify sequences of steps in instructional tasks. One can ask learners to introspect during, or after, task performance. There are questionnaires that also yield processing protocols. Various experimental arrangements can be made to yield task-analytic information. Eye movement records can sometimes be helpful. Computer simulation methods provide detailed programs and flow diagrams to represent sequences of processing operations in problem-solving. And Carroll (1976) has been developing a method that maps ability tests onto a general process model.

At present there is no one best way to gain initial hypotheses about processes in task performance. This is, in many ways, the crux of the whole problem. By one means or another, one seeks a listing of component processes hypothesized to account, in some combination, for individual differences in the task of interest.

Componential Analysis.   Several aspects of the discussion in previous sections of this paper parallel ideas offered by R. Sternberg (1977). Though developed independently, the two views converge on several common distinctions and emphases. Sternberg has gone on, however, to construct a methodology based on these views which he calls "componential analysis." This seems the best place to summarize his approach. The strategy incorporates many of the principal strengths of information-processing, factor-analytic, and psychometric models. He has applied it to the analysis of several forms of analogical reasoning problems, of the kind typically found in general mental ability tests. For a full discussion of the approach and application, the reader should consult Sternberg (1977). Only an outline can be presented here.

A componential analysis includes the following steps:

1. Any task or test is composed of items (whether test items or the particular problems used in successive trials in an experiment). Each item is regarded as a composite of subtasks, yielding a composite score for each of a number of individuals. The first step is to identify these subtasks. In Sternberg's work with analogy items, the subtasks are defined by the parts of an analogy. A true-false analogy of the form "A is to B as C is to D" has three subtasks in addition to the total problem process: given an understanding of A, process B-C-D; given A-B, process C-D; given A-B-C, process D.

2. Given an identification of the subtasks, an experiment is designed to obtain what are called "interval" scores for each subtask. In the analogies' example, total solution time is regarded as a composite of the solution time needed after A is understood, after A-B is understood, and after A-B-C is understood by the subject. The experiment can be arranged to provide information in the form of cues separately for each successive part of the task to create these conditions. Four time-interval scores (counting total time) are thus obtained. Error, as well as latency, scores can be used for this purpose.

3. The experimental procedure for breaking up the task item to derive the interval scores is assumed not to have altered the task, psychologically. The interval scores are also assumed to be additive, i.e., the composite score contains the interval score for the first subtask, as defined above, which contains the score for the second subtask, etc. This latter assumption is tested by fitting the correlations among scores to the Guttman simplex model.

4. From the interval scores, component scores are estimated, using one or more information-processing models of the task for each subject. The alternative models are examined in terms of amount of total variance accounted for. The component scores for the best fitting model(s) are adopted as the basic measures of individual differences in information processing for that task.

5. The component model is then internally validated by examining correlations among component scores using the concepts of construct validity, and by experiments designed to test implications of the model.

6. The component model is externally validated by examining correlations of component scores, and interval scores, with reference-ability factor scores, derived from established reference tests. A structural regression analysis is used to examine the network of relations among component, interval, and factor scores.

7. The previous steps lead to what Sternberg calls an "intensive task analysis" of one task. Such analyses of a series of related tasks then comprises an "extensive task analysis." This aims to demonstrate that the components and models established for one task generalize to account for performance in other, related tasks.

Thus, Sternberg has taken a major step toward formalizing a procedure that incorporates most of the concepts and methods reviewed in the present paper. Some reservations remain regarding the generality of the procedure, however. While Sternberg applies it to a variety of analogy items, with other tasks the identification of convenient subtasks to obtain a starting point may not be so readily apparent to the investigator or to the subject. In items from tasks such as the Embedded Figures Test, the Street Gestalt Completion Test, and various spatial ability tests, similar segmentation of subtasks may require considerable experimental work initially. Furthermore, the experimental designs employed to segment analogies and obtain interval scores may not be applicable to all kinds of items, so other experimental designs may have to be invented for some kinds of tasks or tests. Finally, extensive task analysis may be the most difficult step, and this step is not yet well specified. It has been shown by the work of many cognitive psychologists, using whatever method, that process models can be built for single tasks. Combining such models will not simply be a matter of correlating their component scores. General models must be assembled that incorporate all specific models, and these cannot simply be patchworks. Nor can it be assumed that LTM simply contains many specific programs, since this ignores the correlational network of tests and tasks, and in the extreme returns to oversimplified S–R views. And, having strong specific models in hand may, in a strange way, actually impede progress toward this step, since their accommodation to more general purposes may be awkward, requiring the relaxing of assumptions and much disassembly. Thus, it would appear that the model-builder ought to have an eye on general purposes from the start. This is probably best accomplished by simultaneous analysis of a range of tasks. But Sternberg's approach clearly merits extensive trial. He has now applied it to the analysis of a broad range of reasoning problems with significant success. (See Sternberg, in press.)

Learning Samples. Process analyses of aptitudes need, at some point, to be brought together with comparable analyses of instructional treatments. A check station is required, close to laboratory conditions, where combined assumptions and hypotheses can be examined and perhaps refined. The miniature instructional experiments that have dominated the instructional psychological literature in recent years may be a useful form for this purpose. They are to be regarded as "learning sample tests," however, on a par with the work sample tests of industrial psychology; they probably do not supply direct generalizations to instruction.

Learning samples can also be extracted from real-school instruction, and this may be preferable in many cases. The investigator strives to trace components of his aptitude process model through to individual differences in actual learning under alternative treatments. Considerable use may be made here also of various forms of task analysis, including learner introspection.

Aptitude Test Revision.   It is likely that conventional aptitude tests will at times need revision to sharpen processing contrasts identified in early analyses. Revision may be minor in some cases, extensive in others. The aim is to ensure that the aptitude measure to be used in field research indeed embodies and displays the processing distinctions important in theory. The test is then made a vehicle to ply between field and laboratory.

Instructional Studies.   The ultimate goal is demonstration that aptitude measures connect to instructional treatment variations in understandable and predictable ways. Aptitude and instructional treatments described with common process models should make this possible. But the proof is in the real-school, long-duration instructional studies. Hopefully, laboratory analyses of aptitude and continuing ATI studies in the field will be conducted as parallel, closely-coordinated transactions.

STUDIES OF SHORT-TERM MEMORY:
A DEMONSTRATION AND CRITIQUE

No area of experimental cognitive psychology has been treated to more research attention in recent years than that of immediate memory. This is reasonable, since experiments on immediate memory gave birth to the history of research on learning, and since it is likely that immediate memory operations provide a foundation on which deeper processing activities are built. Differential psycholgists, too, have long made a place for a "memory span" factor in taxonomies of human ability and have often used paired-associate tests as well. The tests used to represent such factors have been the only cognitive tasks in common use in both psychologies, until recently.

Short-term memory is thus a natural site for initial exploration of relations between cognitive process measures and cognitive test scores. It is a good place to demonstrate application of some of the points explicated in previous sections of this report. But a word of caution is in order: although immediate memory may be basic to cognitive functioning, it is unlikely to be comprehensive in its yield of concepts of value in theorizing about individual differences in cognition. Aptitude constructs are unlikely to reduce to memory functions, so a broad perspective needs to be maintained.

Ever since Galton and J. McK. Cattell, there have been sporadic investigations of individual differences in short-term learning and memory tasks and the degree to which such differences were correlated with mental tests. Among the more programmatic efforts were those of Woodrow (1946) and of a group headed by Gulliksen (1942, 1961; see also Allison, 1960; Duncanson, 1964; Stake 1961). Although these authors reported little relation among tests and learning tasks, their results actually support the view that general ability and simple learning correlate. (For discussion, see Cronbach & Snow, 1977.) The early findings fail, however, to give a more detailed picture of the bases for such correlations.

The Hunt Studies

E. B. Hunt's program of research relating ability variables to speed and sequence of immediate memory processing has reopened this issue and raised many new questions. The first study reported in the Hunt program (Hunt, Frost, & Lunneborg, 1973) examined the performance of 40 college students on a continuous paired-associate task. This task provided estimates of four parameters, as defined in the work of Atkinson, Brelsford, and Shiffrin (1967). The parameters, defined by Atkinson, Brelsford, and Shiffrin (1967) for their continuous paired-associate task, are the following: α, the probability of entry of an item into STM; r, the number of items that can be held in STM at one time; Θ, the rate of transfer of information into ITM; and τ, the rate at which information becomes unavailable from ITM. Since Hunt's subjects represented extreme groups on verbal (V) and quantitative (Q) ability (as measured by college admissions tests), it was possible to compare means on each parameter among groups of students labeled "high" or "low" on each ability. Herein lie two initial problems that will confuse further research, unless recognized.

By convention, extreme groups blocked by partitioning an aptitude continuum are described by terms such as "high," "medium," and "low." But these are absolute terms applied to groups defined on a relative standard. Hunt's "lows" may turn out to be equal to another researcher's "highs," or vice versa. At the least, studies using extreme-groups designs will need to report normative ranges on the tests used, to qualify the abbreviated labels. In the case of Hunt's subjects (whose admission to college was, in part, based on these tests), we should prefer the term "medium" as probably a more accurate description for his "low" groups.

A more serious difficulty concerns the meaning of V and Q. Extreme groups, formed on the basis of V and Q distributions, differ also on all personal variables correlated with V and Q (but left unmeasured in the study).

As mentioned previously, there is likely to be a whole network of correlates for any individual difference distribution. Interpretation of results in terms of V and Q is thus tenuous at best. A difference in some information-processing parameter associated with V might be associated also with differences in G, verbal fluency, or achievement motivation, or sex, or even in Q itself. In less selected populations, for instance, V will tend to correlate with Q and show mean differences favoring females. This difficulty becomes evident in another way below.

The Hunt analysis concluded that differences on two parameters α and τ, were associated with Q. No statistically significant differences were found for the other two parameters (r and Θ) or for any parameters on the V contrast. Apparently, students with high quantitative ability showed a higher probability of placing items in STM (α) and a lower rate of loss of information from ITM (τ) than did students scoring at a medium level of quantitative ability.

However, a plot of the reported means (see Fig. 2) suggests a different story, and this underscores several of the methodological preferences stated previously. There are three implications to be drawn from the figure, none of which were apparent in the statistical tests applied to means or given attention in the authors' interpretation.

1. Both V and Q ability appear to relate to both parameters, though admittedly the relation of Q is clearly the stronger. This implies that a more general ability, not Q alone, underlies the correlation with both parameters. Considering that V and Q are probably correlated in the population, taking a hierarchical view of ability organization, both abilities are subordinate to G_c and G. The principle of parsimony demands that special ability interpretations be adopted only when general abilities can be ruled out. They cannot be here, because no general ability measures were included. One could have been approximated, however, by forming two composites, V + Q and V-Q. The first composite then represents G, while the second gives an independent linear contrast to test the special-ability hypothesis. Normally this is best done in continous distributions rather than in extreme groups, but it could have clarified interpretation here.

2. If some general ability relates to both parameters, we should expect the two parameters to be intercorrelated. If one approximates the G continuum by attending only to the high-high and medium-medium groups (the general dimension), the plot clearly suggests this, and Hunt et al. (1973) reported a correlation of 0.42 between α and τ later in their chapter. Unfortunately, the matrix of intercorrelations did not include the ability tests, so the relative strength of these various relations could not be studied.

3. In the plot, Q appears to moderate the relation between V and the two parameters. Among high quantitative students, V relates to α. The vertical line is nearly parallel to the ordinate, suggesting that this correlation is almost perfect, at least when means rather than individual scores are examined.

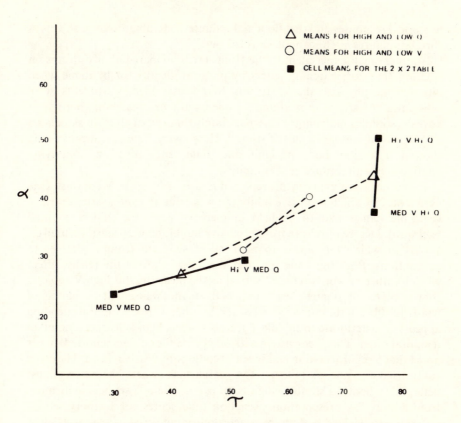

FIG. 2   Plot of means on two parameters (α and τ) of the Atkinson–Shiffrin model for groups of subjects differing in verbal (V) and quantitative (Q) ability (after Hunt, Frost, & Lunneborg, 1973).

Among medium quantitative students, V relates to τ. The mean slope here approaches the horizontal, again suggesting high positive correlation. In the Hunt analysis, row and column means were tested for statistical significance; apparently this moderator relationship (an interaction) was not. These relations may be weak, so conclusions are unwarranted. But overly conservative statistical analyses, which minimize Type I errors at the expense of Type II errors, are also unwarranted at this stage of research. This moderator trend is an example of the subtleties with which one must deal in combining experimental and correlational methods and concepts. Such a finding deserves to be kept as an hypothesis for research, and not swept aside by the insensitivities of conventional modes of hypothesis testing. If confirmed, the hypothesis would state that verbal ability is associated with entry of information into STM among learners of high quantitative ability, but is associated more with the rate of loss of items from ITM among learners middling in quantitative ability. It is noted here that the task involved largely numerical responses and that floor and ceiling effects, ubiquitous problems in correlational research, cannot be ruled out.

Another small experiment in the Hunt series compared ability groups on reaction time for matching letters by physical identity, or by name when different in physical shape. It was found that high V students were substantially faster than medium V students in name matching, but not in physical stimulus matching. This would imply that verbal ability is associated with speed of coding linguistic stimuli. Here again, however, means for Q showed a similar but nonsignificant trend, suggesting an underlying relationship with a more general ability.

Two other Hunt experiments reported results *only* for the V contrast. One used a task in which proactive inhibition was built up over a series of trials: vegetable names had to be held in memory while the subject counted backward. Degree of release from proactive inhibition was then measured on a trial in which the words to be recalled switched from vegetables to occupations. Both high and medium V subjects showed the release effect when number of words recalled served as the measure. But high V subjects showed markedly greater release when performance was scored for number of words recalled in the correct serial order. In other words, temporal encoding appears to deteriorate in middle V learners, while high V learners maintain temporal order. This is consistent with other data the authors reported. It was noted that temporal coding and speed of coding are closely related. The other study used Sternberg's (1969) STM search task, where the subject must determine whether a stimulus digit is, or is not, one of a set held in memory from a previous presentation. Reaction time scores for memory sets of differing size yielded a slope parameter reflecting speed of search. High V subjects showed faster search speeds than did medium V subjects.

Summarizing these and related studies, Hunt et al. drew the conclusion that verbal ability is associated with speed of coding, temporal-order preserving, and search operations in STM. Given the uncertainties introduced by the V and Q extreme-groups design, a more likely hypothesis for further work might be that differences in these processes relate to G, at least within its middle to high range.

The Seibert–Snow Studies

It is appropriate now to discuss some earlier research conducted in the traditional correlational mold. This will show some of the powers and also some of the weaknesses of such studies, relative to the Hunt approach. Two studies (Seibert & Snow, 1965; Snow & Seibert, 1966; and Seibert, Reid, & Snow, 1967) were designed to explore individual differences in some temporal features of initial stimulus processing in the visual system and their relation to tested abilities. Their general purpose was to test and extend the Guilford taxonomy by demonstrating that motion-picture tests tapped abilities that could not be fitted into existing categories. It was reasoned that the factor analytic conception of human intellect was based almost solely on printed tests. The dynamic character of film, and the control of temporal and spatial features of stimuli that it provided, would allow not only a more comprehensive survey of human abilities but one that might come closer to process descriptions of ability than traditional measurements via printed media. In particular, motion pictures might be used to present experimental stimulus arrangements as group tests.

A large number of motion-picture tests were constructed. These were combined with several existing motion-picture tests available from wartime work in the Aviation Psychology Program (see Gibson, 1947), as well as a battery of printed reference tests, and investigated in a series of exploratory factor analyses. While some specific hypotheses were built into the tests, these were not precisely stated or tested in the exploratory phase (and as it turned out, the only phase) of the research. Discussion will be limited here to one particular exploratory hypothesis.

Several motion-picture tests were constructed to allow group test administration of experimental conditions like those used by Averbach and Coriell (1961) to study the "erasure" or visual backward-masking phenomenon. They had followed Sperling's (1960) early work on information-processing hypotheses in the visual system, but had not noticed individual differences among their three subjects. We thought that there might well be important individual differences in the effects of backward masking, and that different abilities might relate to performance at different points in a backward-masking curve. The test was designed to present randomly-constructed letter arrays tachistoscopically. In each item, one letter of the array was marked by an adjacent bar or circle appearing simultaneously, or at a short interval later. Eight delay intervals, ranging up to 510 msec, were included with each item incorporating one delay interval. A score for each delay interval showed the number of marked letters correctly recorded on items at that interval. Following Averbach and Coriell, the condition in which the letter was marked simultaneously by a bar marker *and* after an interval by a surrounding circle, should give the effect called "erasure."

A sample of 100 male freshmen engineering students at Purdue University served as subjects. With a delay interval of 94 msec, average performance was quite inaccurate. At shorter or longer delay intervals, average performance was relatively accurate. These findings replicate the results of Averbach and Coriell. But there were marked individual differences at each delay interval. Correlating these differences with ability factors drawn from a factor analysis of other motion-picture and conventional tests, it was possible to project ability factors into the delay interval space to show how much variance in performance could be accounted for by each ability factor. It was found that subjects with high scores on an ability factor called "perceptual integration" (PI) did well at intervals shorter than 94 msec; subjects with low scores on this factor did poorly. The factor represented tests requiring identification of pictures of common objects presented on the screen, with parts masked and/or with parts distributed as bursts, over a short time span. Measures of closure speed and visual acuity also correlated with this factor. Subjects high on a factor called "verbal facility" (V), including conventional vocabulary tests as well as measures of tachistoscopic letter and word recognition, did well at intervals longer than 94 msec; those scoring lower on this factor did poorly here. Figure 3 shows the percent of variance accounted for by these factors at each delay interval. It also suggests that a third ability factor, perceptual speed (PS), may be relevant to performance at about 260-msec delay, and that PI may become relevant again at later delay intervals. Categorizing subjects as high–high, high–low, low–high, or low–low on the PI and V factors, respectively, yielded the four average curves shown in Fig. 4.

Since the subjects were freshman engineers, they were probably more similar to the high Q than to the medium Q subjects of the Hunt et al. studies.

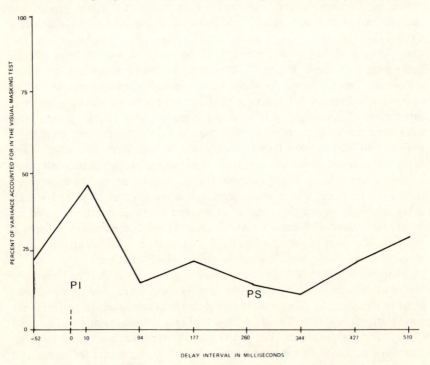

FIG. 3   Percentage of variance accounted for at each delay interval in the visual masking test by the perceptual integration (PI), verbal (V), and perceptual speed (PS) ability factors. $N = 100$ Purdue engineering students.

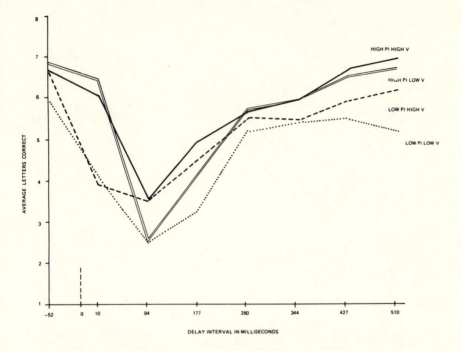

FIG. 4   Average number of letters correct at each delay interval for groups of students (N = 25) defined as high PI and high V, high PI and low V, low PI and high V, and low PI and low V.

The verbal factor, however, was not defined by a college admissions test, and included some STM measures in addition to vocabulary. It might be reasonable to equate Hunt's high V subjects with the high V subjects of the Seibert–Snow research. But a similar equation for medium versus low subjects in the two studies might not be safe. The two ends of the Seibert–Snow peceptual factor are fairly described as "high" and "low," since engineering students are probably unselected on such a variable.

Treating abilities as continua in multidimensional space is superior as an exploratory strategy to the extreme groups procedure used by Hunt. With the multivariate analysis completed, one can then always produce mean curves of the sort shown in Fig. 4, if these are considered more descriptive or understandable than the "geological," percentage-of-variance chart of Fig. 3. In another respect, however, the Seibert–Snow study suffers from a problem exactly like that of Hunt. The factor analysis was conceived in the Guilford tradition, and relied on varimax rotation to define a long list of special abiilty factors. Hence, no general ability construct was defined; so one cannot be sure that V is the key ability here, as opposed to G or G_c. The perceptual factors, PI and PS, suffer similarly from uncertainty of interpretation.

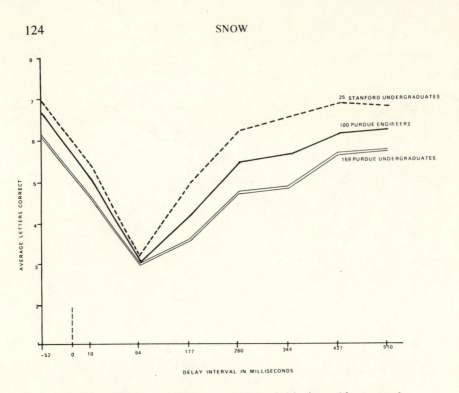

FIG. 5   Average number of letters correct at each delay interval for groups of
Stanford undergraduates ($N = 25$), Purdue engineering undergraduates ($N =$
100), and Purdue undergraduates ($N = 159$).

The possibility that a more general ability may be implicated is apparent in
Fig. 5. This shows the overall mean curves on the backward-masking task for
three samples of college students. The 100 Purdue engineering students used
in the previous analyses are shown as a solid curve. Another 159 subjects from
a later study were relatively unselected Purdue undergraduates in humanities
and sciences. Their average curve is shown as a blank core curve. Recent data
on the same task have also been collected from 25 Stanford undergraduates;
their average is the small-dash curve. (For details on this study, see Snow,
Marshalek, & Lohman, 1976.) It is likely that these three samples differ on
general scholastic ability. Certainly they differ in the selectivity exercised at
admission by their respective academic programs. These differences
correspond to the differences in elevation of the curves shown in Fig. 9, and
can be seen on both sides of the 94-msec point. In short, general ability cannot
be ruled out as the basic correlate of performance on this task.

   Other problems plague virtually all correlational surveys of this sort. Test
administration is typically conducted with the group of subjects together in a
large auditorium. Order of test administration is the same for all subjects, and
interaction among subjects, while controlled, can never be ruled out

altogether. Order effects, and sources of error common to tests adjacent in time, can influence the pattern of correlations obtained. In addition, studies that present experimental conditions on film under such conditions must deal with the confounding effects of viewing distance, viewing angle, and visual acuity. Seibert and Snow assigned subjects to seats randomly, and included an individual administration of a visual acuity test. These variables could then be included in the analysis and/or controlled statistically. The PI factor discussed above included individual differences in viewing distance and visual acuity in its definition. All these problems lead to doubts about adequacy of controls and replicability of conditions.

There is, on the other hand, a benefit to be derived from the relative lack of controls in correlational as opposed to experimental studies. Figure 5 displays curves obtained from three different large group administrations of a film designed to approximate the exacting experimental conditions applied by Averbach and Coriell (1961) to three laboratory subjects. the form of the curves is similar enough to that obtained by Averbach and Coriell to suggest that the phenomenon of backward masking is generalizable over substantial variations in task and administration conditions, and subject samples.

Despite the limitations of the Seibert–Snow research as an exploratory correlational survey, the findings do lead to hypotheses worth further test, and these connect loosely to the Hunt, et al. results. The implication of Figs. 3, 4, and 5 is that subjects differ in the severity with which the backward-masking effect occurs and the temporal location at which it occurs. These differences are associated with differences on tests of perceptual and verbal abilities. Perhaps masking at about 100 msec delay marks the point where in the average subject information is being transferred from a sensory buffering operation, designed to register and accumulate bits of percept, to one designed to code sums of these in STM.

This would associate the result with the first Hunt finding relating parameter α, the probability of entry of an item into STM, to V among high Q subjects (if the engineering students used by Seibert and Snow are assumed to be high Q). But there are two alternative interpretations for such a finding. Both can be understood within a three-component model consisting of (1) an iconic sensory buffer or store, (2) a symbolic recognition-encoding mechanism, and (3) STM.

One view would hold that individual differences arise from two p-variables: differences in strength (or resistance to decay) of the initial iconic image, reflected by the PI score; and differences in speed of encoding into STM, reflected by the V score, assuming Hunt's hypothesis is correct. Then, we assume that the masking stimulus causes erasure only if it occurs *during* transfer (coding) of information from iconic to STM store; it is perceived as superimposed on the array if it occurs while the array is in iconic store, and is coded by array position if it occurs after the array is coded into STM. Thus, subjects who are high in V (and have high Q in this sample) are able to code letters into STM more rapidly than are low V subjects, so erasure occurs at shorter delay intervals for them. Subjects who are high PI retain a more lasting iconic image on which their encoding processes can work, so erasure occurs later for them. Encoding, and erasure, then would occur early if a subject is high V–low PI and later if a subject is low V–high PI. The high–high subject has the benefit of both lasting iconic images and fast encoding. He would show the best overall performance. The low–low subject's performance would show more pronounced erasure effect through a wider range of delay intervals. Figure 4 seems to bear this out.

An alternative view posits a single q-variable as the source of process differences. Subjects high in V code the array symbolically into STM from iconic store, and the masking effect operates as before. However, subjects high in PI transfer the iconic image directly to STM as an image; symbolic encoding occurs at output from STM during response, rather than at input to STM. The masking effect still operates on the symbolic encoding process, but it comes later for these subjects because the encoding step comes third, rather than second, in the model. Perhaps the masking stimulus "catches up" to the array image in STM, interfering only if encoding has started.

Thus, this alternative hypothesis, though less plausible than the first in today's parlance, is more parsimonious with respect to individual differences; it posits a single process difference concerned with the order in which a series of three processing steps are carried out, and suggests that the aptitude score difference, V–PI, would index that process difference. It avoids hypothesizing individual differences in iconic image decay and speed of encoding, or associating these directly with separate aptitudes. The two alternatives are depicted schematically in Fig. 6. Further research will need to contrast these alternatives experimentally, and to distinguish V and PI and G correlationally.

The masking or erasure effect appears to be useful in probing for individual differences in the initial visual processing system. Research on visual masking has grown substantially in the past decade, and there are now sophisticated cognitive, as well as sensory physiological explanations for the phenomenon. (See Breitmeyer & Ganz, 1976; Kahneman, 1968; Turvey, 1973.) But individual differences have not been considered in this work.

It was noted above that one of Hunt's studies showed V (or G) related to speed of search in Sternberg's (1969) STM task; that is, the individual slopes relating memory set size to reaction time (RT) for each subject were shallower among more able subjects and steeper for less able subjects. This seems also consistent with the Seibert–Snow data. Each 8-letter array is a memory set. The subject must somehow fix as much of it in STM as fast as possible, to be able to match the marker to one of the letters when it appears. Averaging across delay intervals, the high ability subjects (high G?) clearly do best. This in turn leads into further research by Chiang and Atkinson (1976).

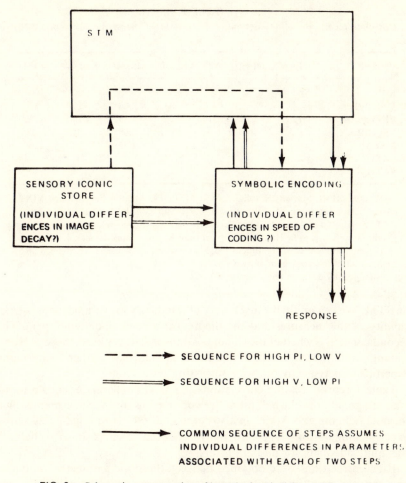

FIG. 6   Schematic representation of hypothesized individual differences in
two *p* variables versus one *q* variable to account for visual masking results.

The Chiang–Atkinson Study

Chiang and Atkinson administered the Sternberg memory-search task, a
visual search task (Atkinson, Holmgren, & Juola, 1969), and a standard digit
span task to a sample of college students, of which half were male and half
female. They also collected SAT–V and SAT–Q test scores from university
records.

There are two points of interest here. First, because the Chiang–Atkinson
design included two search tasks, and assessed reliability for each of the
measures derived from these tasks, it is possible to conduct a more
penetrating correlational analysis of their data than is typical in experiments

TABLE 1
Correlations and Reliability Estimates Reported by Chiang and Atkinson (1976)
$(N=30)$[a]

Variable	MINT	MSLOPE	VINT	VSLOPE	MSPAN	SAT–V	SAT–Q
MINT	(.96)	.11	.97[b]	.43	−.33	.20	−.39
MSLOPE		(.89)	.04	.83[b]	.04	.19	.03
VINT			(.95)	−.29	−.35	.14	.29
VSLOPE				(.91)	−.08	.34	−.05
MSPAN					(.95)	−.18	−.09
SAT–V						—	.44[b]
SAT–Q							—

[a]Where: MINT=Memory Search Intercept, MSLOPE=Memory Search Slope, VINT=
Visual Search Intercept, VSLOPE=Visual Search Slope, MSPAN=Digit Span Average,
SAT–V=Scholastic Aptitude Test Verbal Score, SAT–Q=Scholastic Aptitude Test
Quantitative Score. Split-Half Reliability, appearing in the main diagonal, was estimated
by the correlation of scores on Blocks 1, 3, 5, with scores on Blocks 2, 4, 6, stepped up by
application of the Spearman–Brown Formula.
[b]Significantly different from zero at .05 level.

on STM. We can apply the machinery of test theory to examine the construct
validity of the measures and the theoretical models underlying them. The
second concern is whether the Chiang–Atkinson data replicate those of Hunt.
Chiang and Atkinson pushed their data analysis further than many
experimenters typically do, with surprising results.

Table 1 reproduces the correlational data. The reliabilities shown in the
main diagonal are split-half estimates corrected using the Spearman-Brown
formula. Chiang and Atkinson also computed test–retest reliabilities across
experimental sessions. These are not reproduced here. As shown, reliability
was quite adequate for all parameters.

High correlations were obtained between the slope parameters, and also
between the two intercept parameters. These, with the relatively low
correlations between the within-task pairs or slope and intercept parameters,
constitute evidence of construct validity following the traditional multitrait–
multimethod reasoning of Campbell and Fiske (1959). In brief, this is that
measures representing the same trait but based on different methods of
measurement should correlate more highly than measures of different traits
based on the same method of measurement. The very high correlations
among like parameters here allowed Chiang and Atkinson to form two
composite scores for overall slope and intercept in their later analyses.
However, the like parameters are thought to represent different components
in the information-processing models of each task. We can pursue the
construct validity question further, using the individual correlations to test
the basic models.

The reliability estimates allow us to correct the observed parameter intercorrelations for attenuation, and thus to see what correlations should obtain in theory among the true parameter scores. The correction formula is simply $r_{TxTy} = r_{xy}/\sqrt{r_{xx}}\sqrt{r_{yy}}$ where r_{TxTy} is the true score correlation between two measures, r_{xy} is the obtained correlation, and r_{xx} and r_{yy} are the reliabilities of the two measures. Using the test–retest reliabilities reported by Chiang and Atkinson in this formula, the theoretical correlations between like parameters exceed 1.00, suggesting that the test–retest estimates were too low. This is likely, since they were based on intersession correlations that displayed practice effects, and Chiang and Atkinson appear not to have adjusted these coefficients by Spearman–Brown as they did the split-half coefficients. Using these latter estimates (see Table 1), the intercept intercorrelation becomes 1.00 while the slope intercorrelation becomes .90. These results suggest that the relation between slopes, and also between intercepts across the two tasks, is close to perfect. According to the underlying models, however, the two slopes and the two intercepts should not reflect exactly the same information-processing components. Further, the observed correlation in Table 1 between VSLOPE and MINT is 0.43, not to be ignored, though of borderline significance statistically. When corrected for attenuation, this correlation becomes 0.45.

These results are examined further in Fig. 7, which shows the presumed model components for each parameter, following Chiang and Atkinson, together with the theoretical correlations obtained by correcting for attenuation. Within-task correlations have not been corrected or shown in the figure, since errors of measurement within the same task are not independent. Note first that the two intercept parameters differ by one component, yet correlate perfectly. Such a result might arise for one of three possible reasons: (1) stimulus encoding might be a constant, indicating that there are no individual differences in this stage of processing; (2) individual differences in stimulus encoding might be perfectly coincident with individual differences in binary decision and/or response production, and thus deserve no status as a separate ability construct; or (3) the models of one or both tasks might be wrong in some way. If one assumes for the moment that the models are

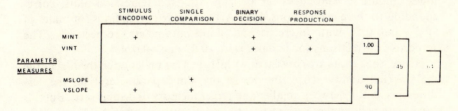

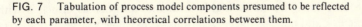

FIG. 7   Tabulation of process model components presumed to be reflected by each parameter, with theoretical correlations between them.

correct, then the three other correlations make sense. VINT and MSLOPE have no process component in common and correlate near zero. MINT and VSLOPE have one process component in common and show a moderate correlation, representing about 20% common variance. But this common component is stimulus encoding! If the intercorrelation arises from individual differences in stimulus encoding, then the first alternative explanation for the results listed above must be incorrect; stimulus encoding cannot be a constant. This produces doubt about the second alternative explanation as well, even though it cannot be logically eliminated. There is, in addition, other evidence that individual differences in stimulus encoding can be measured reliably and correlated significantly across independent tasks (see Ward, 1973, below). We are left with the conclusion that one or the other model must be changed. The only change consistent with the data is to say that individual differences in stimulus encoding are present also in VINT. This makes the perfect correlation between VINT and MINT reasonable, while preserving the reasoning associated with the zero correlation obtained between VINT and MSLOPE. Note, finally, that the earlier estimate that 20% of the variance in MINT and VSLOPE was due to stimulus encoding is corroborated by the correlation of 0.90 between the slope parameters; this correlation indicates that 81% of the variance of these parameters is due to individual differences in the comparison stage, and thus 19% is due to stimulus encoding.

A second point is the hypothesis derived from Hunt that the slope parameter should correlate with V. Table 1 shows nonsignificant correlations between the slope parameters and SAT-V, though the correlation for VSLOPE is high enough to be of marginal interest. Also, the correlation of SAT-V and SAT-Q is significantly positive, suggesting that the hierarchical model is correct; a raw V measure is not an isolate. Thus, the data seem to fail here. But Chiang and Atkinson took their analysis a step further. Combining the two slope parameters and also the two intercept parameters, they computed all the correlations separately for males and females. A striking sex difference emerged. Correlations between SAT-V and the combined slope were 0.72 for females and –0.36 for males. A similar pattern was noted for SAT-Q, though the respective correlations were 0.3 and –0.44, somewhat lower. Figure 8 reproduces the Chiang–Atkinson regression plots, corresponding to these correlations. MSPAN also gave correlations for males of –0.54 and 0.56 with intercept and slope parameters, respectively. The respective correlations for females were –0.02 and –0.024.

Hence, the results are consistent with Hunt's for males only: the higher the male verbal ability score, the lower the slope parameter (i.e., the less difference in RT between smaller and larger memory or display sets). But this same statement applies with respect to quantitative ability; SAT-V and SAT-Q are correlated about as highly with one another as either is with the parameters, and none of the correlations are extremely large. If one extracted a general factor combining V and Q, it would probably account for the result.

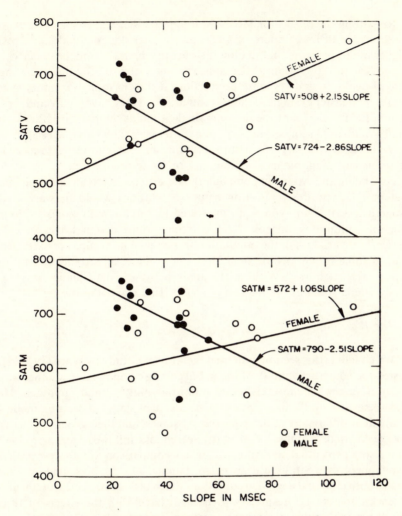

FIG. 8   Relation of SATV and SATM scores to slope in msec for males and females (from Chiang and Atkinson, 1976).

The opposite pattern appeared for females: the higher the verbal ability score (and to a somewhat lesser extent, quantitative ability also), the higher the slope parameter (i.e., the more difference in RT between smaller and larger memory or display sets). The findings for females are somewhat uncertain, however, since inspection of the scatterplots shows one, and perhaps two, female outliers who may have had a marked effect on the regression lines. Removing one or both of these subjects would lower the female correlations, but would not change the overall trend of results. (See Snow, 1977, for other notes on the significance of outliers.)

Regarding the results for MSPAN, it appears that higher span scores are associated with lower intercept scores and steeper slopes in males, but with higher intercept scores and shallower slopes in females. Using the underlying model for interpretation, males appear to be faster at stimulus encoding, binary decision, and response production, if they have high memory span scores, and faster at single stimulus comparison, if they have high V and/or Q scores. Females appear to be slower at single stimulus comparison if they have high V and/or Q scores. Memory span for females shows a slight relation to speed at single comparisons in this same direction, but is unrelated to speed in stimulus encoding, binary decision, and response production.

As Chiang and Atkinson point out, the sex difference was an unanticipated outcome. It requires replication before conclusions would be warranted. Nonetheless, it is an hypothesis uncovered by careful multivariate exploration of continuous variables. An extreme-groups design leaves out the network of variables in the population from which its groups are extracted. Unless some provisions are made to explore these, important moderating effects are left buried. Without the analysis by sex, the Chiang–Atkinson study would stand as a failure to replicate Hunt's hypothesis.

The Ward Study

We conclude this section with brief mention of a study by Ward (1973). He tested the construct validity of the initial coding component in another way, using a somewhat more elaborate multitrait–multimethod approach. His data bear also on the assumption of independent stages in decision models. Individual differences at three processing stages, and their generality across two tasks, were examined. A memory search task followed Sternberg (1969) and also a perceptual matching task, where comparison stimuli were present simultaneously; both used drawings of familiar objects, presented on slides under both clear and degraded conditions. Each task allowed measurement of latencies for correct responses to be associated with the effects of three conditions: stimulus degrading, category membership (i.e., match vs. mismatch was correct), and response probability (i.e., match vs. mismatch had high vs. low probability of occurrence). These experimental variables were hypothesized to affect the process stages of stimulus encoding, match–mismatch decision, and response production, respectively. On the memory task, significant main effects occurred for all three experimental variables, and there were no interactions, so the Sternberg hypothesis of independent stages was supported. On the matching task, all main effects were again significant in expected directions, but the interaction of category membership and response probability was also significant. Here then, stimulus encoding could be assumed independent of the next two process stages, but these latter operations seemed not independent of one another.

The parameter estimates associated with each stage were similar in the two tasks: stimulus degrading led to an increase in latency of about 200 msec; a difference of about 70 msec arose from manipulating stimulus category membership, and change to a lower response probability setting caused an increase in latency of about 55 msec. Correlations between pairs of parameters across the two tasks were 0.75, 0.34, and 0.21, respectively, implying that individual differences in the encoding stage at least were consistent across tasks. The cross-task correlation for encoding became 0.84 when disattenuated. Several correlations also suggested that the stimulus-encoding parameter of one task predicted matching and response production parameters of the other. Thus, while individual differences in the latter parameters seem not to be correlated across tasks, they may represent systematic variance within tasks. Ward's data are partially consistent with our expectations, noted in a previous section, that early stages would be independent, later stages would not, and individual differences would be cumulative across stages.

Future Research

There is other relevant literature, but this is not the place for a comprehensive review. Some brief notes on possible next steps for research in this area will serve as summary.

Hypotheses. Several related hypotheses deserve attention in further research on individual differences in short-term visual memory. First is the question of whether individual differences here should be regarded as a function of two (or more) independent parameter differences, or of a single difference in the sequencing of component processing steps. Second, the independence of individual differences in iconic decay, symbolic encoding, single-item comparison, and decision and response production must also be checked further. The data so far suggest that the first three steps may be independent, and the last two not.

Design of Laboratory Experiments. A next study in this direction could be conceived as a correlational survey, including measures of all of the above. But a crucial issue concerns the two p-variable versus one q-variable hypothesis. This appears to require the design of task conditions that can be manipulated to clarify such a distinction, and its inclusion with the above measures in an experiment. R. Sternberg's componential analysis may provide a format for the conduct of this work.

The design of such studies will need to include multiple measures of each process construct of interest. And statistical analysis will need to examine possible interactions with sex.

Relevant Instructional Conditions. The area of short-term visual memory was chosen for demonstration here because data on this were in hand. In general, however, aptitude process analyses should be linked somehow to likely instructional alternatives. Thus the question: Assuming, say, that differences in iconic decay and symbolic coding processes are associated with ability test scores of the PI and V sort, what instructional situations might provide sites where this information is relevant? We might speculate that skilled performance in receiving coded messages visually, in speed reading, and in rapid comprehension of complex figures, pictures, or sequences of these, might depend in part on such individual differences in the short-term temporal characteristics of visual processing. Rapid arithmetical computation might also depend on such individual differences, as might various psychomotor skills. Instruction designed to promote learning of these skills could be adapted differently for the high V–low PI learner and the low V–high PI learner, by attempting to capitalize on speedy coding or lasting iconic imagery. In general, however, process analysis ought to be guided by an ATI hypothesis from the start, if it is to feed instructional research and development. (See Cronbach & Snow, 1977, for related discussion of strategy in ATI research on instruction.)

CAPITALIZATION AND COMPENSATION: A CHALLENGE

There is no fitting conclusion for the present paper. It has projected one form of suggested further research based on one view of the starting points. There are certainly other views and other starting points. The proof will be in the production of a coherent, useful theory of aptitude based on the orientation provided here, or on one that is demonstrably superior.

In several sections of this paper, various hypotheses have been stated briefly, or implied without explication. There is no sensible alternative at this stage of work. This is after all, only a prospectus for further research. But one theme deserves a clearer identification. While introduced late in this paper, it is an overriding theme in all ATI research, and thus a fitting point with which to conclude.

Individual differences among human beings come into play upon situational demand. Individuals seem to meet these demands by capitalizing on their aptitudes, and by compensating for their inaptitudes. Where possible, in effect, they substitute aptitudes they possess for those they lack. In the same sense, situations can be said to capitalize on some individual differences and to compensate for others. The practical problem to which all research on aptitude is ultimately addressed is the design of situations in such a way as to capitalize upon and/or to compensate for the existence of these individual differences. Capitalization and compensation thus seem to be general functions of persons, of situations, and of person–situation interactions. Research on aptitude will need to build a process theory powerful enough to control these functions for practical use.

REFERENCES

Allison, R. B. Learning parameters and human abilities. Unpublished report (NR 151-113). Princeton, N.J.: Educational Testing Service, 1960.

Atkinson. R. C.. Brelsford. J. W., & Shiffrin. R. M. Multiprocess models for memory with applications to a continuous presentation task. *Journal of Mathematical Psychology*, 1967, *4*, 277–300.

Atkinson, R. C., Holmgren, J. E.,& Juola, J. F. Processing time as influenced by the number of elements in a visual display. *Perception & Psychophysics*, 1969, *6*, 321–326.

Averbach, E., & Coriell, A. S. Short-term memory in vision. *Bell System Technical Journal*, 1961, *40*, 309–328.

Breitmeyer, B. G., & Ganz, L. Implications of sustained and transient channels for theories of visual pattern masking, saccadic suppression, and information processing. *Psychological Review*, 1976, *83*, 1–36.

Calfee, R. C. Sources of dependency in cognitive processes. In D. Klahr (Ed.), *Cognition and instruction*. Hillsdale, N.J.: Lawrence Erlbaum Assoc., 1976.

Campbell, D. T., & Fiske, D. W. Convergent and discriminant validation by the multitrait-multimethod matrix. *Psychological Bulletin*, 1959, *56*, 81–105.

Carroll, J. B. Psychometric tests as cognitive tasks: A new "structure of intellect." In L. Resnick (Ed.), *The nature of intelligence*. Hillsdale. N.J.: Lawrence Erlbaum Assoc., 1976.

Chiang, A., & Atkinson, R. C. Individual differences and interrelationships among a select set of cognitive skills. *Memory & Cognition*, 1976, *4*, 661–672.

Cronbach, L. J. The two disciplines of scientific psychology. *American Psychologist*, 1957, *12*, 671–684.

Cronbach. L. J. Beyond the two disciplines of scientific psychology. *American Psychologist*, 1975, *30*, 116–127.

Cronbach, L. J., & Snow, R. E. *Aptitudes and instructional methods: A handbook for research on interactions*. New York: Irvington, 1977.

Duncanson, J. P. Intelligence and the ability to learn. RB 64-29. Princeton, N.J.: Educational Testing Service, 1964.

Estes, W. K. *Learning theory and mental development*. New York: Academic Press, 1970.

Estes, W. K. Learning theory and intelligence. *American Psychologist*, 1974, *29*, 740–749.

Ferguson, G. A. On learning and human ability. *Canadian Journal of Psychology*, 1954, *8*, 95–112.

Ferguson, G. A. On transfer and the abilities of man. *Canadian Journal of Psychology*, 1956, *10*, 121–131.

Flammer, A. *Individuelle unterschiede im lernen*. Weinheim, West Germany: Belz, 1975.

Gagné, R. M. (Ed.). *Learning and individual differences*. Columbus, Ohio: Merrill, 1967.

Gagné. R. M. *The conditions of learning* (2nd ed.). New York: Holt, Rinehart & Winston, 1970.

Garrett, H. E. A developmental theory of intelligence. *American Psychologist*, 1946, *1*, 372–378.

Gaudry, E., & Spielberger, C.D. *Anxiety and educational achievement*. New York: Wiley, 1971.

Gibson, J. J. (ed.) *Motion picture testing and research*. Washington, D. C.: U.S. Government Printing Office, 1947.

Glaser, R. Some implications of previous work on learning and individual differences. In R. M. Gagné (Ed.), *Learning and individual differences.* Columbus, Ohio: Merrill, 1967.

Glaser, R. Individuals and learning: The new aptitudes. *Educational Researcher,* 1972, *1*, 5–12.

Glaser, R. Components of a psychology of instruction: Toward a science of design. *Review of Educational Research,* 1976, *46*, 1–24.

Glaser, R., & Resnick, L. Instructional psychology. *Annual Review of Psychology,* 1972, *23*, 207–276.

Guilford, J. P. *The nature of human intelligence.* New York: McGraw-Hill, 1967.

Guinaugh, B. J. An experimental study of basic learning ability and intelligence in low-socio-economic populations. Unpublished doctoral dissertation, Michigan State University, 1969.

Gulliksen, H. O. An analysis of learning data which distinguishes between initial preference and learning ability. *Psychometrika,* 1942, *7*, 171–194.

Gulliksen, H. O. Measurement of learning and mental abilities. *Psychometrika,* 1961, *26*, 93–107.

Hunt, D. E., & Sullivan, E. V. *Between psychology and education.* Hinsdale, Ill.: Dryden, 1974.

Hunt, E. B., & Lansman, M. Cognitive theory applied to individual differences. In W. K. Estes (Ed.), *Handbook of learning and cognitive processes,* Vol. I. Hillsdale, N.J.: Lawrence Erlbaum Assoc., 1975.

Hunt, E. B., Frost, N., & Lunneborg, C. E. Individual differences in cognition: A new approach to intelligence. In G. Bower (Ed.), *The psychology of learning and motivation,* Vol. 7. New York: Academic Press, 1973.

Hunt, J. McV. *Intelligence and experience.* New York: Ronald Press, 1961.

Jacobs, P. I., & Vandeventer, M. The learning and transfer of double-classification skills by first graders. *Child Development,* 1971, *42*, 149–159. (a)

Jacobs, P. I., & Vandeventer, M. The learning and transfer of double-classification skills: A replication and extension. *Journal of Experimental Child Psychology,* 1971, *12*, 240–257. (b)

Jensen, A. R. *Genetics and education.* London: Methuen, 1972.

Kahneman, D. Method, findings, and theory in studies of visual masking. *Psychological Bulletin,* 1968, *70*, 404–425.

Klahr, D. (Ed.) *Cognition and instruction.* Hillsdale, N.J.; Lawrence Erlbaum Assoc., 1976.

Koran, M. L., Snow, R. E., & McDonald, F. J. Teacher aptitude and observational learning of a teaching skill. *Journal of Educational Psychology,* 1971, *62*, 219–228.

McGeogh, J. A., & Irion, A. L. *The psychology of human learning.* Toronto: Longmans Green, 1952.

McGuire, W. J. The Yin and Yang of progress in social psychology: Seven koan. *Journal of Personality and Social Psychology,* 1973, *28*, 446–456.

Mischel, W. Towards a cognitive social learning reconceptualization of personality. *Psychological Review,* 1973, *80*, 252–283.

Owens, W. A. Toward one discipline of scientific psychology. *American Psychologist,* 1968, *23*, 782–785.

Reitman, J. S. Computer simulation of an information-processing model of short-term memory. In D. A. Norman (Ed.), *Models of human memory.* New York: Academic Press, 1970.

Resnick, L. (Ed.) *The nature of intelligence.* Hillsdale, N.J.: Lawrence Erlbaum Assoc., 1976.

Seibert, W. F., & Snow, R. E. Studies in cine-psychometry I: Preliminary factor analysis of visual cognition and memory. Lafayette, Ind.: Purdue University Audio Visual Center, 1965.

Seibert, W. F., Reid, J. C., & Snow, R. E. Studies in cine-psychometry II: Continued factoring of audio and visual cognition and memory. Lafayette, Ind.: Purdue University Audio Visual Center, 1967.

Snow, R. E. Research on aptitudes: A progress report. In L. S. Shulman (Ed.), *Review of research in education*, Vol. 4. Itasca Ill.: Peacock, 1977.

Snow, R. E., Marshalek, B., & Lohman, D. Correlation of selected cognitive abilities and cognitive processing parameters: An exploratory study. Technical Report No. 3, Aptitude Research Project, School of Education, Stanford University, Stanford, Calif.: 1976.

Snow, R. E., & Seibert, W. F. Exploratory factor analysis in cine-psychometry. Paper presented at the meeting of the American Psychological Association, New York, September 1966.

Sperling, G. A. The information available in brief visual presentation. *Psychological Monographs*, 1960, 74, Whole No. 498.

Stake, R. E. Learning parameters, aptitudes, and achievement. *Psychometric Monographs*, 1961, Whole No. 9.

Sternberg, R. *Intelligence, information processing, and analogical reasoning: The componential analysis of human abilities*. Hillsdale, N.J.: Lawrence Erlbaum Assoc., 1977.

Sternberg, R. Deductive reasoning. In R. E. Snow, P.-A. Frederico, & W. Montague (Eds.), *Aptitude, learning, and instruction: Cognitive process analyses*. Hillsdale, N.J.: Lawrence Erlbaum Assoc., In press.

Sternberg, S. Memory-scanning: Mental processes revealed by reaction-time experiments. *American Scientist*, 1969, 57, 421–457.

Taylor, D. A. Stage analysis of reaction time. *Psychological Bulletin*, 1976, 83, 161–191.

Terman, L. M. *The measurement of intelligence*. Boston: Houghton Mifflin, 1916.

Turvey, M. T. On peripheral and central processes in vision: inferences from an information-processing analysis of masking with patterned stimuli. *Psychological Review*, 1973, 80, 1–52.

Underwood, B. J. *Psychological research*. New York: Appleton–Century–Crofts, 1957.

Underwood, B. J. Individual differences as a crucible in theory construction. *American Psychologist*, 1975, 30, 128–140.

Vale, J. R., & Vale, C. A. Individual differences and general laws in psychology: A reconciliation. *American Psychologist*, 1969, 25, 1093–1108.

Ward, W. C. Individual differences in information processing units (Research Bulletin 73–70). Princeton, N.J.: Educational Testing Service, 1973.

Whitcomb, W. A., & Travers, R. M. W. A study of within-test learning function as a determinant of total score. *Educational and Psychological Measurement*, 1957, 17, 86–97.

Woodrow, H. The ability to learn. *Psychological Review*, 1946, 53, 147–158.

6

Toward a Theory of Intelligence: Contributions from Research with Retarded Children

JOSEPH C. CAMPIONE
AND
ANN L. BROWN
University of Illinois

One approach to the understanding of intelligence is through research with retarded children and adults. Any characterization of the way(s) in which they differ from nonretarded individuals results in a specification of important components of intelligence. In this paper, we deal with two general areas of research. In one, centering on the role of control processes in memory and problem-solving situations, we argue that research with the retarded has succeeded in identifying a major component of intelligence. The results from a large number of experiments lead us to the conclusion that a hallmark of intelligence is the ability to generalize information from one situation to another, and that this ability in turn depends upon effective "executive control." In areas where less research with retarded individuals has been done, we suggest that comparative/developmental work is necessary to gain a better understanding of the processes in question. We illustrate this point by discussing some work aimed at locating individual differences in parameters representing basic components of general information-processing systems.

I. INTRODUCTION

While the topic of intelligence has been of central interest to many workers for a long time, there seems to have been a recent upsurge in relevant research and theorizing (e.g., Detterman, 1977; Resnick, 1976). This renewed interest is no doubt due to many factors, but at least two seem obvious: an increase in the tendency of researchers to work in areas of societal concern, and the recent advances in theory and research in the area of general cognitive psychology. These theoretical developments have encouraged a number of individuals to believe that we now have available analytic devices capable of

Preparation of this manuscript and conduct of the research reported in it have been supported by PHS Grants HD–05951, HD–06864, and HD–00111 from the National Institute of Child Health and Human Development.

dealing with so complex a problem. One chief result of this social and intellectual climate is the emergence of a number of different approaches to the problem of understanding intelligence, some of which are nicely illustrated in this symposium.

One approach to the problem, and the one we have chosen, is through the study of research in the area of mental retardation. Our attempt here will be to describe how research in retardation can contribute to the development of theories of intelligence, and to highlight some recent aspects of intelligence which have been emphasized as a result of some of our own work with educable retarded children (IQs around 70). In that program, which is about ten years old, the questions guiding the research concern (a) the nature of process differences underlying performance disparities in a variety of "cognitive" tasks, and (b) ways of ameliorating, or at least reducing, the differences.

The relevance of such research to issues regarding intelligence seems obvious. If it is possible to identify characteristics which are lacking or reduced in retarded individuals relative to nonretarded individuals, and which are wholly or in part responsible for observed performance differences in a class of cognitive tasks, we will also have identified some important components of intelligence. Essentially, a partial definition of intelligence, and one which is at least implicit in our work, is that it consists of processes which are lacking or reduced in effectiveness in the population of retarded children. Viewed in this way, it is possible to argue that a major goal of those interested in the experimental or instructional psychology of the retarded child is to contribute to the development of an empirically-based theory of intelligence (although this goal is seldom stated explicitly).

The approach to intelligence through research with retarded children also leads one to think about the developmental aspects of intelligence or its components. One virtue here is that this leads to the identification of some troublesome problems, and raises some interesting questions which otherwise might be overlooked. In this paper, we would like to outline the implications of research with the retarded for general views concerning the nature of intelligence. In the main part of the paper, we will describe two types or areas of research. In one area (described in Section III, A), there is a considerable amount of data, and as there is not enough space here to do justice to the richness of that literature, we will be content to abstract what we see as central to the problem of defining one major component of intelligence. We will also try to point to the kinds of questions which need to be attacked before we will be in a position to elaborate on the picture we currently see. In the other main area (Section III, B), there are fewer data, and the treatment will be more speculative. Our aim there is to argue that it is in these areas that research with retarded children can provide information essential for better understanding of both intelligence and retardation.

At this point, we would like to pause and emphasize two points: we do not believe that the set of "educable retarded children" is a homogeneous one, and we do not believe that there is any single factor which might define intelligence. To simplify our discussions, however, we will not explicate these points again. We center on one facet of intelligence here because we believe that a variety of data converge to indicate its centrality to the problem. Further, we will write as though the set of educable children were homogeneous; and, in fact, if we were to restrict our attention to their performance on the specific processes we want to emphasize here, they may well be quite homogeneous. However, this does not in any way rule out the possibility that they may be extremely heterogenous if other aspects of intelligence were being discussed.

II. AREAS OF RESEARCH AND THE PROBLEMS OF DEFINITION

A. The Distinctions and Problems

In terms of some general conception of the human information-processing system, there are two areas in which to search for individual difference constructs. One area is in the functioning of the basic hardware of the system that we assume, and here the variations are likely to be in terms of quantitative parameters describing the system's efficiency or adaptability. The second is in terms of the effects of development of the individual's knowledge base, and in this domain individuals can vary quantitatively in terms of how much information they have acquired, and qualitatively in terms of the types of information, routines, and operations represented in memory.

To elaborate this view and to then make some substantive comments about intelligence requires a clear nomenclature system, and this represents our first problem. Many of the key terms we would like to use have been used loosely and interchangeably in the developmental/comparative literature (we have contributed here ourselves), but in order to facilitate communication we think that it is necessary to define each term as precisely as possible. We have found this exercise helpful, and hope that the attempt to deal with the confusion will be of value to others.

A chief problem is encountered when the terms structure (or structural limitation) and process (or control process) appear. Even in the simplest case of dealing with a stable system, a computer, it is by no means trivial to decide what is structure and what is process; the complexity increases dramatically when the thinker is human (e.g., Winograd, 1975). In many instances, it is assumed that the adult thinker is also a (relatively) stable organism, even though this is clearly untrue (e.g., Reese, 1976). Cognitive growth is a continuous process which progresses throughout the life span. For the avowed developmentalist, however, the problem of change or growth simply cannot be avoided (Brown, 1978b). The organism is in a constant state of flux, and both its structural and process features undergo fundamental changes with development. Or at least some of them do, or may—a point to which we will return shortly. In any event, it is clear that the structure/process distinction is a particularly troublesome one for developmental psychologists (Case, 1974; Cellerier, 1972; Newell, 1972).

In the area of retardation, we have elsewhere (Brown, 1974; Campione & Brown, 1977) used the distinction between the structural features of an information-processing system and its associated control processes as a way of classing intelligence-related differences. Following Fisher and Zeaman (1973), we used structural to refer to basic, invariant, unmodifiable components of the system, and process to refer to optional, trainable routines and strategies. In this view locating structural correlates of intelligence is the aim of those interested in seeking a theory-based definition of retardation. To quote Fisher and Zeaman (1973), "since individual differences in intelligence are highly stable traits in our retardate population, only stable parameters, those representing structural features, are meaningfully relatable to intelligence" (p. 251). Thus, structural features are stable and untrainable, whereas control processes are modifiable; or, alternatively, a structural limitation is one which is impervious, or relatively impervious (see Campione & Brown, 1977) to training. While this distinction is in principle simple enough, it was treated as analogous to another distinction, thus leading to confusion. Based on the computer metaphor underlying the original Atkinson and Shiffrin (1968) theory and the Fisher–Zeaman adaptation of it, structure was equated with the hardware of the system and process with its software. The problem is simply that these distinctions are not the same. For example, if it turned out to be impossible to train retarded children to employ memory strategies effectively, this inability would pinpoint a structural characteristic of that population, but it would not implicate any of the hardware of the system. Memory strategies are exactly the things Atkinson and Shiffrin termed control processes.

Because of this confusion, we need another set of terms to use in reference to the hardware/software distinction and also to further breakdowns or refinements of that dichotomy. Again, some specificity would be nice, and we will first consider some problems and ambiguities which have cropped up in the developmental literature. Much of the discussion will be based on general developmental work, rather than work specifically in retardation; however, we believe that any treatment of issues involved in "developmental" research is relevant to considerations of "comparative" research. Borrowing from Chi (1976), we begin with the assertion that discussions of development, capacity, and performance are frequently confusing, if not irrational, because the key capacity referents are used loosely and interchangeably. To understand "capacity" discussions, a necessary condition would seem to be that the theorist's underlying metaphor be made explicit. Not only is this condition rarely satisfied, it also appears that some authors lack any consistent metaphor.

B. A Nomenclature System

The first terms to be considered, or reconsidered, are "structure" and "structural limitation," which have been used to refer to (a) the hardware of the system, as in a computer metaphor (STS, LTS, etc.); (b) the schemes of the intelligence in Piaget's sense; (c) limitations to the efficiency of various parts of the hardware (e.g., capacity limitations in STM, speed of encoding); (d) any untrainable component of an individual's thought; and (e) others. The picture is even more confusing if viewed in the context of development, for some of these various "structures" are assumed to undergo no development (e.g., the hardware), clear development (Piagetian schemes), or may or may not change with age, ability and experience (limitations to the efficiency of the hardware).

We now turn to the use of "capacity" itself, again a term whose uses vary quite widely. As Chi (1976) has pointed out, it is frequently equated with performance, in which case the relation between capacity and performance becomes simple, if uninteresting. It is sometimes used interchangeably with structure to refer to developmental limits on the effects of training, and less frequently to stage type limits inherent in models dealing with qualitative changes in thinking. A different use, and probably the most frequent, is in reference to some limitations on the basic hardware of the information—processing system, e.g., the number of bins or slots in STM.

While we do not believe we can eliminate such problems, we would at least like to define the way we use some of the key terms, and then make suggestions about their possible relations to development and intelligence. As a beginning point for this discussion, we will adopt the distributed memory model described by Hunt, Frost, and Lunneborg (1973) or the modal model outlined by Craik and Lockhart (1972). Such a system includes a very short-term memory which has a large immediate capacity, but from which information is rapidly lost if it remains unattended. The second major "stage" in the system is short-term memory, which is a limited capacity system (finite number of slots) from which information is also lost unless maintained by strategic processing. The final major store in the system is long-term memory, an apparently unlimited store of experience.

Within this system, we would like to use the term *architecture* to refer to the major stores, or the system's hardware. We are also interested in some quantitative properties of the various architectural units: capacity, durability, and efficiency. By *capacity* we mean the amount of space available in the units, e.g., the number of slots in STM or the amount of filing space in LTM. *Durability* refers to the relative permanence of the information in each unit, indexed most clearly by the rate at which unattended information is lost. Finally, we use *efficiency* somewhat generically to refer to other temporal characteristics associated with the selection and manipulation of information with the system, e.g., speed of encoding, rate of memory search, rapidity with which attention is switched, temporal duration of alertness effects, etc. This set of parameters would reflect the efficiency with which the system's resources can be marshalled and manipulated.

We now consider the contents of LTM, along with some areas in which quantitative and/or qualitative changes may be found. The subsets of LTM identified are not presumed to be mutually exclusive, and the distinctions are made to highlight particular classes of information. First, we use the term *knowledge base* to refer to the existing semantic networks and data structures, the individual's organized knowledge of the world. The term *scheme* is used to refer to Piagetian rules of thinking, both figurative and operative. Finally, we use *control processes* to mean the rules and strategies available to the thinker for memorizing, understanding, solving problems, etc.

Within this system, we would make the following generalizations about development. With regard to architecture, there is no compelling evidence that any fundamental changes take place. Turning to control processes, schemes, and the knowledge base, these are all areas in which we are certain that dramatic development occurs. The interesting questions concern the extent to which capacity, durability, and efficiency vary as a function of developmental level, and mediate some of the well-documented changes in performance which come about with increases in both experience and intelligence. The difficulties are to rule out the effects of variations in the availability and use of LTM contents. That is, performance on any complex task is influenced by the properties of the architectural system, the set of control processes in LTM, and any of a number of interactions among the two. Furthermore, there are a number of other possible interactions which may complicate our analysis of the determinants of performance in a given situation, e.g., between the knowledge base and some efficiency parameters, between the knowledge base and use of control processes, etc. Thus, making inferences about developmental differences in architectural efficiency requires that we institute controls for variation in the effects attributable to the contents of LTM, a problem rendered more difficult by the dramatic array of strategies and tricks mature problem-solvers bring to bear on the typical laboratory task (Reitman, 1970). There are a number of ways of approaching the problem. One is to devise extremely simple tasks in which there is little room for LTM variation to be important (e.g., to attempt to guarantee that the information is equally familiar to all subjects), a second is to experiment in such a way that strategies are likely to be either difficult to implement or unlikely to be of help, and a third is to develop a precise mathematical model of the task in question in which specific parameters reflecting different processes can be reliably estimated.

III. AN OVERVIEW OF THE RESEARCH

Having attempted to provided a framework within which we can look for correlates of intelligence, we would now like to outline what we will do in the remainder of the paper. In the next section (III, A), we will concentrate on research dealing with the role of control processes in a variety of situations, emphasizing the work from our laboratories. It is in the area of control process use that we would like to argue that the data obtained with retarded children provide clear information for those interested in describing the intelligence of any system, a child, a college student, or a machine. To anticipate our final conclusion, we will endorse a view of intelligence based on executive functioning. We will arrive at this position by focusing on a number of general components of efficient problem-solving: the invention or production of plans and strategies; the generalization of those routines; and the role of metacognitive factors (Brown, 1978a; Flavell & Wellman, 1977) in both production and generalization. The experimental paradigm involved in the research is that of transfer of training. Individual projects consist of baseline periods, where we look for the spontaneous production of strategies; training periods, where we train strategy use; and maintenance and generalization phases, where we investigate the extent of any subsequent nonprompted use of the instructed activities. From a consideration of such research conducted both in our laboratories and those of others, we will argue that it is within the domain of invention and deployment of planful activities that a significant part of intelligence can be described.

We do not believe that this is the only area in which retardation research can illuminate the development of general theory, nor do we believe that the defining psychological/cognitive features of retarded children lie wholly in the use of control processes. There is evidence to suggest that properties of the architectural system also reflect differences. We will consider that area in the subsequent section (Section III, B). But, since there are few retardate data available, in that section we will simply point out the need for additional research and indicate why we think such research is necessary for students of either retardation or intelligence.

To lead into our discussion, it seems appropriate to provide at least a little background. While there has been a long history of research with retarded individuals, it is clear that one major impetus to research with the retarded came from the publication of the *Handbook of Mental Deficiency* (Ellis,

1963), in which many of the field's leaders summarized their views. That volume also provided a reasonably concise summary of the state of the art at that time. To characterize the aims of the contributors, the goal of a number of the chapters was to specify processes or parameters which were general enough to account for performance differences between retarded and nonretarded children in a variety of areas. Some of the more notable treatments dealt with attention (Zeaman & House), STM durability (Ellis), and speed of cortical response (Spitz). A major increase in research addressed to issues of intelligence and mental retardation followed the publication of this book (see Detterman, 1977), and much of that research was influenced by the ideas outlined in it.

In general, the processes singled out were presumed to be invariant features, or defining features, of the subject's system, reflected in part in the tendency of theorists to seek physiological explanations underlying the differences (Campione & Brown, 1977). Fairly quickly, however, the invariance position came under attack. The role of active strategies became a central concern in the area (as was also the case in the more broadly-defined field of cognitive psychology), and led naturally to a number of training studies in which attempts were made to improve the performance of retarded children. The vast majority of this research involved the use of memory paradigms, and one of the early papers instrumental in bringing about this change in emphasis was provided by Belmont and Butterfield (1969). They argued there that comparative differences in STM performance could not be attributed to variations in the durability of information in STM but rather to the differential employment of, e.g., types of acquisition strategies.

Since the late 1960s, a considerable proportion of the research in mental retardation has included training components, and a number of thorough reviews of various aspects of this literature have appeared recently (Belmont & Butterfield, 1977; Borkowski & Wanschura, 1974; Brown, 1974, 1978a; Butterfield & Belmont, 1977; Campione & Brown, 1977). We do not intend to go into detail here, but rather aim to review the general progression of this type of research and ask what kinds of inferences about intelligence we can draw from it.

A. Research on the Role of Control Processes

1. *Background.* The early studies in this domain were designed, following the production versus mediation deficiency model (Flavell, 1970), to see if teaching memory strategies to retarded children would result in enhanced performance. It is interesting to note that this research was prompted by a number of theorists incuding Ellis (1970) and Spitz (1972), who had revised their earlier (Ellis, 1963) positions. These theorists proposed that major sources of difficulties encountered by retarded children stemmed from their

failure to employ generally applicable strategies, such as rehearsal and chunking. The answer to these training studies was invariably "yes," and one simple conclusion could thus be drawn—performance levels were not completely determined by limitations in the architectural system. In a number of subsequent studies (Belmont & Butterfield, 1971; Brown, Campione, Bray & Wilcox, 1973), clearer evidence about the role of particular strategies was provided. Specifically, the sets of authors set out to show that IQ-related variation in the use of rehearsal strategies was a major determinant of recall differences. In those experiments, four groups of subjects were typically investigated: retarded adolescents, either left to their own devices (and presumably not rehearsing) or trained to use rehearsal strategies, and nonretarded adolescents given straightforward learning instructions (and hence presumably rehearsing) or prevented from rehearsing. The same pattern of results was obtained in the two sets of experiments. Stated most simply, the rehearsal-trained retarded subjects showed the same pattern of performance as did the uninstructed nonretarded children; and the nonretarded adolescents prevented from rehearsing performed like the noninstructed retarded children. Thus, in terms of the patterns of performance, retarded children could be made to look like nonretarded children, and conversely, by manipulating rehearsal use within each population. These studies showed most clearly that a failure to use rehearsal strategies did characterize the performance of retarded children, and thus highlighted a way in which they differed from nonretarded children of comparable chronological age. At the same time, they also demonstrated the extent to which instruction could serve to reduce the performance differences. As a final point, it should be mentioned here that training did not eliminate differences in terms of overall accuracy levels; retarded children still performed more poorly, even after training, than nonretarded children given no strategy training.

2. Current trends. Following this initial work, research has proceeded in a number of directions, and we will indicate three here. One direction, exemplified most elegantly by Butterfield, Wambold, and Belmont (1973), was to attempt more detailed training, with the aim of eliminating performance differences entirely. We see two reasons for undertaking this kind of research. First, it is clearly relevant to questions regarding whether or not performance is limited by architectural properties; if differences can be eliminated under conditions *optimal for all subjects*, the answers must be "no." Second, attempting more detailed training is analogous to trying to simulate complex behavior with a computer—the processes and steps involved in the execution must be specified in detail. As retarded children do not spontaneously fill in gaps left in training, their performance gives clues to the kinds of "gap-filling" which is automatic, or relatively so, for the more intelligent problem-solver. We will return to this point later. Next, on a more theoretical level, a characterization of the retarded child in more general terms has come forward. While theorists had emphasized the role of specific strategies (such as rehearsal, chunking, elaborating, etc.), it became more reasonable to think of "production deficiencies" in the use of these routines as manifestations of a more general limitation. Borrowing from Miller, Galanter, and Pribram (1960), Brown (1974) argued that the overriding feature was that moderately retarded children simply lacked any "plan to form a plan," with the consequence that they perform relatively poorly on *all* tasks which require strategic intervention for them to achieve optimal efficency. This notion has also contributed to the third direction research has taken: work addressed to generalization of training effects. If the deficiency of the retarded child is due to a general factor rather than to the lack of a specific routine, then the effects of training aimed at that specific routine cannot be of much importance unless at least some kinds of generalized effects of that instruction can be obtained. The analogy is to treating a specific symptom of a more pervasive problem and leaving the problem itself unattended (not to mention the other symptoms). As an example, if the problem of the retarded child stems from a general failure to be strategic, training a specific rehearsal routine will not help overcome that more general limitation, unless the student does show evidence of some form of generalization. Without that, performance on all other "strategic" memory tasks will remain unaffected, and the overall benefits to be derived from the training will be trivial.

What are the aims of research concerned with the problem of generalization? We raise the question because there appear to be a number. For example, one type of generalization would be demonstrated if children who were instructed to rehearse on a particular task would continue rehearsing in other tasks where such behavior would be appropriate. Training, however, might be more broadly addressed to the problem of inculcating strategy use in general, and generalization here would be demonstrated if subjects trained to rehearse would also behave strategically in situations where other routines, say chunking, were required. The distinction is between generalizing rehearsal strategies and generalizing strategic processing. The latter is what we might aim for ideally, but at the present time, we would settle for the former as there is as yet no convincing evidence indicating generalization of a specific strategy by retarded children (Campione & Brown, 1977).

3. Data and interpretation. At this point, we can summarize briefly what has been found in this research area, and ask what the data might mean both for theoretical views of intelligence and for practical considerations regarding special education. To summarize the results, while mildly retarded children are unlikely to produce mnemonic or problem-solving strategies spontaneously, relevant strategies resulting in enhanced performance can be taught relatively easily, and the effects of this training can be maintained over appreciable time periods (e.g., Brown, Campione & Murphy, 1974); however, generalization of specific strategies to new situations is almost never obtained. While the "program" can be entered into LTM, it seems to remain unaccessed unless the precise conditions of storage are reencountered, and even this is not always sufficient to elicit the use of previously trained strategies, as we will describe shortly.

Using this data base as a starting point, we wish to ask what, if anything, we can say about intelligence. Alternatively, given that we characterize the retarded as showing neither spontaneous invention or generation of strategies nor generalization following training, what more can be said about how to conceptualize these failures? We begin by asserting that the two aspects (lack of production and lack of generalization) are the same one in different guises, specifically, that both represent generalization failures, a point we have argued elsewhere (Campione & Brown, 1974a, 1977; see also Belmont & Butterfield, 1977). We will provide some empirical justification for this claim shortly, but first we want to consider the assertion and its implications in slightly more detail. The main assumption needed to justify the presumed equivalence of production and generalization failures is that the components of the various strategies already exist in memory before any training takes place. Thus, the failure to produce a strategy in response to task demands reflects a failure to retrieve and sequence those specific components in order to employ them as a means to an end, i.e., a failure to use those components in an inventive and flexible way, or a failure to generalize the use of those components to the new situation. There are some simple explanations for these production failures, which would imply that failure to produce a strategy originally are different in kind from failures to generalize trained outlines. For example, it might be assumed that retarded children are not aware of the necessity and possibility of constructing such routines, and that this alone is responsible for their poor performance. If that were the only problem, however, simple training might be expected to lead to generalized effects, as both the need and possibility would have been demonstrated.

Given the actual data, such a conception can readily be dismissed, and we then must ask what other aspects of the overall process must be trained *explicitly*. While we cannot provide a thorough and well-documented answer, we can proffer a few informed guesses. We presume that anything which must be explicitly trained in retarded adolescents, but which occurs spontaneously in nonretarded children, represents an important component of intelligent behavior. If one statement could summarize our conclusion, it would be that it is not the presence or availability of the components of the target activity that is at fault in the retarded child, but rather it is the ability to select, modify, and sequence these components into an overall plan of procedure, and then to oversee and evaluate the effectiveness of the approach selected.[1] Alternatively, it is not specific knowledge per se that is lacking, but rather the understanding of that knowledge as assessed by its appropriate use. To quote Moore and Newell (1974), "S understands K if S uses K whenever appropriate" (pp. 203–204). We assume that knowledge (K) can typically be taught (see footnote 1), but that it is the "understanding" of K, or the general use of K, that is the hallmark of intelligence.

We can now consider the evidence that it is use, rather than availability, of components that is the crucial factor. There are a number of paradigms in which we find evidence for this conjecture. While the inference is more straightforward in some situations than others, the evidence does appear to converge rather nicely. First, consider the typical production deficiency experiment. While subjects do not spontaneously employ, e.g., a simple memory strategy, giving only simple and brief instructions is sufficient to get them to use it, and performance improves. It seems clear here that, given the trivial amount of intervention involved in most successful training studies, no new components have been instilled and that subjects did not use their resources well unless prompted to do so. Turn next to the longer-term effects of explicit training. Even when training has been successful in bringing about the use of a particular strategy, it may be the case that subjects fail to use it on successive opportunities. As the strategy training was successful originally, it seems safe to assume that "K exists," and hence that it is its use which has become the problem.

In some recent research in our laboratory (Brown & Barclay, 1976; Brown, Campione, & Barclay, 1978), we obtained the following pattern with a group of moderately retarded children with IQs around 70 and mental ages of around 6 to 7 years. While they failed to produce the target activity originally, they responded well to training and continued to perform acceptably on a *prompted* posttest in which they were instructed to continue the instructed activity. On a subsequent posttest where no prompting was given, they failed to produce the strategy. One year after training, they returned to the lab and were given the same experimental task, at which time they failed to show

---

[1]We are aware that this is no doubt oversimplified. In many cases, the components or basic knowledge must also be taught explicitly. Clear examples would be formal, decontextualized systems which seem to require schooling for their appearance in thought. In these instances, our claim would be that it would be easier to communicate the principles of the system than it would be to arrange for its flexible use, and the latter would be more clearly related to intelligence. In the case of the strategies which have been the subject of much of the research we have reviewed, we do not believe our interpretation is very likely to lead us far astray.

Also, we have ignored the effects due to scheme variation. Given the assertion that the contents of LTM limit what can be known (at least at a given time), it follows that not all knowledge can be instilled.

evidence of strategy use and performed at their original, prior to training, level. After this, they were given another series of prompts and performance improved immediately and dramatically, indicating that the routine itself had not faded from LTM. On the following day, prompting was withdrawn, and performance again declined to match pretraining levels. The important point is that use periods were sandwiched between nonuse periods, showing that failure to employ the activity occurred, even when it was clear that the knowledge required was still available in LTM.

Another bit of evidence comes from the research reported by Butterfield et al. (1973). In that work, they were interested in training retarded children to study a six-item list in preparation for some recall tests. Without going into too much detail, the strategy (dubbed a 3–3 active–passive strategy) consisted of looking at the first three items and then stopping to rehearse that set, the "active" component, followed by looking briefly at the last three items, the "passive" component, and then responding to the test quickly. While the precise recall requirements varied in different phases of training and transfer, they were all such that this strategy would be an appropriate one. What is important for our purposes is that subjects who were taught the active and passive components separately (and were demonstrably able to use them) did not spontaneously combine them to produce the overall strategy. They had to be taught both the pair of components and the precise way of combining them; as such, it is clear that guaranteeing that the components were available was far different from arranging for their appropriate use, *even in what might be called optimal circumstances.*

It is important to note that the condition did appear to be extremely conducive to obtaining proper integration in the Butterfield et al. experiment, for that underscores the difficulties one might have in trying to elicit such behavior. Assuming that training procedures could be designed to elicit the requisite sequencing in optimal circumstances, the problem might still not be solved. To illustrate, in a study with young nonretarded children, we (Campione & Brown, 1974b) were interested in the effects of successively training two components of an oddity problem. In one condition, for example, the target task required children to learn to choose the odd-colored object on each trial. They were given two training experiences prior to administration of this final transfer task: on the first, they learned to choose the odd object from an array; and on the second, they were trained to pay attention to the color aspects of the objects (rather than their shape or size). When given the final problem, the majority of these nonretarded children solved the problem immediately, i.e., they combined the two components into the overall rule, "choose the odd color." The finding of interest is that, if the format of the oddity training problem was different from that of the final task, such nice transfer did not occur. That is, under the most favorable conditions, performance was excellent, but it deteriorated when an additional complexity was introduced. Retarded children seem to run into problems under even the best of conditions, and these data suggest that even if this difficulty could be overcome, they might still require further instruction before they could deal with less than optimal situations.

Finally, the failure of retarded children to show generalization following successful initial training again affirms the importance of use, rather than availability, of information.

4.Summary. Having in this review emphasized the centrality of generalization, we can attempt to summarize our views by specifying what it is that we think underlies successful generalized use of knowledge and routines. i.e., identifying the processes involved in generalization. A more precise characterization of intelligence would result if we could indicate exactly what these processes are, and a still more accurate picture would emerge if we could indicate which areas cause particular problems for the retarded individual.

To do this, we need a model of the generalization process, and we have outlined the skeleton of such a model elsewhere (Campione & Brown, 1977). In that treatment, heavy emphasis was placed on the role of metacognitive activities, where metacognitive refers to the subject's awareness of his own cognitive machinery and operations. Briefly, it was assumed that the first step in achieving generalization of some routine to a novel situation was for the subject to realize the need for some strategy. The factor important here is the ability of the subject to predict the limits of the architectural system. If, for example, the number of items to be recalled exceeds the capacity of STM, some strategic intervention would be required for successful performance. Given such a statement, the subject would then have to evaluate the task requirements and consult his array of routines to determine which one or ones might be appropriate. Having thus selected one, the subject would then have to execute the strategy and monitor both the efficacy with which it was being carried out and the extent to which it was leading to acceptable performance levels. The information realized here would then govern decisions about future actions, e.g., whether to continue with that approach or to switch to some alternative.

These processes map nicely onto the functions assigned to the executive in many contemporary memory models. Theorists have come to agree that an important requirement of any functioning system is that it include the capacity for self-awareness, or accurate knowledge and understanding of its own weaknesses and properties (Becker, 1975; Bobrow, 1975; Bobrow & Norman, 1975). In such systems, some specific executive responsibilities include recognizing its own limitations, being aware of the routines available, being able to characterize the current problem, planning and scheduling strategies, and monitoring the effectiveness of the chosen routine. Given the correspondence, an alternative statement of our conclusions is that intelligence differences are attributable to variations in the efficiency of the executive, or in the quality of control that executive exerts. It is interesting to note in this context that these executive functions are among the most difficult to instill in a computer. While retarded children may not be as aware of the contents of their memory as nonretarded children, as assessed by the accuracy of their "feeling of knowing" reports (Brown & Lawton, 1977), many machines programmed to act intelligently can make no judgments at all about whether some bit of information is available to them (Newell, 1977).

Having favored a definition of intelligence in terms of the functioning of the executive, we would like to be able to state more precisely which of the many functions of an executive are most important. In keeping with our general approach, if we were able to locate the processes most difficult to introduce into the retarded individuals' executive functioning, we would have more to say about intelligence. We cannot do that at this time, but we can make some tentative guesses and suggest the kind of research necessary to fill in the picture which is developing. we can also make some more practical suggestions about the kinds of training attempts which should be undertaken. It is to these considerations that we now turn.

5. *Implications for research and practice.* We have argued that a failure to generalize is one clear indicator of intelligence. Further, our analysis of generalization failures led to an explanation emphasizing the role of basic metacognitive skills. As such, we would expect retarded children to experience problems in this domain, and this does appear to be the case. For example, they do not (1) predict their capacity limitations well (Brown, Campione & Murphy, 1977), (2) modify the allocation of their memory accurately (Brown & Lawton, 1977), or take steps necessary to be able to assess the state of their current degree of knowledge in order to know when to terminate processing (Brown & Barclay, 1976). This represents only the barest beginning to systematic research in this area, however, and the question then becomes, where do we go from here?

A number of implications follow from the conclusions we have reached. Considering first practical aims, it seems clear that training attempts should be aimed at the executive functions we have described. If this is where the problem lies, efforts should be aimed directly at the problems of the executive, rather than at training specific routines and hoping that simply making information available to the learner will somehow lead to understanding of that information.

There is another implication for instruction which, while not following directly from the views we have outlined here, is consistent with them. It may be possible to achieve generalization by training routines or skills which are truly transsituational themselves. Generalization is a problem in the areas we have considered because the strategies being trained are specific to a small class of situations. Continued use in novel situations does consequently require complex processing. Some metacognitive skills, however, do have the property of being very broadly applicable; we are thinking of simple checking and self-testing skills (Brown, 1978a; Brown & DeLoache, 1978) that could be used in almost any problem situation. Since they are generally applicable, they (in some sense) place fewer demands on the subject, who is not required to discriminate situations where their use would be appropriate from situations where it would not.

The obvious suggestion is to look at the effects of training these general routines, and it is in this area that we have achieved our only training success to date. We attempted to train a simple "stop-check-and-study" routine in the context of having educable retarded children study and recall a supraspan list of items (Brown & Barclay, 1976). Their task was to study the items until they were sure they could recall all of them. They were taught strategies for dealing with the task, and one feature of those routines was a self-testing component in which the children were to test themselves before deciding whether or not to terminate study and tell the experimenter they were ready to attempt recall. The training was successful in bringing about much improved performance, and, more to the point, the subjects showed subsequent generalization to a different task requiring gist recall of prose passages (Brown, Campione, & Barclay, 1978).

Turning to theoretical considerations, the aim is to extend the generalization model and relate the processes therein to variations in intelligence. It may be instructive here to think about the role of training studies. In one sense, they provide one relatively direct way of gaining some of the information we need if we are to make any more specific statements about intelligence. Obviously, they can tell us the extent to which the various executive functions are trainable, or if the different functions vary in trainability. Can we instill general knowledge of the system's working and limits? Can we teach retarded individuals to evaluate task demands adequately? Can we teach them to monitor their stage of learning? Or comprehension (cf. Markman, 1977)? We expect that some components are harder to instill than others, and having identified those, we would be prepared to make stronger statements about the definition of intelligence.

There is also one other advantage to be derived from attempting to design training studies of this type. They force the theorist or trainer to specify exactly what is meant by "executive function." Devising specific training routines forces us to come to grips with some of these problems in the same way as do the programming requirements placed on the artificial intelligence theorist. In fact, in many cases it is not clear where training attempts should be aimed, because we do not know exactly how to specify the problem we are trying to remediate. This is perhaps because we have only a rough characterization of how people generalize. Before we can design training procedures, we need to add further substance to the models and specify the processes in more detail. Essentially, we are back in what might be termed the beginning state of the task analyze-train cycle, although dealing with more complex phenomena.

As an example of the kind of research which follows from this orientation, consider one aspect of the generalization process we have described. The learner is advised to evaluate the task demands, consult his repertoire of available routines, and find the best match possible. Retarded children do not do this, and we might aim to train them to do so. The obvious problem then is, exactly how do we proceed? We do not know what steps are involved, nor do we know which ones are difficult for the immature learner. Our approach to this problem is to consider the "simple" case in which a specific rehearsal routine has been trained in a given task. For the subject to generalize that strategy to a different task requires that he or she at least (a) detect the similarity of the two tasks in terms of the processing demands, and (b) modify the rehearsal strategy to fit the new situation more closely. Unless both occur, no evidence for generalization is likely to be obtained (Campione & Brown, 1974a). We might begin by asking whether retarded children can do either if prompted, and the first phase of the experiment would involve training the strategy in Task A and then presenting Tasks $1 - N$ and asking the subjects to rate the likelihood that rehearsal would clearly help (prototypical tasks) to those where it would probably help (near tasks) to those where it would be inappropriate (far tasks). If subjects could not carry out the categorization readily, training attempts aimed at this processing would be indicated. In another phase of the experiment, subjects given training on Task A would be presented some subset of the prototypical and near tasks, and told that some rehearsal strategy should be used. They would also be advised that it might be necessary to modify the specific strategy they were taught in order to deal most effectively with the new problem. In this way, we could determine how capable they were of making the necessary modifications, and from there get some ideas about the kind of training which might be indicated.

The kind of procedure outlined is, of course, the same as the one we have been using and advocating all along. A task or process analysis of some domain is made, research is designed to determine the areas in which problems occur for retarded children, and then attempts to train the weak components are investigated. As the general outline of the research remains constant, someone might ask how we determine whether any progress is being made. The criterion we apply is that progress is being made to the extent that the specific projects address more directly what we believe to be important components of intelligence. Using this criterion, we are convinced that research in the area of retardation is progressing, and will make substantive contributions to theories or views of intelligence.

B. Properties of the Architectural System

While we believe research in retardation has emphasized the role of strategy invention and use in intelligent behavior, we do not believe that this respresents the whole story. As we have mentioned earlier, it is not clear that training on even specific tasks is sufficient to eliminate individual differences in performance. Although the retarded subjects involved in the Butterfield et al. (1973) research were able to achieve performance levels equal to those of nontrained adults, no attempt was made to train the adults. It seems clear that such training would increase adult performance also, and the main question concerns how much improvement would come about if we did undertake to train adults. In one study with college students, for example, Lyon (1977) reported that individual differences were unaffected by intervention. While everyone improved, those who performed relatively poorly before training also did so after training. The ready conclusion is that there are limitations imposed elsewhere in the system, specifically in properties of the architecture.

As the data base here is not extensive, we can summarize briefly what we know about individual differences in the development of properties of the architectural system. Of the three properties we have identified, capacity, durability, and efficiency, the most thoroughly researched is durability. At least since Galton (1887) there has existed the belief that retarded individuals suffer from some type of short-term memory deficit relative to their nonretarded counterparts. The specific form of that hypothesis which has been subjected to experimental analysis is the notion that there are intelligence-related differences in the rate of forgetting from STM, a position espoused clearly by Ellis (1963). The specific prediction which follows from this view is that IQ and retention interval should interact to determine performance levels, i.e., the drop-off in accuracy over time should be more pronounced the lower the subject's IQ. Again, statements about forgetting rate, or durability, can be made only when differences due to variations in strategic behavior (most typically rehearsal) have been eliminated. A number of other potential problems which can be encountered in this area have been pointed out by Belmont and Butterfield (1969). There have been a number of reviews of this literature (Belmont & Butterfield, 1969; Chi, 1976), and the conclusions appear to be straightforward; there is no compelling evidence to indicate that durability of items in STM varies with either age or intelligence. While less work relevant to the question of durability of items in LTM has been conducted, what evidence is available would suggest the same conclusion—the rate of loss of LTM information does not appear to vary with age or development (Belmont, 1966; Wickelgren, 1975).

Turning to capacity, we have nothing to add to Chi's (1976) arguments and simply state that, as with durability, there are no data which force us to the conclusion that there are developmental differences in capacity, conceived as the number of slots in STM. While performance in memory span tasks clearly varies with age and intelligence, there are adequate explanations for these differences which do not require assumptions about capacity changes. In this regard, Chi seems to reach the same conclusions as Huttenlocher and Burke (1976), who argue that developmental differences in memory span performance may reflect what we have called here the efficiency of the system, specifically the rate at which incoming items can be identified. We will return to this point after making some comments about efficiency and its development.

While we see no reason to expect durability and capacity to be related to intelligence, there is evidence to suggest that efficiency parameters will differentiate children of varying IQs. In this area, the results obtained by Hunt and his colleagues (Hunt, in press; Hunt, Frost, & Lunneborg, 1973; Hunt, Lunneborg, & Lewis, 1975) are extremely instructive for those interested in retardation, as they highlight areas and processes in need of attention. In fact, a case can be made that these kinds of processes both lend themselves well to comparative/developmental research and are of particular interest to students of retardation, and we will shortly list a number of reasons for these beliefs. At the same time, the kind of developmental and comparative research which is suggested is, in our view, necessary to gain a more complete picture of the processes in question.

While this is not the place to describe specific experimental paradigms, we would like to outline one in order to illustrate a number of points. Specifically, consider the name/physical identity task introduced by Posner (Posner, Boies, Eichelman, & Taylor, 1969) and employed in both adult (Hunt, in press) and developmental (Keating & Bobbitt, in press) work. In this paradigm, the main dependent variable of interest is the difference between the times required for subjects to identify nominal identity (e.g., the pair Aa consists of elements which have the same name) versus physical identity (e.g., AA). The difference presumably reflects the amount of time required for the subject to retrieve the names of the letters from memory and thus the speed with which items can be identified. The logic is that the nominal identity decision involves all the components of the physical identity decision plus retrieval of the letters' names. Thus, the difference gives the time required for that particular component. Two points are of interest, one conceptual and one methodological. First, the parameter involved here (the difference score) presumably varies only quantitatively. Retrieval of well-learned items from memory remains fundamentally the same across individuals differing in age and intelligence; only the rate at which it is carried out varies. In terms of dealing with issues concerning development, such purely quantitative variation at least simplifies the analysis of any change. Methodologically, the use of a difference score as the main metric lends itself well to comparative and developmental research. In any attempts aimed at assessing the temporal limits of information processing, it is safe to assert that the subject's reaction time (to choose one popular dependent variable) includes a number of components any proportion of which might vary with developmental status. Thus, changes in overall reaction time as a function of age or intelligence would be extremely difficult, if not impossible, to interpret. The use of a difference score methodology provides one way of getting around this problem, as the effects we are not interested in can be "subtracted out."

We now turn to a consideration of the ways in which developmental and comparative research addressed to questions of efficiency can contribute to the attainment of both theoretical and practical objectives. Theoretically, information about the development of individual differences would provide an additional way of classifying the different parameters. Knowing, for example, that college students of varying aptitude differ in terms of how rapidly they identify incoming information does not tell us anything about the "history" of either those parameters or the variation between individuals. When did the differences first emerge? Have the parameters varied with maturation? Is the rate of change dependent upon intelligence? Are parameter values influenced by cultural or instructional variations? Different processes or parameters may lead to different answers to these questions, and their role in a theory of intelligence would presumably vary accordingly.

To illustrate, the four panels in Fig. 1 illustrate different patterns which might be obtained. The simplest, and possibly the most relevant to a theory of intelligence, is shown in panel (a). The parameter varies with intelligence but not with age, and is in this sense directly comparable to IQ. In panel (b), there are additive effects of age and intelligence. Parameter values change at a constant rate, with the result that differences due to ability are of the same magnitude throughout development. In panels (c) and (d) are examples of a pair of cases in which processing parameters are an interactive function of age and ability. In (c), ability groups diverge over time, a pattern consonant with a "cumulative deficit" notion of retardation; and in (d), ability differences are minimized with increasing maturation. It is at least possible that such a classification would shed light on the meaning of the adult differences. For example, parameters showing patterns (c) and (d) may be more sensitive to, or influenced by, environmental factors than those illustrated by (a) or (b).

While there are not enough data currently available to determine the relative frequencies with which the different patterns may occur, there is evidence that variations are obtainable. For example, Keating and Bobbitt (in press) employed the Posner task described above to investigate speed of encoding and a STM task borrowed from Sternberg (1969) to obtain estimates of memory scanning rate as a function of age and ability (average and above average). In the Posner task, additive effects due to age and ability were found, i.e., pattern (b). The memory scanning data, though not overly clear, indicated differences due to ability but not age, a pattern similiar to (a).

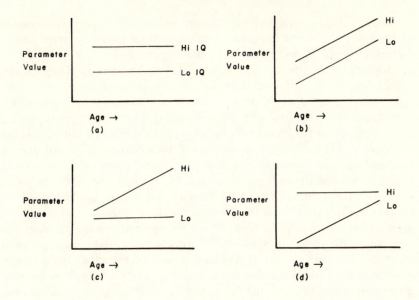

FIG. 1. Some of the possible patterns relating central processing parameters, age, and ability.

This latter pattern holds up fairly well, but not perfectly, over a number of experiments. For example, Harris and Fleer (1974) found that STM scanning rates were slower in retarded children than in children of average intelligence, and slower still for brain-injured retarded children; they did not find any age-related differences in scanning rate. In a number of other studies, rates have been found to decrease slightly with increasing age, although the changes have not been statistically significant; and Hermann and Landis (1977) reported a significant age effect using this same measure.

Presuming that enough individual difference parameters can be found, and that there is an acceptable amount of pattern variation, these differences would be interesting in at least one other way. In the retardation area, there has been a debate about the extent to which IQ should lead to any performance differences when the mental ages (MAs) of the contrasting groups are equated and motivational factors are adequately controlled (e.g., Zigler, 1969). Without going into detail, it appears to be the case that sometimes matching for MA is sufficient to eliminate individual differences, but at other times it is not. (Where differences exist after matching groups on MA, it may still be difficult to rule out motivational differences.) In any event, some of the research suggested here might provide an alternative way of conceptualizing the different kinds of tasks. For example, if performance depended upon processes whose development looked like Fig. 1(b), it would seem possible that retarded and nonretarded children matched for MA, and hence differing in chronological age, would perform at comparable levels, as there are occasions when such groups would be equated with respect to the parameter representing that process. If, however, performance depended on a process where development was mirrored by a Fig. 1(a)-like pattern, there would also be IQ-related differences, again presuming all other factors were equal.

As one example, we might consider a task like digit span, in which performance does increase with age and ability. As we have already pointed out, it does not appear acceptable to "explain" this development by positing changes in STM capacity. A number of investigators have recently argued that performance in such a task does not depend upon use of mnemonic strategies when material is presented rapidly (Huttenlocher & Burke, 1976; Lyon, 1977), but rather that it may depend upon the rate at which the items can be identified (this is not their only suggestion). A similar conclusion has been arrived at by Chi (1976), although her approach to the problem was somewhat different. The point is that encoding rate, the parameter upon which these writers suggest digit span depends, does show a corresponding relation to age and ability (Keating & Bobbitt, 1977). Although we know of no direct attempt to assess the correlation between span and encoding rate, such an experiment can easily be done.

Finally, we would like to put forth one other reason why research in this area would seem indicated. As we mentioned earlier, the variations in parmeters representing the processes are quantitative ones, and hence comparatively simple in terms of relations to development. If these parameters do relate well to IQ variations, they may lend themselves well to inclusion in batteries of items aimed at early detection of retarded children. This is certainly an area of extreme interest currently, and one in which the number of successes remains remarkably low. We know of no attempts to adapt the procedures employed in "efficiency research" to the problem. While there are many problems to be solved before such an enterprise could pay off, it seems to justify some effort, and we are beginning to collect some relevant data.

IV. SUMMARY

In this paper, we tried to abstract some of the main findings from research in two different areas, one dealing with the role of control processes in mediating performance differences between groups of retarded and nonretarded children, and the second concerned with the extent to which individuals of varying ability might differ in terms of the properties of the architectural units of an assumed information-processing system. We reviewed the literature selectively, with an eye toward finding ways in which research in retardation could inform those interested in developing theories of intelligence, and areas in which developments in cognitive psychology might suggest directions in which retardation research should proceed.

We believe we have found good examples in both cases. In the major part of the paper, we considered the implications of research with the retarded. Here we concentrate on the role of control processes. A considerable amount of evidence here converges to show that the ability to produce and invent strategies, and the ability to generalize the effects of training comprise a prime component of intelligence. While specific routines can readily be instilled, the use of those routines in novel situations presented subsequently is remarkably lacking. This conclusion also meshes well with the ideas expressed by others. As one example (see Brown, 1978a, for further discussion), Resnick and Glaser (1976) have argued that intelligence is that ability to learn in the absence of direct or complete instruction; the failure of retarded children to generalize effectively clearly limits their ability to evade the necessity for direct and complete training.

In the second area considered, the properties of the architectural system, we noted that in two of the three areas which we identified (durability and capacity) there was no compelling evidence to indicate that these parameters may be related to intelligence. In the third area, efficiency, there are fewer data but some suggestions that interesting relations with intelligence might exist. Given that, we simply pointed out the need for research on these topics with retarded children, and tried to indicate a number of reasons why such research might be profitable.

REFERENCES

Atkinson, R. C., & Shiffrin, R. M. Human memory: A proposed system and its control processes. In K. W. Spen & J. T. Spen (Eds.), *The psychology of learning and motivation.* New York: Academic Press, 1968.

Becker, J. D. Reflections on the formal description of behavior. In D. G. Bobrow & A. Collins (Eds.), *Representation and understanding: Studies in cognitive science.* New York: Academic Press, 1975.

Belmont, J. M. Long-term memory in mental retardation. In M. R. Ellis (Ed.), *International review of research in mental retardation* Vol. 1 New York: Academic Press, 1966.

Belmont, J. M., & Butterfield. E. C. The relation of short-term memory to development and intelligence. In L. P. Lipsitt & H. W. Reese (Eds.), *Advances in child development and behavior,* Vol. 4. New York: Academic Press, 1969.

Belmont, J. M., & Butterfield, E. C. Learning strategies as determinants of memory deficiencies. *Cognitive Psychology,* 1971, *2,* 411–420.

Belmont. J. M., & Butterfield, E. C. The instructional approach to developmental cognitive research. In R. V. Kail, Jr. & J. W. Hagen (Eds.), *Perspectives on the development of memory and cognition.* Hillsdale, N.J.: Lawrence Erlbaum Assoc., 1977.

Bobrow, D. G. Dimensions of representation. In D. G. Bobrow & A. Collins (Eds.), *Representation and understanding: Studies in cognitive science.* New York: Academic Press, 1975.

Bobrow, D. G., & Norman, D. A. Some principles of memory schemata. In D. G. Bobrow & A. Collins (Eds.), *Representation and understanding: Studies in cognitive science.* New York: Academic Press, 1975.

Borkowski, J. G., & Wanschura, P. B. Mediational processes in the retarded. In N. R. Ellis

(Ed.), *International review of research in mental retardation*, Vol. 7. New York: Academic Press, 1974.

Brown, A. L. The role of strategic behavior in retardate memory. In N. R. Ellis (Ed.), *International review of research in mental retardation*, Vol. 7. New York: Academic Press, 1974.

Brown, A. L. Knowing when, where, and how to remember: A problem of metacognition. In R. Glaser (Ed.), *Advances in instructional psychology*. Hillsdale, N.J.: Lawrence Erlbaum Associates. 1978. (a)

Brown, A. L. Theories of memory and the problems of development: Activity, growth and knowledge. In L. Cernak & F. I. M. Craik (Eds.), *Levels of processing and memory*. Hillsdale, N.J.: Lawrence Erlbaum Associates, 1978. (b)

Brown, A. L., & Barclay. C. R. The effects of training specific mnemonics on the metamnemonic efficiency of retarded children. *Child Development*, 1976, *47*, 71–80.

Brown, A. L., Campione, J. C., & Barclay. C. R. Training self-checking routines for estimating test readiness: Generalization from list learning to prose recall. Unpublished manuscript, University of Illinois, 1978.

Brown, A. L., Campione, J. C., Bray, N. W., & Wilcox, B. L. Keeping track of changing variables: Effects of rehearsal training and rehearsal prevention in normal and retarded adolescents. *Journal of Experimental Psychology*, 1973, *101*, 123–131.

Brown, A. L., Campione, J. C., & Murphy, M. D. Keeping track of changing variables: Long-term retention of a trained rehearsal strategy by retarded adolescents. *American Journal of Mental Deficiency*, 1974, *78*, 446–453.

Brown, A. L., Campione, J. C., & Murphy, M. D. Maintenance and generalization of trained metamnemonic awareness in educable retarded children. *Journal of Experimental Child Psychology*, 1977, *24*, 191–211.

Brown, A. L., & DeLoache, J. S. Skills, plans, and self-regulation. In R. Siegler (Ed.), *Children's thinking: What develops*. Hillsdale, N.J.: Lawrence Erlbaum Assoc., 1978.

Brown, A. L., & Lawton, S. C. The feeling of knowing experience in educable retarded children. *Developmental Psychology*, 1977, *13*, 364–370.

Butterfield, E. C., & Belmont, J. M. Assessing and improving the cognitive functions of mentally retarded people. In I. Bailer & M. Steinlicht (Eds.), *Psychological issues in mental retardation*. Chicago: Aldine, 1977.

Butterfield, E. C., Wambold, C., & Belmont, J. M. On the theory and practive of improving short-term memory. *American Journal of Mental Deficiency*, 1973, *77*, 654–669.

Campione, J. C., & Brown, A. L. The effects of contextual changes and degree of component mastery on transfer of training. In H. W. Reese (Ed.), *Advances in child development and behavior*, Vol. 9 New York: Academic Press, 1974. (a)

Campione, J. C., & Brown, A. L. Transfer of training: Effects of successive pretraining of components in a dimension-abstracted oddity problem. *Journal of Experimental Child Psychology*, 1974, *18*, 398–412. (b)

Campione. J. C., & Brown, A. L. Memory and metamemory development in educable retarded children. In R. V. Kail, Jr., & J. W. Hagen (Eds.), *Perspectives on the development of memory and cognition*. Hillsdale, N.J.: Lawrence Erlbaum Assoc., 1977.

Case, R. Structures and strictures: Some functional limits on the course of cognitive growth. *Cognitive Psychology*, 1974, *6*, 544–573.

Céllerier, G. Information processing tendencies in recent experiments in cognitive learning theoretical implications. In S. Farnham-Diggory (Ed.), *Information processing in children*. New York: Academic Press, 1972.

Chi, M. T. H. Short-term memory limitations in children: Capacity or processing deficits? *Memory and Cognition*, 1976, *4*, 559–572.

Craik, F. I. M., & Lockhart, R. S. Levels of processing: A framework for memory research. *Journal of Verbal Learning and Verbal Behavior*, 1972, *11*, 671–684.

Detterman, D. Is *Intelligence* necessary? *Intelligence*, 1977, *1*, 1–3.

Ellis, N. R. *Handbook of mental deficiency*. New York: McGraw–Hill, 1963.

Ellis, N. R. Memory processes in retardates and normals. In N. R. Ellis (Ed.), *International review of research in mental retardation*, Vol. 4. New York: Academic Press, 1970.

Fisher, M. A., & Zeaman, D. An attention-retention theory of retardate discrimination learning. In N. R. Ellis (Ed.), *International review of research in mental retardation*, Vol. 6. New York: Academic Press, 1973.

Flavell, J. H. Developmental studies of mediated memory. In H. W. Reese & L. P. Lipsett (Eds.), *Advances in child development and behavior*, Vol. 5. New York: Academic Press, 1970.

Flavell, J. H., & Wellman, H. M. Metamemory. In R. V. Kail, Jr., & J. W. Hagen (Eds.), *Perspectives on the development of memory and cognition*. Hillsdale, N.J.: Lawrence Erlbaum Assoc., 1977.

Galton, F. Notes on prehension in idiots. *Mind*, 1887, *12*, 79–82.

Harris, G. J., & Fleer, P. B. High speed memory scanning in mental retardates: Evidence for a central processing deficit. *Journal of Experimental Child Psychology*, 1974, *17*, 452–459.

Hermann, D. J., & Landis, T. Y. Differences in the search rate of children and adults in short-term memory. *Journal of Experimental Child Psychology*, 1977, *23*, 151–161.

Hunt, E. B. Mechanics of verbal ability. *Psychological Review*, 1978, *85*, 109–130.

Hunt, E., Frost, N., & Lunneborg, C. Individual differences in cognition: A new approach to intelligence. In G. Bower (Ed.), *The psychology of learning and motivation*, Vol. 8. New York: Academic Press, 1973.

Hunt, E., Lunneborg, C., & Lewis, J. What does it mean to be high verbal? *Cognitive Psychology*, 1975, *7*, 194–227.

Huttenlocher, J., & Burke, D. Why does memory span increase with age? *Cognitive psychology*, 1976, *8*, 1–31.

Keating, D. P., & Bobbitt, B. L. Individual and developmental differences in cognitive processing components of mental ability. *Child Development*, in press.

Lyon, D. R. Individual differences in immediate serial recall: A matter of mnemonics? *Cognitive Psychology*, 1977, *9*, 403–411.

Markman, E. M. Realizing that you don't understand: a preliminary investigation. *Child Development*, 1977, *48*, 986–992.

Miller, G. A., Galanter, E., & Pribram, K. H. *Plans and the structure of behavior*, New York: Holt, Rinehart, & Winston, 1960.

Moore, J., & Newell, A. How can Merlin understand? In L. W. Gregg (Ed.), *Knowledge and cognition*. Hillsdale, N.J.: Lawrence Erlbaum Assoc. 1974.

Newell, A. A note on process-structure distinctions in developmental psychology. In S. Farnham-Diggory (Ed.), *Information processing in children*. New York: Academic Press, 1972.

Newell, A. Production systems and the notion of an architecture colloqium. Paper presented at Stanford University, November 1977.

Posner, M. I., Boies, S. J., Eichelman, W. H., & Taylor, R. L. Retention of visual and name codes of single letters. *Journal of Experimental Psychology* (Monograph) 1969, *79*, 1–16.

Reese, H. W. The development of memory: Life-span perspectives. In P. B. Baltes (Chair), Implications of life-span developmental psychology for child development. In H. W. Reese (Ed.), *Advances in child development and behavior*, Vol. 11. New York: Academic Press, 1976.

Reitman, W. What does it take to remember. In D. A. Norman (Ed.), *Models of human memory*. New York: Academic Press, 1970.

Resnick, L. B. *The nature of intelligence*. Hillsdale, N.J.: Lawrence Erlbaum Associates, 1976.

Resnick, L. B., & Glaser, R. Problem solving and intelligence. In L. B. Resnick (Ed.), *The nature of intelligence.* Hillsdale, N.J.: Lawrence Erlbaum Associates, 1976.

Spitz, H. H. Consolidating facts into the schematized learning and memory systems of educable retardates. In N. R. Ellis (Ed.), *International review of research in mental retardation,* Vol. 6. New York: Academic Press, 1972.

Sternberg, S. Memory scanning: Mental processes revealed by reaction-time experiments. *American Scientist,* 1969, *57,* 421–457.

Wickelgren, W. A. Age and storage dynamics in continuous recognition memory. *Developmental Psychology,* 1975. *11,* 165–169.

Winograd, T. Frame representations and the declarative/procedural controversy. In D. G. Bobrow & A. Collins (Eds.). *Representation and understanding: Studies in cognitive science.* New York: Academic Press, 1975.

Zigler, E. Developmental versus difference theories of mental retardation and the problem of motivation. *American Journal of Mental deficiency,* 1969, *73,* 536–556.

7

Detterman's Laws
of Individual Differences Research

DOUGLAS K. DETTERMAN

Case Western Reserve University

A system of laws is presented which is intended as a guide for individual differences research in human intelligence. Formulation of these laws was based on previous research efforts in the area. Perhaps most important of these laws is Law IV—It can't be done. These laws were suggested as a starting point for the unification of the two disciplines of scientific psychology.

The preceding papers have addressed the question of what methodology should be used to study individual differences in human intelligence. The authors of these papers have been so thorough that no criticism or preference has been left unexpressed or at least none has been left unimplied. What can a discussant do when everything has already been discussed? Admit that everything worth saying has been said? Never!! After considerable thought and consultation, it finally dawned on me that a discussant with nothing to discuss must systematize.

To the casual observer, systemization might seem an impossible task since none of the authors agreed on anything. Nor did they agree with previous writers on the topic, who, it should be pointed out, did not agree with each other. (The one exception might be Carroll's statement that little progress has been made thus far in understanding mental abilities in terms of processes. There seems to be some agreement on this point. However, even here there is substantial disagreement concerning optimism about the future.) General disagreement should not be taken as a serious obstacle to deriving general principles, though. As every good scientist realizes, everything is complicated until it is understood at which time it seems very simple indeed. All that needs to be done is to specify the principles underlying the disagreement and it will be clear that all of those who have addressed methodological issues in individual differences research are actually in substantial agreement.

What I propose to do is to develop a set of laws which will guide those wishing to participate in individual differences research. I am immodestly forced to call these *Detterman's Laws of Individual Differences Research* in

The preparation of this manuscript was supported by a Mental Retardation Research Training Grant—NIH Grant #HD-07076.

order to avoid the expense of extended litigation that I have been advised would result if I assigned the names of others more deserving to these laws. Please be assured that I have every confidence of victory in a court test of accuracy of assignment but it is simply another case of unaffordable justice.

Once Detterman's Laws have been accepted by the community of researchers, they will greatly simplify communication. For instance, a paper concerning methodology might be condensed to a few lines: Law XIV; Law III, Corollary 1; Law XV. Published research papers could be reduced to absurdity in a single line: Jones (1984), Law IV. Manuscripts submitted for publication could be easily dispatched in the same way by any reviewer familiar with the system. In fact, I am optimistic enough to see the day when actual laboratory research becomes unnecessary. Instruction in individual differences research will consist of a seminar in which brash, first-year graduate students attempt to propose research projects to be carried out. Most of these proposals will die a speedy death from the citation of one or the other of Detterman's Laws. But a few of the proposals will breed real interest among the eager students. These proposals will generate a wave of contagious enthusiasm, sweeping up the students until they are brought crashing back to reality by the gray-haired professor seated at the head of the table. In an impatient, tired voice he says, "Law IV! Law IV! When will you students ever learn to use Law IV?" This is an image that sends chills down my spine. Individual differences research methodology will have ripened to its fullest potential.

Although the laws I am about to set forth form an integrated system, I will present them in three sections. The first deals entirely with statistical methodology, the second with research strategies, and the third with the interpretation of empirical results. For the most part, the laws will be presented without supporting evidence. In most cases, the proof will be immediately evident to the clever student. Other students might wish to substantiate the reasoning for each law to sharpen their methodological sophistication.

DETTERMAN'S LAWS OF STATISTICAL INERTIA

There are four basic laws that form the foundation of this portion of the system. From these basic laws, numerous more specific principles are derived. These laws have such an important place in the system that it would probably be wise to commit them to memory (particularly Law IV).

Law I. Individual differences exist. This is perhaps the weakest part of the entire system. Some may wish to regard this as an hypothesis, rather than a law, pending definitive evidence.

Law II. Anything which exists can be measured incorrectly. If error were eliminated from measurement there would be no uncertainty. If there were no uncertainty, Truth would be obvious, and science as a systematic way of discovering Truth, would be unnecessary. Error, therefore, is the heart of science, the very reason for its existence. Futher, those branches of science having the most error require the best science.

Law III. Incorrect measurements require intelligent application of appropriate statistics to be interpretable.

Law IV. It can't be done. The proof for Law IV may not be obvious to even the best students of individual differences research methodology. That is because several corollaries to Law III have been omitted. You may wish to attempt to discover them for yourself before reading further.

Law III, Corollary 1. All statistics are the same except for minor differences in form and assumptions. It can easily be shown that every statistic is related to every other. For example, F-statistics can be related to eta, the curvilinear correlation coefficient, which can be related to the Pearson product-moment correlation coefficient which can be related to chi-square which can be related to F. Selection of a statistic to be used is a somewhat arbitrary matter depending on the form of the data and the assumptions the data meet. Selection of the appropriate statistic to satisfy the form of the data is a simple matter and almost always correct. The one exception is the case in which the data meet all of the assumptions of the statistic selected, in which case the form of the data will be inappropriate and another statistic should have been selected. This simplifies matters greatly since the only concern a researcher must have is that his data meet all of the assumptions of the particular statistic selected.

Law III, Corollary 2. Application of statistics to psychological data requires that some assumptions be ignored, some violated, and still others ravaged completely. This corollary is supported by a hundred years of research.

Law III, Corollary 3. There will always be someone to point out Law III, Corollary2. The guiding dictum of individual differences methodologists is the New Testament injunction, "Let he who casts the first stone be without sin." Despite other beliefs, methodologists express true ecumenicism in the whole-hearted adoption of this principle.

Law III, Corollary 4. NORTON1952, BOX1953. The NORTON1952, BOX1953 corollary is an important one because it makes research not concerned with individual differences easy to do. The studies referred to in this law show that the assumptions of analysis of variance are resistant to violation. This law is sometimes known as the "it doesn't matter" law.

Nomothetic researchers ALWAYS use analysis of variance designs. Whenever Law III, Corollary 3 is operative, they simply cite Law III, Corollary 4. Many methodologists regard this law much as the John Birch Society regards the Miranda Decision, as a license for mayhem. In protest, they have refused to practice on the nomothetic side of the street, instead devoting their full attention to individual differences research. *Note:* This law does not apply to individual differences research because it is superseded by later laws.

The four corollaries of Law III should make the validity of Law IV evident. They show that is quite impossible to perform any statistical test without violating its assumptions. In case it has not been made clear, there are a number of more specific laws derivable from the first three which make Law IV incontestable.

Law V. Correlations are always wrong. A euphemistic way of expressing this law is that the computed value of the sample correlation coefficient will always be within ±2 of the population parameter.

However the law is stated, its meaning is clear. Whenever a correlation is computed, one of the following conditions will obtain to make it uninterpretable: non-normality, heteroscedasticity, curtailed range, or extreme outliners. If one of these conditions is not present in the data, then some other debilitating condition will be.

There is an occasional brave soul who will claim to have computed a correct correlation coefficient. Laws VI and VII cover this situation. Either may be used or, for full effect, use both.

Law VI (Special Form). Correlation does not imply causation. This law will be cited in a condescending tone of voice in such a way as to give the impression that the speaker really doesn't believe the correlation is correct but even if it were it is trivial if it does not imply causation. This law is never stated in its more general form.

Law VI (General Form). No statistic implies causation. Implication of causation is a logical process and has nothing at all to do with the statistic employed. I have always wanted to meet the clever nomothetic researcher who developed the Special Form of Law VI. Not only did it place the burden of guilt on individual differences researchers but also diverted attention from other statistical methods by suggesting that all statistics except correlation do imply causation.

Law VII. Everything is correlated with everything else. As for Law VI, when the violated assumption of an alleged correct correlation is not immediately obvious, Law VII may be invoked. This law will reduce any correlation (as well as the correlator) to insignificance. A startled expression suggesting that only a ninny would expect to find other than significant correlations is often employed when invoking this law. More complex forms of this law are frequently used in debates concerning the advantages of orthogonal as compared to obtuse factor rotation.

Although a number of other laws could be stated concerning correlation, Laws V–VII cover every possible situation. Additional laws would be superfluous.

Law VIII. Never factor analyze anything. This law can be derived from Law V. Since all correlations are wrong, no factor analysis can be worth doing. However, there are a number of other pieces of evidence which support this law. First, it is impossible to conduct a factor analysis correctly on data which are completely suitable. The reason for this is that there are no data or methods which are completely correct or suitable. Common infractions include too few subjects, inappropriate methods of factor extraction, and inappropriate criteria for factor termination to mention just a few. Second, even if it were possible to extract factors correctly, determining an acceptable rotation has never been accomplished by anyone in the history of Western civilization. Third, it is impossible to name factors and still have friends. Any attempt at naming factors produces instant hostility. I once witnessed an altercation between co-investigators over which factor should be called "Factor I" and which should be called "Factor II." I cannot tell you how the argument ended because I have not yet seen the research in print. I assume they are still arguing. After all, they extracted eight factors, giving them 8! possible namings to discuss.

Law VIII, Corollary 1. No two reviewers will ever agree on the correctness of a factor analysis. This corollary follows naturally from Law VIII. If you ever have data which have been tainted by the application of factor analysis and wish to publish them as cathartic therapy, there are only two possibilities. You may take your chances and submit to a journal using only single reviewers or you can include all possible reviewers as co-authors.

Law IX. Analysis of variance is unacceptable. The underlying reason for this law is that analysis of variance has become identified as the major technique of nomothetic researchers. Some individual differences researchers feel that anyone using this method should be forced to wear a scarlet "A." This seems rather extreme to me, though, since I cannot see how this would contribute to the person's rehabilitation. I think it would be far more constructive to require the hand calculation of several large correlation matrices and hand factor analysis and rotation for particularly hard cases.

There are several more specific reasons for this law. Most of these have been developed to close loopholes enterprising scofflaws have found in the original formulation. One clever technique involves dividing groups on the basis of ability and entering ability as a factor in the analysis of variance design. This approach is sometimes known as the aptitude-treatment interaction approach. It is also employed to discover differences between normal and mentally retarded subjects. An obvious problem is that the midrange of ability is often omitted and the results are, therefore, not representative of the entire population. Another problem is that task difficulty will vary over ability groups. In the extreme case, floor or ceiling effects result. But even without these extreme effects, artifactual interactions may result simply from differences in task reliability in the ability groups.

Another technique used to attempt to circumvent this law is the use of change scores. There is probably nothing more entertaining in psychological research than to watch a novice attempt to use change scores from a pre- and post-test design to analyze individual differences. I am convulsed by laughter every time I see the expression that results when, after months of studying journal articles and methodological discussions, they realize that Law IV applies. It is particularly good fun when the novice is someone doing a thesis or dissertation. At this point in the development of the system, clever students often suggest the possibility of analysis of covariance. The best way to handle this situation is to have them do a blackboard demonstration of a test of homogeneity of covariance. Do this late in the semester, though, as it may take several months for them to realize that Law IV applies.

Law X. The less frequently used multivariate techniques (e.g., multivariate analysis of variance or covariance, canonical correlation, discriminant analysis, pattern analysis) must be left to the expert. These techniques are so filled with potential pitfalls that they should only be attempted by an expert.

Law X, Corollary 1. There are no experts in the less frequently used multivariate techniques. And if there are, they wouldn't admit it.

Law XI. Multiple regression is unnecessary. It has recently been shown that the application of multiple regression to correlation matrices in which all variables are moderately correlated (as they always are in individual differences research—see Law VIII) is about as good as adding the predictors together and correlating the total with the criterion. In this case, Law V (correlations are always wrong) applies.

In other cases, beta weights will be uninterpretable, cross-validation will be impossible because of small sample size, the matrix will be singular, or the solution will be entirely determined by error variance. I have a personal fondness for multiple correlation because I like the authoritative look of the capital "R" and so it was with a sense of great personal sacrifice for the sake of science that I included this particular law in my system.

Law XII. Law XI concludes the present development of Detterman's Laws of Statistical Inertia. However, I have reserved Law XII for any statistics invented at some future time. Given the perverse ingenuity of the statistical mind, I probably should make allowance for many more than one future law. Perhaps the numbers over one thousand should be reserved for this purpose.

There is no question that these laws require some practice in application. The experienced researcher should have little difficulty but someone new at the game may, on rare occasions, be tempted to bring data and statistics into proximity. I have therefore condensed the laws of this section into one law to serve as a general guide for the neophyte.

Law XIII. The potential usefulness of any statistical technique is directly proportional to the impossibility of its correct application.

DETTERMAN'S LAWS OF RESEARCH STRATEGY

This set of laws is concerned with the etiquette and procedures for carrying out proper individual differences research. This was, without question, the most difficult set of principles to discover. I liken my efforts to Amy Vanderbilt attempting to discover the protocol governing a fraternity stag film.

Law XIV. There are no individual differences researchers. This law is counter-intuitive but true none-the-less. You will not find a single person claiming to be a scientist in the area of individual differences in human intelligence. There are cognitive psychologists interested in individual differences. There are developmental psychologists interested in individual differences. And there are information processing and mental retardation psychologists interested in individual differences. There are not even any graduate programs training students to be researchers in individual differences.

The apparent exceptions to this rule are psychometricians. They unabashedly claim that they are individual differences scientists. The error in this reasoning is readily apparent. They are not scientists at all. They demonstrate a perverse fixation on the elimination of error. By Law II, error is the heart of science. Psychometricians are therefore antiscientific. This is a fundamental point which must be kept in mind at all times.

Law XV. My area is best. Always maintain your allegiance to the area in which you were trained. After all, that's where your friends are and that is where the reviewers of your manuscripts are. In the researcher's utopia, friends and reviewers are one and the same. Remember also that you must only use research methodologies native to your basic area of interest. To do otherwise would be an expression of contempt to those to whom you owe your loyalty.

Law XVI. Always remember that you are bringing religion to the heathen. Friends will regard your interest in individual differences as peculiar. By maintaining the attitude that you are going to take the superior methods developed in your basic area of interest and solve, at last and once and for all, the problems of individual differences research, you will garner real sympathy for your eccentricities. Many will regard you as casting pearls before swine, but they will respect you for trying to convert the heathen.

Law XVI, Corollary 1. Never cite other areas. Citation of other areas will be taken as a sign of approval of that area. Never approve of other areas. Strict adherence to this law will greatly reduce the amount of reading to be done. On rare occasions, a pesky reviewer or editor will require a citation from another area. In these cases, the 97–2–1 rule is considered synonymous with this corollary. The following list must be used in conjunction with this rule:

Psychophysics
Information Processing
Cognitive Psychology
Educational Psychology
Developmental Psychology
Mental Retardation
Psychometrics

The 97–2–1 rule is employed by finding your basic area on the list above. Ninety-seven percent of the citations in any publication should come from this area. Two percent of the citations should come from the area immediately above yours on the list. Citations from areas more than one above you on the list will smack of arrogance. These citations should be accompanied by phrases such as "the very excellent work of" or "the classic study by." The final part of the rule specifies that one percent of the citations in a published paper should come from areas no more than one position below your basic area on the list. These citations should be qualified by phrases such as "the promising work of" or "a line of research with easily correctable deficiencies by." If citations come from areas more than one below you on the list, you will be accused of giving credence to utter nonsense.

The one exception to this rule is the area of psychometrics. Researchers in the area of psychometrics are free to cite, praise, or criticize individual differences research from any area they wish. But since they are antiscientific, all other areas have agreed to ignore them.

The ordering of the above list is completely rational. Psychometricians are antiscientific so they must be placed at the bottom of the list. Mental retardation researchers attempt to bring scientific methods to bear on an antiscientific, psychometric classification system. They are an equal blend of science and antiscience and, therefore, represent the absolute zero point of the scale. Developmental psychologists have a keen desire to do something practical and aspire to be educational psychologists. Educational psychologists have given up the hope of ever doing anything practical and would be content with an abstract understanding of the rules of the mind. They are latent cognitive psychologists. Cognitive psychologists are attracted by the precision of information-processing models, but they don't know enough math to practice in this area. Those in information processing would really like to be psychophysicists but all they know is math.

Law XVII. Explain psychometric traits in terms of basic processes. This law describes how religion should be brought to the heathen. What could be more noble than to explain away scientifically an antiscientific classification scheme?

Law XVIII. Basic processes are processes basic to your area. For example, if you are in mental retardation, explain psychometric traits in terms of rehearsal, rehearsal strategies, or meta-something. If in information processing, any parameter of the Atkinson and Shiffrin model is a good bet.

Law XVIII, Corollary 1. Use models at least ten years old. By adhering to this law, you may be certain that the model used will have wide acceptance in your area of research.

Law XVIII, Corollary 2. Never blame the model. If, by some quirk of fate, parameters of the model employed do not account for the psychometric trait in question, never blame the model for this. It would be viewed as ingratitude. Always blame the intractability of psychometric traits. After all the model was developed by nomothetic researchers and they regard individual differences as error. They are therefore more scientific since they have more error to work with than individual differences researchers (see Law II).The fact that no consideration was given to individual differences in developing the model means nothing.

Law XIX. Never integrate areas. Attempts to integrate areas are regarded as grave social blunders. For example, it would be inappropriate to attempt a developmental study of the relationhip between information processing parameters and psychometric traits.

Law XX. Collect as few data as possible. After all, data limit interpretation.

Law XX, Corollary 1. Those data which afford maximum freedom in interpretation are best. This should be the ultimate guiding principle in the planning of all individual differences research.

This concludes the portion of the system dealing with research strategy. Strict adherence to these laws will catapult you to instant fame as an individual differences researcher. Attempts to violate them might lead to infamy, though I can't be sure of that since I know of no one who has tried.

DETTERMAN'S LAWS OF CREATIVE
RESEARCH INTERPRETATION

The problem with doing research is that you always have to interpret it. Some scientists believe that it is simply enough to say that X is a function of Y and leave it at that. However, none of these scientists is an individual differences researcher. The trouble is that in individual differences research,

X is so seldom a function of Y or anything else included in the experiment that creative interpretation is essential.

Law XXI. Lacking reliability and/or validity, theorize. A good example of the application of this law occurs in the area of infant intelligence. Since none of the extant infant intelligence is either reliable or valid, numerous theories explain why this should be so. Quite frankly, this law is not mine. It was discovered by the originators of personality tests who have since built an entire discipline on it.

Law XXII. Having obtained reliability and/or validity, theorize elaborately. Some people are surprised to find that reliable and valid experimental findings require more elaborate theories than those lacking these "virtues." The reason for this is simple. The imposition of reliability and validity creates restrictions on the data. These restrictions require more elaborate theorizing. There are two corollaries which guide the construction of elaborate theories.

Law XXII, Corollary 1. When changes in experimental conditions produce no changes in performance, refer to the underlying psychological process as a structure or capacity.

Law XXII, Corollary 2. When changes in behavior occur without changes in experimental conditions or contrary to predictions, refer to the causative psychological process as a strategy, plan, or metaprocess. These two corollaries are sufficient to cover the outcome of nearly all of the individual differences research that I know about. They are elegant in their simplicity and universal in scope. There is only one additional law in this portion of the system that needs to be considered.

Law XXIII. Never define anything more precisely than absolutely necessary. Sometimes known as the law of minimum definition. The reason for this law is that precise definition limits explanatory power. Where would we be if there were exact definitions of terms like structure, capacity, strategy, trait, process, or cognition? I prefer to contemplate a regression to Watsonian behaviorism than the possibility of exact definition.

It should be pointed out that the invention of new terms is applauded under the authority of Law XXII. When new terms are invented, however, the restriction of Law XXIII should be kept firmly in mind.

These, then, are the 23 laws which constitute *Detterman's Laws of Individual Differences Research.* They are sufficient to guide even the most inexperienced researcher on his initial foray into individual differences research. I owe an enormous debt of gratitude to the unrecognized many who have made the formulation of this set of principles possible. They have inspired me by their example and, by their encouragement, have spurred me to codify a system that I hope will stand as testimony to their wisdom. It might even provide the basis for unification of the two disciplines of scientific psychology. But then again, it might not.

After discovery of these principles I found, with some consternation, that there was a slight flaw in the system. Although this flaw probably has little effect on the integrity and cohesiveness of the system, I would be less than honest if I did not mention it. I refer to this flaw as *Detterman's Paradox*. Everyone I have shown these laws agrees that they apply to everyone but him. Therefore, by consensus, the laws apply to $N-1$ individual differences researchers. On the other hand, a tally of those who thought the laws applied to themselves would indicate that they apply to no one. It would appear that the laws simultaneously apply to almost everyone and no one! This paradox is most unsettling. I have every faith that it is an artifact representing a minor oversight that will be easily resolved with some additional work.

EPILOGUE

If the truth were known, there is only one "law" that I would advocate— Control your conditions and you will see order—but Pavlov said that some time ago. I do not think that there are any magic "laws" which will lead to an explanation of individual differences in human intelligence. In fact, such laws might be counterproductive.

The major strength of research in individual differences is the multiplicity of approaches to the problem. Each approach has the potential of making a unique contribution. And each approach has its unique limitations. Perhaps from the results of these different methodologies, a coherent picture of human intelligence can be pieced together.

It has always seemed to me that the unity in approach demonstrated by nomothetic researchers has been a detriment rather than a strength. Although in many ways it makes life much simpler to have a consensus even when that consensus is incorrect, it can lead ultimately to stagnation.

Perhaps if we learned to tolerate cultural diversity, the research methodologies employed to investigate individual differences in human intelligence would come to be the predominant approaches, or at least the most productive.

ACKNOWLEDGMENTS

I would like to thank Joseph Fagan and Gary Szakmary for reading portions of this manuscript. Many of the less important ideas contained in it are theirs. Since I followed all of the suggestions they gave me, any remaining errors in style or logic must be their responsibility.

II

PERSPECTIVES
ON MEASUREMENT

If there is any consensus at all among the authors contributing to Part I, it is that research on intelligence done in the near future will differ in major respects from research that has been done in the not-too-distant past. In particular, research will be more theoretical in its underpinnings, and more experimental in its execution. One might wonder whether this new vision in intelligence research will have any impact upon the technology of intelligence testing. Unfortunately, a developing close connection between the two cannot be taken for granted: Many intelligence tests of the past have exhibited only the most casual theoretical underpinnings. Explanations of the tenuous link between theory and practice have abounded: Whether it was the demands of the marketplace, the inadequacies of the existing theories, the possibly premature success of the test leading to a reliance upon the tried-and-true, or some combination of these factors, will probably never be truly known.

A panel of scholars in the field of intelligence and intelligence testing was asked to answer the following question regarding the future of intelligence tests: What forms will intelligence tests take in the year 2000, and what purposes will the tests serve? The answers of these scholars appear in the following pages. Neisser suggests a reconceptualization of the nature of intelligence in terms of a "Roschian" prototype, and suggests that the ideal way to measure intelligence will be to combine all of the relevant attributes of the prototype into an overall index. Horn speculates that changes in our culture as well as changes in our theories of intelligence may lead to modifications in our current testing procedures; he believes that response-time measurement, computerized testing, and oral presentation of test items via audio-visual media will become more prominent in the tests of the future. Resnick foresees the functions of testing undergoing considerable modification, with future tests more often being used to monitor instructional outcomes so that instructional processes can be adapted to individual differences in learner abilities; she suggests that learning ability, neglected for some time now, will again be seen as a key to the understanding of individual differences in intelligent performance. Brown and French predict that Soviet psychology will begin to influence our notions about intelligence testing; they suggest, for example, that Vygotsky's "zone of potential development" will become an important construct in the tests of the future. Turnbull foresees replacement of conceptually vague terms such as "IQ" with terms referring to the kinds of skills required of children and adults in the classroom; he further believes that the tests of the future will yield more separate scores on a variety of abilities. Finally, Detterman suggests that new practices in testing will evolve from theories that genuinely integrate their accounts of task and subject differences; he believes that such an integration is still some way off.

8

The Concept of Intelligence

ULRIC NEISSER
Cornell University

Rosch's theory of concepts, applied to the concept of intelligence, suggests that one's intelligence is just the degree to which one resembles a prototypically intelligent person. Because no single characteristic defines the prototype, there can be no adequate process-based definition of intelligence. In principle, a combination of many empirically derived measures into a single index—as in a Binet test—would be appropriate. In practice, many of the relevant characteristics are simply impossible to measure.

The last few years have seen a resurgence of interest in the nature of intelligence—in what intelligence *is*. This revival can be conveniently dated to 1974 when Lauren Resnick convened the Pittsburgh symposium. She expressly invited the participants to discuss the real nature of this magical essence rather than its distribution or its heritability: "... what *is* it, rather than who *has* it" (Resnick, 1976, p. 4). The hope of that symposium (as of this one) was that recent advances in cognitive psychology may make such questions more tractable than they had proved to be in the early days of the mental testing movement. The first generation of intelligence testers was deeply concerned with the problem of definition, but did not make much headway with it. In 1921, for example, the *Journal of Educational Psychology* asked 17 "leading investigators" what they conceived intelligence to be. Fourteen were bold enough to reply, but their answers reflected little agreement and had little practical influence. This lack of consensus on what was being measured apparently did not shake the confidence of the psychometricians, however; they kept right on measuring. The tests were unquestionably reliable and predictive, so they must be measuring *something*.

The editors of the *Journal* hoped that their symposium would provoke vigorous discussion, and it did. Unfortunately, the discussion generated more heat than light. I will show later that this was inevitable. The concept of intelligence *cannot* be explicitly defined, not only because of the nature of intelligence but also because of the nature of concepts. While that source of difficulty was not fully appreciated in the 1920s, it was clear that the definitions being offered by the leading investigators were of little value. In the end, the only important consequence of the J.E.P. symposium may have been to increase general exasperation with all discussions of the nature of intelligence.

Among those most exasperated was Edwin G. Boring, who was not a psychometrician at all but an experimental psychologist. Boring resolved to cut the Gordian knot. He effectively ended the squabble over definitions by announcing that " . . . intelligence as a measurable capacity must at the start be defined as the capacity to do well in an intelligence test. Intelligence is what the tests test" (1923, p. 35). Psychometricians have never been comfortable with this *tour de force*, which seems to trivialize their work. Indeed, Terman had warned against such a move in the 1921 symposium: "We must guard against defining intelligence solely in terms of ability to pass the tests of a given intelligence scale" (1921, p. 131). Critics of testing don't think much of Boring's move either, and often claim that it demonstrates the intellectual bankruptcy of the entire enterprise. Although that judgment may be too harsh, there is no doubt that the circular definition has serious flaws. For one thing, it leaves out a great deal.

My own concept of intelligence includes many abilities that the tests definitely do *not* test. Moreover, the operational definition traps us in 1923: how can we tell if a new test is any good except by correlating it with old ones? Despite such weaknesses, Boring's proposal at least had the merit of cutting off an unproductive debate. Whether the resumption of that debate under the auspices of cognitive psychology will lead to a more rewarding outcome is still an open question.

Modern cognitive psychology consists, in large part, of a collection of methods for the analysis of problem solving and rapid judgment. These analyses are typically incorporated in models of processing that postulate various components and various strategies. Such an analysis can be, and has been, applied to intelligence test items in the hope of modeling the actual procedures by which the items are solved. In this way, it is suggested, information processing psychology may deepen our understanding of the tests and of the skills they measure. Even if the enterprise succeeds, however—which is far from certain—it will not necessarily deepen our understanding of intelligence itself. If we are to address *that* problem more successfully than Boring's generation, we need a better notion of what we are looking for: of what the models are to model, and the tests are to test.

To see the need for such an analysis, imagine what will happen when present research efforts reach their climax. Some day soon, psychologist *P* may claim that intelligence is really *X*, a particular amalgam of cognitive components and strategies. How will *P* support this claim when it is challenged? There are really only two ways. First, *P* will probably report that there is a high correlation between scores on X and scores on tests. Unfortunately, such a correlation cannot prove that X is *intelligence* unless we have already accepted Boring's doctrine about what the tests test. Second, P may simply try to persuade us. Look, says P, there are these and these good reasons to identify X with intelligence. (A high correlation might be among P's reasons, or it might not.) Such a reasoned argument is the more appealing alternative, but its success will depend critically on what we include in the concept to begin with (that is, what pre-existing notion P can appeal to). X mustn't be height or weight or strength, for example; they may be important, but they aren't intelligence. What is?

In attempting to describe the existing concept of intelligence, we have one great advantage over the early psychometricians. That advantage, like the new information processing methodologies, stems from recent progress in cognitive psychology. In this case, however, the advance is conceptual rather than methodological: we understand concepts themselves better now than anyone did in 1921, or for that matter in 1971. The imaginative work of Eleanor Rosch and her associates has clarified the structure of many natural concepts like *bird* and *chair*, and offers a number of insights into the basis of that structure (Rosch, 1978; Rosch & Mervis, 1975; Rosch, Mervis, Gray, Johnson, & Boyes-Braem, 1976). I believe that her analysis applies with almost equal force to the concept of *intelligent person*, and by extrapolation to the notion of intelligence itself. Before undertaking that extrapolation, I will review the changes in the concept of *concept* on which it will be based.

Rosch's analysis deals with only one kind of concept: the kind that categorizes the objects and events of the ordinary environment. *Chair, bird, game, person, kitchen chair, blackbird, football game, intelligent person* are concepts of which we can encounter instances, saying to ourselves or to others "Aha, there's a chair." Indeed, she prefers the term "category" and rarely speaks of "concepts" at all. (I will be less inhibited here.) Those categories to which her analysis applies may appropriately be called "Roschian." Among their characteristics are: absence of decisively defining features, existence of "best" or "prototypical" instances as well as marginal ones, hierarchical arrangement of categories with one level being "basic," and various special characteristics of that basic level.

Rosch was not the first to suggest that the category concepts of daily life may lack decisive defining features. That insight is generally attributed to Wittgenstein (1953), who illustrated it with the example of *game*. There is no single feature that all games have in common; instead, they resemble one another much as different members of a family do. No sharp boundary separates games from non-games. Wittgenstein did not suggest that category membership is determined by resemblance to a prototype, perhaps because this method would not work for his favorite example. But while *game* has no single prototype, many familiar categories do. "Chair," "house," "fish"—these terms are confidently applied to some objects and with much less certainty to others. A dining room chair is certainly a chair, but is a stool? A carseat? A beanbag chair? We all know about the little house on the prairie, but is an igloo a house? A trout is a fish but are minnows, whales, lampreys? In the case of an apparently biological category like *fish* we may be tempted to turn to science for advice. We will get a straight answer about minnows (yes) and whales (no), but not about lampreys. They are *cyclostomata* and not *osteichtyes*; whether that makes them *fish* is not really a biological question.

The central exemplars of Roschian categories are called "prototypes." What establishes them? By hypothesis, no particular set of properties defines the category precisely; otherwise it would not be Roschian. Nevertheless, some properties must be common to several members; otherwise there would be no category at all but only a list. The prototype is that instance (if there is one) which displays *all* the typical properties. A prototypical chair, for example, is something like this: it has a horizontal surface about half a meter off the floor with a vertical back rigidly attached to it; four legs support the seat; it is man-made out of relatively permanent material, portable, and was built to be sat on. Note that the size of a prototypical chair is roughly the *average* of real chair sizes; an object that was too small or too large would seem less definitely a chair. Other properties of prototypes may be maxima rather than averages, however. The surer we are that an object was built to be sat on, for example, the better it qualifies as a chair.

Why do so many natural categories exhibit organization around a prototype? As Rosch (1975) points out, it is partly because of the distribution of real properties of real things. Such distributions are not random: objects that have some chair-relevant properties are likely to have others as well. In other words, there are a lot of chairs around. I do not mean that concepts are formed by some blind statistical aggregation of features, but that conceptual activity is at least partially responsive to the conceiver's environment. It is not merely a reflection of that environment, however. We can easily imagine things we have never encountered, and in particular we can imagine *prototypes* that we have never encountered. I shall argue below that the ideally intelligent person is one such imaginary prototype.

Rosch's account of natural concepts does not stop with the observation that they are prototype-organized. She has also noted that many categories form natural hierarchies of class inclusion, usually at least three levels deep. In her view, categories at the middle level of these hierarchies are more "basic" than those above or below them. Thus *chair* is a basic-level concept with *furniture* as a superordinate and *armchair* as a subordinate. Other familiar hierarchies include *tools–pliers–nose–pliers, clothing–coat–raincoat,* etc. The middle level is said to be basic because it offers the most information. Assigning an object to a superordinate category says relatively little about it, while assigning it to a basic level says a great deal. Little more is then added by further refining the description to the subordinate level. Indeed, when people are asked to list the attributes of superordinates like *furniture* or *tools*, they find surprisingly little to say, while *chair* or *pliers* bring forth a flood of putative attributes. Moreover, one can superimpose pictures of chairs and still get something recognizably like a chair, but nothing coherent results from superimposing pictures of all sorts of furniture; one can list distinctive movements that one tends to make in using chairs but hardly any for furniture in general. When these operations are moved down to the subordinate level, only slight increases in specifiability result (Rosch, Mervis, Gray, Johnson, & Boyes-Braem, 1976).

The notion that there is a basic level of categorizing the things of the world is intuitively appealing. Basic-level concepts like *chair* and *bird* are the ones that languages tend to denote by single nouns, the ones that children learn first, and the ones we use most often in talking about the objects around us. They are formed on the basis of consistent correlations among enduring, concrete properties. Nevertheless, other properties and other levels of classification must not be ignored. Rosch's operations for determining the basic level are literally "superficial"—they depend on appearances. Members of a category *look* more or less like the prototype, having roughly the same shape and size. Their shapes and sizes also dictate that they are handled more or less as the prototype is, and share many listable attributes with it. Yet appearances aren't everything—even children soon mature beyond basic-level perception to realize that two objects may look much alike and yet behave differently. Some chairs are sturdy and others soon break; some birds eat worms and others eat seeds. These differences generate concepts that may be "subordinate" to the basic level, but are of fundamental importance.

Person is certainly a basic-level category. (Its subordinates *man* and *woman* are probably basic too, but this poses no special problem. Most biological taxonomies have more than one basic level; see Rosch, *et al.*, 1976.) You meet prototypical persons every day. There is also an abundance of marginal cases, although they are encountered less often—fetuses, for example, and individuals in permanent comas. (The number of marginals is much larger where people still believe in ghosts or totemic animals; supernatural beings are almost all quasi-persons.) *Person* also meets basic-level criteria of physical resemblance among class members—people pretty much all look like people. The same cannot be said for many subclasses of *person*, however; categories like *introvert* or *simpleton* don't depend on the appearances of their members at all. Contrary to the views of old-fashioned aristocrats and present-day racists, one cannot predict much about an individual's personality or intellectual ability from how he looks. In dealing with people we try to go deeper than appearances, below the basic level at which they differ visibly from chairs and birds. And we do so, I think, by forming Roschian (albeit not basic level) concepts—prototype-organized categories with fuzzy boundaries.

Intelligent person is such a concept, but by no means the only one. The English language includes several thousand adjectives for different kinds of people, from *aboveboard* to *zany* (Goldberg, 1978). Each of them can be regarded as a kind of hypothesis that the corresponding Roschian category really exists; that there are prototypically *aboveboard* and *zany* people, as well as other people who have some but not all of the relevant properties. Concepts like these help us to organize and communicate what we know about people, just as concepts like *chair* and *house* perform these functions for objects. Whether such psychological concepts are arranged in a hierarchical structure is an open question at present; see Cantor and Mischel (1977, 1979) for a possible Roschian analysis of personality traits. But to the extent that a category is embodied in natural language and frequently used, we must take it seriously as a hypothesis about correlations among human behaviors. Such hypotheses are not always true; *unicorn* and *centaur* have all the characteristics of basic-level categories, and terms like *psychic* and *telepathic* define types of people that probably don't exist. (If they did exist, I am sure there would be prototypical and marginal centaurs or telepaths, just as there are prototypical and marginal chairs.)

The notion that some people are intelligent (or clever, or cunning, or bright, or smart, or wise, or insightful, or brilliant, or intellectual, or...) is widespread indeed. I suspect that every language must have some such galaxy of cognitive terms. It is at least certain that the existence of intelligence-related words does not depend on technology or education or testing. E. F. Dube (1977) recently conducted an inquiry into the meaning of such concepts among non-literate traditional villagers in Botswana. He used 13 Setswana words which had been suggested by translators as possible equivalents of "intelligent" and other related trait words in English. The elders of the villages were easily able to "define" these terms, by giving examples of the behaviors and characteristics that justify using a given word. Moreover, their attributions were genuinely predictive of behavior. At Dube's request, the elders pointed out which of the village children were definitely "botlhale" (the Setswana word closest to "intelligent") and which ones were not. These attributions were powerful predictors of the children's subsequent performance in an experiment on memory for stories. (For another study of African conceptions of intelligence, see Wober, 1974.)

So far as I know, there has been no systematic study of the everyday concept of *intelligent person* in America (but see Bruner, Shapiro, & Tagiuri, 1958). It is a complicated notion. When I recently asked Cornell undergraduates to list characteristics of *intelligent people*, they produced an immensely variegated array ranging from "able to think logically" to "realizes there is a lot he doesn't know." In the absence of systematic data on the scope of the category, I will have to speculate about it.

In my opinion, then, *intelligent person* is a prototype-organized Roschian concept. Our confidence that a person deserves to be called "intelligent" depends on that person's overall similarity to an imagined prototype, just as our confidence that some object is to be called "chair" depends on its similarity to prototypical chairs. There are no definitive criteria of intelligence, just as there are none for chairness; it is a fuzzy-edged concept to which many features are relevant. Two people may both be quite intelligent and yet have very few traits in common—they resemble the prototype along different dimensions. Thus, there is no such quality as *intelligence*, any more than there is such a thing as *chairness*—resemblance is an external fact and not an internal essence. There can be no process-based definition of intelligence, because it is not a unitary quality. It is a resemblance between two individuals, one real and the other prototypical.

I am not the first to propose this view of intelligence. E. L. Thorndike, perhaps the most open-minded of the early psychometricians, once made a similar suggestion.

> For a first approximation, let intellect be defined as that quality of mind (or brain or behavior if one prefers) in respect to which Aristotle, Plato, Thucydides, and the like, differed most from Athenian idiots of their day, or in respect to which the lawyers, physicians, scientists, scholars, and editors of reputed greatest ability at constant age, say a dozen of each, differ most from idiots of that age in asylums. (1924, p. 241)

Here Thorndike specifies the prototypes precisely indeed. To be sure, he also postulates the existence of a single "quality of mind" differentiating Aristotle from those Athenian idiots, but elsewhere, he was more careful on this score:

> ...to assume that we have measured some general power which resides in [the testee] and determines his ability in every variety of intellectual task in its entirety is to fly directly in the face of all that is known about the organization of the intellect. (1921, p. 126)

If intelligence is a resemblance and not a quality, how can it be measured? That depends, of course, on the dimensions involved. If we wished to quantify resemblances among chairs, for example, we might make about a dozen observations of each one and combine them in an additive index. We would probably get two or three lengths, a couple of angles, indices of color and pattern and comfort, and some conventional codes for type of material, skill of workmanship, and date of manufacture. Combined in some standardized fashion, these items would reliably characterize any given chair, and specify its similarity to the prototype. An index of *chairness* could even have predictive validity—properly transformed, it might correlate .50 (say) with the chair's retail price. Those who opposed its use might well argue that despite the reliability and validity of the index, no satisfactory definition of "chairness" had ever been offered. They would be right, but none *can* be offered; *chair* is a Roschian category. The only thing available for measurement is resemblance to the prototype, and it is indeed best measured by cumulating similarities over many dimensions. Because the same thing applies to *intelligence*, no satisfactory verbal definition of that concept is possible either.

The ideal way to measure intelligence, then, would be to combine all the relevant dimensional measurements into an overall index. Such an index would inevitably be somewhat arbitrary in the weights given to various components, but in principle it might be a reasonable standardization of intellectual differences. In practice, however, this ideal is unattainable; many of the relevant dimensions cannot be measured in any standard way. The characteristics of the prototypical intelligent person include not only verbal fluency, logical ability, and wide general knowledge but common sense, wit, creativity, lack of bias, sensitivity to one's own limitations, intellectual independence, openness to experience, and the like. Some of these characteristics (which were all suggested by the Cornell sample) manifest themselves only in unique or practical situations; others cannot be evaluated except by considering the individual's life as a whole. Thus there are really only two possibilities: not to measure intelligence at all, or to measure it inadequately. Much could certainly be said for the first alternative, but for various reasons psychology and society have adopted the second. *Some* of the properties relevant to the Roschian prototype of intelligence are measurable, and we measure them.

Considered from this point of view, the basic structure of Binet-type tests makes sense. A typical intelligence test consists of a large number of separate items, selected for mutual correlation and criterion validity rather than on theoretical grounds. The individual items function like the individual dimensions of chairs in my hypothetical example. Combined into a total score, they measure the testee's resemblance to a prototypical intelligence-test smartie who would get all the items right. (One might argue that Binet's prototype was the *average* rather than the smartest child; it is the average who is used as the standard in calculating mental ages. But this seems awkward. There are apparently no nouns or adjectives meaning "person of average intelligence," and no one speaks of IQ tests as if they measured "averageness.") The effective prototype of measurable intelligence, then, is someone who scores high on tests. He or she also does very well in school and other academic enterprises; this correlated property convinces the psychometrician that the test is indeed measuring similarity to the proper prototype.

Do such prototypes exist? Is the category real, or are we dealing with centaurs and telepaths? No and yes— there are no perfectly intelligent persons (even Aristotle would have flubbed a few scale items), but the category itself is surely as real as chairs. This is established directly by the empirical results. All tests of intellectual functioning are positively correlated with one another, even if the correlations are often low; they form a "positive manifold." Moreover, they are also correlated with academic criteria. It is just such patterns of correlation that (in Rosch's view) mark the existence of natural categories.

This argument suggests that the founders of psychometrics were perfectly right—their tests *were* measuring something, even though no one could articulate just what it was. It was, and is, similarity to a certain prototype. Unfortunately, however, the success of the tests has led to the establishment of two prototypes where there was only one before. The natural category *intelligent person* has been effectively divided into subcategories, one pertaining to academic intelligence and the other to intelligence in general. Boring's definition was a kind of self-fulfilling prophecy: psychometrics has *created* a concept of intelligence which is exactly what the tests test. (Like other Roschian categories, that concept itself has fuzzy boundaries. No one can say exactly what academic performances are criterial for it; the correlations just get lower as one leaves the center.) I have discussed the distinction between academic and general intelligence elsewhere (Neisser, 1976), and so will not dwell on it here. It should be obvious, however, that the two are different. All of us can think of highly "intelligent" acquaintances who are nevertheless "stupid" about a lot of things, or vice versa. Such judgments do not involve any real contradiction. One characterization is being made with respect to an academic prototype, the other with respect to a more mundane one.

In summary, I have suggested that intelligence itself does not exist except as a resemblance to a prototype, but that the concept *intelligent person* is based on fact, i.e., on genuinely correlated human characteristics. An individual's similarity to the prototype can be measured, but only with partial success; not all the relevant attributes lend themselves to standardized measurement. Such partial measurement tends to create its own prototype and its own category—also Roschian but necessarily less inclusive. Any future claim about the real nature of intelligence will be evaluated with both of these prototypes in mind. If the claim specifies particular processes or mechanisms which are said to underlie general intelligence, it will certainly meet with strong opposition. Such a notion cannot do justice to the concept of intelligence that we already have.

I am aware that this analysis leaves several questions unanswered. For one thing, I have not faced the fact that some correlated characteristics seem less fundamental than others. Verbal fluency is correlated with income as well as with reasoning ability; does a highly verbal pauper seem less intelligent because of his poverty? Perhaps he does ("If you're so smart, why aren't you rich?"), but it is not in the same sense in which he would seem less intelligent because he reasoned badly. Note, however, that this is a very general problem of Roschian concepts. As a rule, not all the characteristics of the prototype are equally important. Even a person who had seen only wooden chairs would agree that a steel chair is a chair, because the construction material is not as essential to *chairness* as, say, having a supporting seat. There is something fundamentally naive about the Roschian categories of everyday life. (That may be why we learn them so early and easily.) Further experience and deeper analysis reveal which correlations are adventitious and which are necesary; they provide the marginal cases that make us think again. Indeed, my own reaction to encounters with beanbag chairs and igloos certainly goes deeper than mere uncertainty about whether they belong to the corresponding categories. What actually happens is that I come to distrust the category itself. With some existential sadness I realize that the correlations are not so perfect, the world not so simple, as I had supposed.

To begin to distinguish essential from nonessential characteristics of intelligence, it would be necessary to face another question that my analysis has ignored. *Why* are the properties that we think of as characterizing intelligent people correlated with each other? Is it nature or nurture; schooling, attitude, opportunity, cultural setting, genes, nutrition, or some channeled interaction? The answer is, of course, that not all the correlations have the same basis. Many attributes of intelligence must co-vary primarily because they are sensitive to cultural and situational factors. Other characteristics of intelligent people are probably rooted more directly in their genes. (No one who claims that intelligence is a Wittgensteinian "family resemblance" can easily dismiss the possibility that it runs in families just as resemblances do!) Unfortunately, these issues tend to bring us back from "What is it?" to "Who has it?", so they are somewhat out of place at this symposium.

Another kind of explanation of the correlations among attributes of intelligence may also be important. In some cases (involving either nature or nurture), different intelligent activities may be based on the same underlying processes. Cognitive research may indeed be successful in identifying those processes, and thus account for some of the observable correlations among the attributes of intelligence. Such research is certainly worth pursuing. We must be wary, however, of believing that it will enable us to define intelligence itself. Otherwise we may find ourselves acting out a new version of Boring's scenario in the year 2000, when someone defines intelligence as what the models model. I hope we don't, because it isn't.

REFERENCES

Boring, E. G. Inteligence as the tests test it. *The New Republic*, June 6, 1923, 35–37.

Bruner, J. S., Shapiro, D., & Tagiuri, R. The meaning of traits in isolation and in combination. In R. Tagiuri & L. Petrullo (Eds.), *Person Perception and Interpersonal Behavior*. Stanford, California: Stanford University Press, 1958.

Cantor, N., & Mischel, W. Traits as prototypes: Effects on recognition memory. *Journal of Personality and Social Psychology*, 1977, *35*, 38–48.

Cantor, N., & Mischel, W. Prototypes in person perception. in L. Berkowitz (Ed.), *Advances in Experimental Social Psychology*. New York: Academic Press, 1979, in press.

Dube, E. F. *A Cross-cultural Study of the Relationship between "Intelligence" Level and Story Recall. Ph.D. Dissertation, Cornell University, 1977.*

Goldberg, L. R. *Language and personality: Developing a taxonomy of personality-descriptive terms. Institute for the Measurement of Personality,* Eugene, Oregon, March, 1978.

Neisser, U. General, academic, and artificial intelligence. In L. B. Resnick (Ed.), *The Nature of Intelligence*. Hillsdale, N.J.: Lawrence Erlbaum Associates, 1976.

Resnick, L. B. *The Nature of Intelligence*. Hillsdale, N.J.: Lawrence Erlbaum Associats, 1976.

Rosch, E. R. Universals and specifics in human categorization. In R. Brislin, S. Bochner, & W. Lonner (Eds.), *Cross-cultural Perspectives on Learning*. New York: Halsted, 1975.

Rosch, E. R. Human categorization. In N. Warren (Ed.), *Studies in Cross-cultural Psychology*. London: Academic Press, 1978.

Rosch, E. R., & Mervis, C. B. Family resemblances: Studies in the internal structure of categories. *Cognitive Psychology*, 1975, *7*, 573–605.

Rosch, E. R., Mervis, C. B., Gray, W., Johnson, D. M., & Boyes-Braem, P. Basic objects in natural categories. *Cognitive Psychology*, 1976, *8*, 382–439.

Terman, L. M. Intelligence and its measurement. *Journal of Educational Psychology*, 1921, *12*, 127–133.

Thorndike, E. L. Intelligence and its measurement. *Journal of Educational Psychology*, 1921, *12*, 124–127.

Thorndike, E. L. The measurement of intelligence: Present status. *Psychological Review*, 1924, *31*, 219–252.

Wittgenstein, L. *Philosophical Investigations*. Oxford: Basil Blackwell, 1953.

Wober, M. Toward an understanding of the Kiganda concept of intelligence. In J. W. Berry & P. R. Dasen (Eds.), *Culture and Cognition: Readings in Cross-cultural Psychology*. London: Methuen, 1974.

9

Trends in the Measurement of Intelligence

JOHN L. HORN
University of Denver

On the assumption that an understanding of the past provides a guide to the future, analyses are directed at explicating major trends of the last 25 years in the scientific study of intellectual abilities. Five major trends are identified. These suggest that in the future several kinds of tests will be used to measure several kinds of basic processes of intelligence; there will be a corresponding decrease in concern to measure a single attribute of general intelligence. There will be emphasis in measuring complex learned capacities of a kind that characterizes adult thinking, in contrast to tests designed for school children. Test items will be presented through the computer, on TV screens, and in ways that permit the individuals' responses to determine which items will follow; responses, including time to respond, will be gathered in the computer and there converted to scores.

CLASSES OF DETERMINANTS

Two major factors produce change in the practices of measuring intellectual abilities: changes in the culture and changes in our theories about human abilities and their development. Also, of course, there is the powerful force of inertia, the trend toward continuing to do tomorrow what we do today and what we have always done.

INERTIA

Perhaps it is true that we learn little from contemplation of that great dust heap we call history. However, if the recent history of the measurement of abilities for practical purposes is any indication of things to come, we might well predict that the ways in which we measure intelligence in the year 2000 will be very similar to the ways we do this measurement today or the ways we did it in 1950 or even earlier. For example, in spite of numerous well established indications that there is more than one form for human intelligence, still today in many clinical and educational applications the major emphasis is on measuring a single conglomerate labeled general intelligence or general aptitude. As early as 1909 Cyril Burt had demonstrated that Spearman's concept of unitary general intelligence must be compromised by recognition of at least a couple of somewhat independent components.

This kind of evidence accumulated over the next 50 years to make it increasingly clear that, at the very least, we should recognize several distinct components of intelligence, and perhaps we should regard some of these components as distinct intelligences. Yet this message from the research literature has had very little influence on the way intelligence has been regarded and measured in clinical diagnosis. The Binet test of today is barely distinguishable from the Binet test that was created in Spearman's time; the form of the Wechsler test has remained essentially unaltered for 40 years. When I took clinical training 24 years ago there was a requirement that I administer and interpret ten Binet's and ten Wechsler's; today many clinical programs still have this requirement in much the same form as it was then.[1] Today, forty-one years after the appearance of Thurstone's pioneering monograph on primary mental abilities, our most frequently used measures of intelligence still have not been constructed to take account of the now voluminous research indicating the multidimensional structure of human intellect. Virtually no technology for multidimensional diagnosis of intellectual capacities has been based on this research evidence.[2] Inertia must be taken into account in any realistic estimation of the form that the measurement of intelligence will take in the year 2000.

This failure to use the evidence on structure is only one of several possible examples of inertia in the measurement of intelligence. Findings from cognitive psychology also have had very little impact. The reader can think of other examples. Consideration of these examples suggests that it is difficult to alter the technology of measuring intelligence. Change is gradual. There is considerable lag between the time when research evidence signals the possibility of changing this technology and the time when such change actually occurs. Perhaps, therefore, intelligence tests in the year 2000 will be very much as they are today. Perhaps, also, they will serve virtually the same purposes.

---

[1]Indeed, more scandalous is the fact that clinical programs still require students to learn the Rorschach and the MMPI. It is not our purpose to consider this bit of inertia here, however.

[2]This is not to say tnat the concepts of general intelligence are theoretically uninteresting or are devoid of research-based support; nor is it to take issue with the evidence that a conglomerate general measure of intelligence often provides better predictive validities than any of the factor components. It is recognized that for many practical purposes of diagnosis, selection and placement, a conglomerate measure may serve adequately. It must be acknowledged also that the Wechsler tests particularly, and other tests to a lesser extent, are often used in diagnosis in a manner that recognizes that performances on different subtests probably indicate different patterns of processes and abilities in individual manifestations of intelligence. Given these qualifications, however, it remains true that the measurement and use of intelligence in clinical and educational settings has been largely uninformed by the evidence indicating independent factors of intelligence. Also, in the construction of intelligence tests there has been very little effort to incorporate the extensive evidence on multiple-factor components of intelligence.

Predictions of little change may be realistic, but they are not terribly interesting. They do little to titillate or engage imagination. It would seem that the purpose of this symposium is to generate something closer to titillation than to dour contemplation of continuance of the status quo. In what follows, therefore, we will take a more venturesome, even if fanciful, view of the matter.

CULTURAL CHANGE INFLUENCES

The measurement of intelligence must reflect the dominant values of the culture in which the measurement occurs. Otherwise, a major feature of intelligence is not assessed. One might measure qualities of intellectual function that do not reflect values of a culture, but to measure only these qualities is to neglect measurement of a part of intelligence that many, particularly in applied settings, regard as most important. For example, suppose we were to measure complex reaction time in ways that introduce practically no systematic between-culture variance. Would such measures be accepted as indicating the kind of intelligence that personnel managers would want to measure in selecting trainees for saleswork or junior executive positions? Probably not. Culture-free tests cannot be accepted and used as indicants of high levels of intelligence in many situations where measures of intelligence are desired. In our society intelligence must involve good reasoning with the contents of our culture. If this is lacking, then a vital component of intelligence is lacking. Other defining attributes of our concepts of intelligence (and there are several such concepts) also pertain to qualities that reflect understanding of, and abilities in dealing with, the dominant culture. Theories of intelligence are, to a considerable extent, accounts of how such understanding and abilities come about. There can be culture-free tests of particular components of intelligence, but there can be no perfectly culture-free tests of intelligence, as such.

This is true not only of our society but also of almost any other society. Intelligence, or the concept that is most similar to this, is defined in part in terms of the values of a given culture, and these vary from one culture to another. The elements that constitute the *sine qua non* of intelligence in our culture are not the same as the corresponding elements of what is, or would be, the concepts of intelligence of other cultures. The abilities involved in finding water are highly valued in the culture of the Australian Aboriginals and thus are an essential part of the intelligence of these people. Those from other cultures perform poorly on Australian Aboriginal intelligence tests. It may be true that the highly intelligent members of our society are the people most likely to become intelligent in the Australian Aboriginal culture if circumstances conspired to make this a necessity, but this is not a known fact and very possibly may not be true. Certainly if adults are to be the subjects of an experiment to test this hypothesis, there is at least a suggestion in the literature that those who are most intelligent in one culture may not be among those who most readily acquire the intelligence of another culture.

Because the concept of intelligence is integrally linked with the values and demands of a culture, a prediction pertaining to the nature and uses of intelligence tests in in the next century must take into account the way our society is changing and is likely to become. Given the complexities involved, the imponderables, and the fact that contingencies about which we can have no knowledge nevertheless will prove to be important, it is extremely difficult to make sensible guesses. Taking our cue from what can be discerned even now, however, a few rough and general predictions seem to be reasonable.

One fairly recent trend of change in our culture seems bound to have an important influence on the future of intelligence testing. This is a trend in the way that information is transmitted and received. The trend is away from use of printed forms—newspapers, books, magazines—toward use of the images of TV and movie screens. This is not to say that printed media publishers need contemplate bankruptcy; printed matter surely will continue to deluge us. It is to say, however, that increasingly in the future, as increasingly in the recent past, transmission of our culture will occur via television and film presentations.

One manifestation of this trend is indicated by the increase in film budgets of educational institutions. Expenditures for educational films in the Department of Psychology at Denver University have increased 400-fold in the last ten years, while over this same period expenditures for books for this department have barely kept pace with inflation. More of our students learn more of the psychology they come to know from film and TV presentaions. This is merely a reflection of what is occurring throughout our educational systems and, more generally, throughout our culture. Whereas in the early days of the cinema and TV these media imitated communication techniques that had been found to work in books, today the illustrations and even the writing styles of books often involve some use of techniques that have been developed from efforts to communicate via TV and film. More of what people are learning is coming to them via the moving images of TV and film.

In the future a large (relative to now or twenty years ago) proportion of what children learn will be based on TV and film presentations. Not only will content come to them in this way, but also techniques for assimilation of material will be derived from use of these media. Just as learning to read, and learning to read rapidly, were major components of education for prior generations of learners, so learning to efficiently deal with information presented via TV and film will become increasingly a part of the education of future learners in our culture. Also, just as reading abilities of a variety of kinds have been prominently involved in 20th Century tests of intelligence, so the abilities that are prominent in comprehending material presented via TV and film will become increasingly a part of the intelligence tests of the 21st Century. If this does not occur, then it seems that inertia in the development of measures of intelligence is nearly pathological, and some very drastic steps should be taken to remedy it. However, I am really not worried. Already there are ample signs of movement toward measuring intelligence with material presented via the CRT.[3]

The shift toward measuring intelligence by means of TV/film presentations will be accompanied by several important changes not only in ability measurements, as such, but also in theories about intellectual capacities. In both practical and the theoretical developments temporal features of presentation and response will become more prominent. Two basic aspects of this development appear to be particularly important. Both reflect important technological changes within our culture.

One temporal feature derives from improved techniques for recording the time it takes to respond to a stimulus. Reaction-time recordings will become more common and important in future measures of human abilities. Time will be recorded in small units with high accuracy. Increased use and accuracy of time recording will come about partly because of advances in computer technology. Minicomputers, microprocessors, and similar hardware will become smaller, cheaper, and better. Presentation of stimuli for measuring abilities and the gathering of responses will be regulated by such devices. Scoring procedures and function models based on ideas about processing time will become increasingly prominent in our theories about intellect and in our practical devices for diagnosing problems and indicating strengths of intellectual capacities.

Time in another sense will become increasingly important in our theories and practical measurements of intelligence. The time to which I refer here is that of time-based flow of stimulation. Tasks presented via TV and film can flow through time in a manner that is not prominent in the materials of present-day intellectual tests. The elements of a problem presented by video tape under computer control can be arranged to occur in a sequence, one after another in a near-continuous flow. Each element can be seen for any specified

---

[3]Incidentally, the widely publicized declines in scores on college selection and educational achievement tests, such as the SAT, may reflect little more than this shift in media of communication of knowledge. The tests that have indicated the decline are tied closely to information transmission by the printed word and the behavior required in the tests, as such, is reading rather than dealing with information presented via TV or film. If, as seems evident, there has been gradual increase during the last couple of decades in the proportion of time and effort students spend in assimilating film-presented information and corresponding decrease in the proportion of time and effort devoted to using the printed word to enhance knowledge, then this could very well show up in a gradual decrease in scores based on the printed-word form of information transmission.

amount of time before being removed from vision. Elements can be allowed to reappear after precisely timed periods. Thus, order and number of repetitions, as well as temporal separation, of elements of problems can be objectively controlled.

These kinds of changes in the technology of observing the phenomena of thinking hold promise for unlocking new understandings of human abilities. Capacities for temporal integration are important features of intelligence, but we know very little about them. The human retains the past, anticipates the future, and brings the past and future together in the present when formulating and solving problems, but we can say little about how such processing is involved in intelligence. Yet it seems that temporal integration is a quality that distinguishes the human intelligence from the intelligence of other animals and also distinguishes the intelligence of mature members of our species from the intelligence of the young. Thus careful study of the processes involved in dealing with the temporal flow of elements of problems can enhance our understanding of the basic features of human intelligence. Moreover, perhaps it is not frivolous to expect that TV and film presentations, controlled by the computer, with computer-gathered responses, will provide measures of temporal integration that are sufficiently accurate to enable us to use them as major components of multiple-component intelligence tests of the year 2000.

Considerably more work will be done in the next few years to build bridges of relationship between auditory and visual abilities. Well before the year 2000 we will have a scientific foundation for measuring intelligence by means of auditory tasks as well as with visual tasks. Perhaps by then we will even know enough to use tactile tasks in this measurement.

Time-based visual presentation of problems can be similar in several respects to auditory presentation, as in tasks designed to measure comprehension of speech. This similarity provides a basis for several approaches to improving measurement of intellectual capacities. Speech can be simulated by temporal-flow visual presentations, and thus be controlled in ways that are not possible in auditory presentations. For example, it seems that when auditory presentations of parts of words and sentences are notably slowed we destroy important qualities of the Gestalt of these stimuli, but that slowed visual presentation of these kinds of materials need not destroy the Gestalt. By thus retaining some of the qualities of the flow of spoken language while controlling some aspects of this flow we can gain insights into how we come to understand spoken language. Comprehension of language is an important feature of the intelligence we measure with our present-day paper and pencil technology, but temporal features of this comprehension are not identified in our measurements, and we do a poor job of describing the elements of language development. These features of language behavior will become more prominent in measures of intellectual capacities as our theories shift toward defining intelligence in terms of abilities in comprehending information that is presented via TV and film.

Expanded use of microprocessors and computers in the administration of test materials and the gathering of responses should also lead to increase in the use of response-contingent tests. These are tests in which one's response determines which of several possible items will appear next. If a subject fails to get a correct answer to an easy item, for example, an even easier item might be administered, whereas if a correct answer is obtained, a more difficult item might be provided. This kind of testing has some of the features of individual testing, as with the Binet or Wechsler. The computer-controlled administration is more objective and more open to study, however. So some additional knowledge about the effects of respondent-determined order of administration can be accrued. Already a considerable amount of work is being done with response-contingent testing.

It can be seen, then, that broad shifts in our culture, in the ways that information is transmitted and changes in the technology of presenting stimuli and gathering responses, should lead to notable changes in that which we measure and call intelligence. However, the model for change that I have suggested with my examples is mainly only one of knee-jerk reaction to cultural change. What about measurement change that comes about because our scientific theories about intelligence are changed, presumably for the better and only partly in consequence of cultural change? More generally, how is the measurement of intelligence likely to be altered by changes in the subject matter of the behavioral sciences?

TRENDS IN THE STUDY OF INTELLIGENCE

We have already noted that one need not be sanguine about the prospect that because scientific theory changes, the technology of measuring intelligence will necessarily change. In spite of the dour predictions that derive from historical precedent, however, I think that in the future theory will more surely determine ability measurement technology. There are several reasons why this prediction seems reasonable even in the absence of support from past performance.

For one thing, an area of academic psychology that has been dominant in the U.S.A. throughout this century, but which heretofore has had little influence in the development of theory about intelligence, now seems to be becoming more involved in the study of intellectual abilities. This is the area that today goes under the heading of cognitive psychology and information processing. Some of the best researchers in psychology are in this field. A considerable amount of knowledge about learning, thinking, and perceiving has been amassed in this area. This is knowledge about intellectual processes, but knowledge which has not been well integrated into theories of intelligence.

In the past most of the research in which the concept of intelligence has been explicitly recognized and studied has been based on analyses of individual differences. In the dominant stream of psychological research, however—particularly in cognitive psychology and its predecessors—the designs and methods of analysis of individual differences research have been actively avoided. There has even been suggestion that two different disciplines of psychology are represented by the differences that distinguish study of individual differences from study in which group means are the units of analysis. This schism within psychology seems to me to be on the way out, however, as indicated in part by the fact that cognitive psychologists are moving into the study of intellectual abilities. Individual differences are being treated as something other than error in more and more of the studies originating in cognitive psychology laboratories. Conversely more and more of the research deriving from considerations of individual differences has used findings from cognitive psychology. This modern trend is well exemplified by the work of the people of this symposium.

A major catalyst promoting this union of cognitive psychology and individual differences psychology is the lure of study of intellectual development. The centroid of psychological research is gradually moving in this direction, aided very considerably by shifts in allocation of funds for research. The trend toward increased funding of research on adulthood development must continue as the proportions of older adults increase in our society. Money will keep those researchers who are already in this field and attract new ones—namely those in cognitive psychology.

Cognitive researchers bring relatively strong theories about particular processes. Although these processes are often very narrow relative to the major abilities of intelligence, they can represent integral parts of the whole. As cognitive theorists work to relate such processes to the abilities of intelligence, there should be notable movement toward describing the interrelationship among processes and thus improved description of the architectonic structure of intelligence. This influential push from cognitive psychology will encourage the development of multiple-process measures of intelligence. The upshot of this work, coupled with what is already known and will become known about the multiple factor nature of intelligence, should result in clinical tests to measure each of several basic intellectual processes coupled with procedures for combining these processes, according to research-based theory, to yield measures of higher-order functions. Thus tests of the future should enable a clinician to accurately diagnose a memory defect of the kind that is produced by alcohol intake—the so-called Korsakoff's syndrome—and also to determine the level of fluid intelligence independent of a memory defect.

Theories about adult development will not only become more important in shaping the form of adult intelligence tests, they will also influence the design of tests that are intended to be used with children. It has been recognized for years that the ultimate developments of intelligence are to be found in the achievements of adults, not in the schoolroom performances of children. It is difficult to be more precise about the matter than this, however, and relatively little research has been directed at providing more precise descriptions. With increased interest in, and funding of, research on adult development, however, the year 2000 should see us making notable advances in identifying just what it is that we mean when we talk about adult intelligence being the quintessence of intelligence. All intelligence tests of that period should reflect this increase in knowledge.

In these speculations I have assumed, implicitly, that the purposes of intellectual assessment will remain largely unaltered. Is this a reasonable assumption? Can we anticipate something drastically different?

PRACTICAL USE OF MEASURES
OF INTELLIGENCE IN THE FUTURE

In this audience I probably needn't stress the fact that intelligence tests are achievement tests and that in most applications the purpose is predictive and descriptive, so the question of the primal course of the achievement is not at issue. In most applications it is largely irrelevant whether ability has stemmed mainly from genetic or mainly from environmental determinants, for example. In selection and placement the question is what can the person do now—what has he achieved—and what is the predictive utility of this information, not what caused the person to be as he is. Similarly, the clinician or educator wants to know a client's level of ability for the purpose of planning a treatment, not for purposes of understanding his ancestry or advising him about what to expect of his progeny. It is true, of course, that it can be helpful in planning a treatment to know the causes of a condition, but such knowledge is not necessary for good treatment. Adequate treatments can be planned in the absence of such knowledge. This must be the case because we know so little about the causes of many conditions that we treat fairly effectively. Also treatments can be the same for conditions that we know to have different causes. No doubt we will learn more about the causes of the achievement failures that can be detected with intelligence tests, but this will not greatly alter the use of these tests because they mainly serve to indicate the achievement failure, as such, not the causes.

Physicians and clinical psychologists often seem to want to use psychological tests for purposes of indicating an organic malfunction or defect. There are good reasons for this desire, but I think it is largely unrealistic. A behavioral test can be convenient and safe relative to other kinds of diagnostic devices, but I suspect that such tests will only very rarely be accepted as the final word on diagnosis of an organic condition. Almost always, it seems, the preferable indicant, if it can be found, is something closer to the malfunction than a behavioral test can ever get—a CAT scan, a chemical analysis, or the like. Psychological tests will continue to serve mainly only rough screening purposes in the identification of organic malfunctions.

We have indicated our guess that in the future there will be decreased emphasis on the measurement of a single general factor of intelligence and increased emphasis on measurement of separate capacities that fall under the rubric of intelligence. Implicit in this prediction is an assumption that those working in clinical and educational settings will continue to want accurate information about their clients' abilities in order to provide better services for these clients. There seems to be little reason to suppose that this application of ability testing will decrease.

The social forces that are directed at curtailing the use of ability tests has not been directed at these clinical/educational uses even as they have, in recent times, often missed their intended marks and have hit these uses. However, it seems that most critics of testing do not really object to ability assessment for purposes of diagnosing and treating problems of the person assessed. This is particularly the case if the test is not simply a global measure but holds promise of yielding useful information about separate processes— the kind of test I expect to see more of in the future. Responsible test critics are mainly objecting to thoughtless, widespread testing in which invidious distinctions are drawn, and motivations are distorted, when there are little or no apparent reasons for making the distinctions. They object to forcing people to take tests, and be invidiously compared, in situations where they have already been forced to be. If one doesn't choose to go into the army, for example, but is forced to do this and then forced to take tests the results of which are used in ways that do not compliment him, then he is likely to complain about testing. Does this also describe the way many students and parents look upon intelligence testing in school systems? I daresay it does. While such use of testing may be necessary for purposes of winning a war, is it consistent with the principal purposes of elementary and secondary education? This is the major kind of question that test critics are asking.

This kind of criticism of testing need not inhibit the use of tests in situations where these criticisms do not apply, although granted that in recent years this has not always been the case. As criticisms of testing become more accurately focused on uses that are unnecessary or improper, the beneficial uses can flourish. Perhaps I'm being overly optimistic, but this is the kind of development I see for the future. By the year 2000 much of the rather meaningless testing we do today will have been abandoned, but offsetting this decrease will be increased use of multiple-component intelligence tests for well accepted diagnostic, selection and placement applications.

On such a note it is difficult to restrain a parting pronouncement that yes, and there will be pie in the sky too! Ah well, optimism is pleasurable.

SUMMARY

Realistic appraisal, based on historical analysis, suggests that in the year 2000 the tests used to measure intellectual abilities in applied settings will be very similar to the tests used today and 40 years ago. However, if the technology of measurement for applied purposes follows advancements in scientific understanding of human intelligence, then we can expect that intelligence tests of the future:

1. will be architectonically structured to provide for measurements of many separate abilities, ranging from very elementary processes to broad but distinct dimensions of intelligence;
2. will involve, perhaps be focused on, abilities to comprehend and assimilate information that comes to one via the continuous flow of TV-like presentations;
3. will contain subtests designed to indicate features of temporal integration of information, auditory organization, and elementary cognitive processing of information;
4. will derive more from the study of adulthood development than from the study of childhood development.

The mainstreams of cognitive psychology will be diverted more and more into the study of intelligence and thus will influence the shape of practical tests. Tests will be used less and less to measure global intelligence just for the sake of measuring it, or to make invidious distinctions, but more testing will be done to help identify particular ability strengths and weaknesses. Theory about intelligence will improve and more test construction will be based on sound theory.

10

The Future of IQ Testing
in Education

LAUREN B. RESNICK
University of Pittsburgh

Will IQ tests as we currently know them be used in schools in the year 2000? Will
they be used as they are now or will they serve different functions? What new kinds
of tests of aptitude and intelligence are likely to be developed in the next twenty
years? In this article, the author attempts to answer the first two questions by
considering the functions that IQ and aptitude tests now serve in schools and the
trends that may modify the present pattern of test use. To answer the third
question, she examines current research on intelligence and aptitude and discusses
the kind of intelligence tests that might prove more useful in instructional
planning.

We are asked as members of this symposium to engage in a form of social
science fiction—predicting what the shape of psychology's most successful
technological development, IQ tests, will be as the century turns. Because it is
social science fiction that we are writing, we must attempt to imagine not only
what is scientifically and technically possible two decades from now but also
what is socially likely. We must, in other words, consider the social
environment in which tests are used, the social functions they are serving, and
the social changes likely to occur over a twenty-year span of time. In
discussing IQ testing, both present and future, I shall confine my remarks to
the role of intelligence and aptitude testing in education. This is not merely a
matter of convenience. As we all know, today's IQ tests are rooted in the
schooling process, having been designed to predict success in academic
situations. This is still where they are most heavily used. For these reasons the
future of IQ tests must depend heavily on the role they play in the educational
context.

THE FUNCTIONS OF IQ TESTS IN EDUCATION

To imagine the social functions of IQ tests in twenty years we must begin
with a clear assessment of their current uses and an examination of today's
trends. It is useful to begin such an assessment by identifying the general

Preparation of this paper was supported by a grant from the Carnegie Corporation of New
York.

functions now served by IQ tests in the educational system. Three general functions for tests in schools can be identified: (1) the management of instruction, (2) public accountability, and (3) legitimization of the schooling process. These functions are intertwined, so that any single testing event may be serving all three functions. Nevertheless, the distinction is useful for analysis. I expand on these functions in the paragraphs to follow, focusing on the particular role of aptitude and intelligence tests.

The Management of Instruction

In the general process of instructional management, tests are used for three purposes which I shall call sorting, grading, and monitoring.

The sorting function. Tests are often used before instruction begins to decide who should be admitted or assigned to particular educational programs. Aptitude, intelligence, and "readiness" tests are heavily used for sorting purposes, as are various other placement and entrance exams.

The grading function. Tests are also given at the end of the instructional process, to measure what has been learned. Such tests often result in a mark or grade awarded to the student. Both the grades students receive for courses and their scores on standardized achievement tests serve a grading function as the term is used here. Intelligence and aptitude tests are not typically used for grading purposes, but IQ or equivalent "expectancy" scores are sometimes used in interpreting end-of-year achievement test scores. Although this is not a widespread practice now, certain social pressures already being felt may lead to substantial growth in the use of IQ tests for this purpose. I will expand on this point below.

The monitoring function. Testing for monitoring purposes is done during the instructional process itself and yields information that allows adjustments to be made while instruction is underway. I use the term *instructional monitoring* rather than *diagnosis* to describe this function because *diagnosis* is often used to refer to aptitude and IQ testing that in fact serves primarily a sorting function, and I believe it is critical to keep these two functions clearly separate in this discussion. At the present time the only tests that directly serve the instructional monitoring function are the curriculum-referenced tests given in some schools to determine what a student has mastered and what specific instruction he or she should receive next. No current IQ or aptitude tests have proven useful for instructional monitoring, as I have defined it. Developing tests that might function as true instructional monitors, allowing relatively short-term and fine-grained adaptation of instruction to individual differences in cognitive processing, seems to me to be the great challenge for scientific research on the nature of intelligence over the next two decades.

Public Accountability

The public accountability function of testing in schools derives from the schools' position as agencies that serve the public and that are funded by it. The public wants information on how its schools are doing and will periodically—as is happening now—put pressure on the schools to raise their "productivity." Typically, the same achievement tests are used for grading and accountability; and this makes it difficult, in practice, to distinguish accountability testing from instructional management testing. Although IQ or aptitude tests are not usually called upon to meet public demands for accountability, public attention to the SAT score decline illustrates how an "aptitude" test, intended to serve the purpose of selection, can come to play an accountability role. More important, strong pressures for higher achievement scores might, under conditions I will discuss below, lead to a protective move by school people to use IQ test scores to set limits on public expectations for student achievement. This phenomenon may keep IQ testing alive in the educational mainstream despite current efforts by many groups to limit its use.

Legitimization of the Schooling Process

Tests play a symbolic as well a practical function in education. Their use lends to the educational process an aura of science and objectivity—often beyond what test-makers believe appropriate. Tests became a standard part of American school practice during the very period, the 1920s, when educators were seeking to establish themselves as "scientific managers" (Tyack, 1974). Tests have remained part of the armamentarium of "scientific" education called upon to buttress, and sometimes to replace, intuitive judgments, particularly in situations where educators feel challenged. In colleges and other selective institutions, relying on standardized admissions tests helps to preserve an image of objectivity. Different perspectives on the real objectivity of IQ and related tests and on their appropriateness for various uses are causing much of today's turmoil over testing. Nevertheless, a recent survey of testing practices in 45 school districts (Salmon-Cox, 1978) suggests that senior school administrators have little doubt that IQ tests are proper and rational ways of discovering children's academic ability. Elusive as this "legitimization" function of tests may be, it will be important to keep it in mind as we attempt to forecast the future, since the fate of tests and the form they take may depend heavily on what is *perceived* as scientific—and how scientific the schools are expected to be.

In the course of this paper, I shall discuss each of the three instructional management functions of intelligence and aptitude tests—scoring, grading, and monitoring—referring to public accountability and legitimization functions as they relate to instructional management. For each function, I will consider what the social demands are that might encourage either the status quo or new developments in IQ testing. Where it seems likely that new kinds of testing are called for, I will consider what scientific and technological developments might be useful and attempt to assess the likelihood of such new developments occurring by the end of this century.

IQ TESTS IN SELECTION AND TRACKING: THE SORTING FUNCTION

In considering the future of IQ tests used for sorting purposes, it is useful to distinguish between the use of such tests to assign children to special education and their use for tracking within the educational mainstream. Because special education laws and funding formulae are currently forcing the schools to treat mainstream tracking and special education assigment in quite different ways, any realistic analysis of trends in these areas must treat them separately, as I will do below.

Assignment to Special Education

As is well known, the first technically successful intelligence tests were designed to predict which children would not do well in mainstream public education. For some (including the founding father, Binet), the tests were part of a humanizing movement, in which education would be adapted to each individual's level of mental functioning. To others, the tests provided a convenient way of solving an economic and social problem—overcrowded urban schools with many underachieving students. Identifying candidates for special educational treatment is still one of the major functions of IQ tests, and the motivations for doing this are as contradictory as in Binet's day. In discussing the use of IQ tests to assign children to special education, I will focus only on identifying the minimally mentally handicapped—those who are labelled educable mentally retarded (EMR) or learning disabled (LD). These children are the ones over whom controversy rages, partly because errors of identification can be made most easily in these "borderline" areas of mental disability, and partly because many people believe that the mildly handicapped can be maintained in the mainstream if it is appropriately altered to accommodate them.

Although many school systems routinely administer group IQ tests periodically to all children in the system, and these tests could in theory function to identify an initial pool of candidates for special education, group-administered tests seem to play a very small role in special education assignment. Instead, difficulties in the classroom (of a behavioral or academic nature) are usually the first signal for "referral" of a child, after which a variety of tests, often individually administered, are given. Thus, it seems likely that special educational placement could proceed without group-administered IQ tests. Individually administered tests—most often the Binet—are, however, central to the process. In the state of Pennsylvania, for example, a child can be labelled EMR only if he or she has an IQ of 80 or less (allowing for a measurement error of 5 points in either direction). A child may be labelled LD if there is a "significant discrepancy" between school work and intellectual potential. The nature and amount of the discrepancy are not specified by law, but IQ is the accepted measure of potential. Thus under current law and practice, selection into special education *could not proceed without IQ tests.*

Can we then expect individual IQ testing for special education placement to continue to be commonplace for the next twenty years? Perhaps not, for a number of reasons. For one thing, the scientific basis for this IQ-dependent process of sorting is weak. There is no strong evidence that separating the mildly retarded from the mainstream helps them achieve better academic performance. (For a brief review of research on this topic, see Leinhardt, 1978). Where programs effective for these children have been identified, they are generally of the same type for both EMR and LD groups and not significantly different from the structured direct-instruction programs that have also been found effective for intellectually "normal" but socially disadvantaged groups such as those served by compensatory education (see, e.g., Bateman, 1979). Thus the instructional basis for continuing the LD–EMR distinction or even for separating either group from the educational mainstream does not seem particularly strong. Nevertheless, placement in special education may have some positive effects. It functions to bring special educational services to at least some of the children who are having difficulty in school (Hobbs, 1975). Probably the most important single feature of these services as they now stand is a very favorable teacher–child ratio, with the result of more individual attention and instruction than these children would receive in larger mainstream classes.

If cost were not an issue, it would be possible to bypass the entire IQ-based selection process for special education by simply offering all children who fell below certain standards of academic performance instruction in such favorable settings. Under these circumstances, individual IQ testing for special education assignment could disappear; the tests would not be needed, because the primary criterion for such placement would be failure to do well in school. This is an attractive future to contemplate, but a very expensive one, since many more children have some difficulty in school than currently receive the LD or EMR label. Because of this cost factor, I believe that we will only be able to shift away from special education for a few, based on labelling through IQ tests, when and if the ratio of children to teachers (perhaps ten or twelve to one) that has long been common in private, nonparochial schools becomes the norm in all schools. Then, everyone would be in a "special" class.

Getting special services would not depend on IQ scores, since there would be time to offer supplementary services to any child who seemed to need them.

What are the chances we will adopt this approach and thus eliminate the need for at least one kind of IQ testing? The chances are small, but I think this kind of vastly improved adult–child ratio in our schools is not a completely absurd scenario for the turn of the century. My very limited optimism is based on two observations. One is that the historical trend is toward generally decreasing class size. Forty or fifty children to an elementary school class used to be considered normal. Now thirty is more or less an outside limit in educators' and the public's thinking, and many schools have only about twenty children in primary classes. Many classrooms also have aides and other adults who play a quasi-teaching role. Second, as our economy increasingly automates production, we will have to absorb more and more of the work force in service occupations. Further, we may well be seeking to create jobs in the public sector, as an alternative to a continually rising public welfare bill. Public service jobs could well include teaching; I can thus envisage an increase in the number of adults in the schools even though the school age population stabilizes or declines. These adults may not all be called teachers, but they may play para-professional roles of importance in the instructional process. If this were to happen—and there is at least a possibility that it might—then we would have sharply reduced need for IQ tests in special education assignment. Of course, many people might still promote the use of IQ-related labelling procedures because they believed that different kinds of instruction were suitable for different categories of children. If all children were offered the best instruction available, however, the question of differential instruction could be explored empirically without the risk of denying instructional help to those who need it. My guess is that, under these conditions, attention would shift from tests useful for selection to tests useful for instructional monitoring. As my discussion of monitoring later in this paper will show, I believe this would mean a turn away from global IQ assessment.

Tracking in the Educational Mainstream

IQ tests came into widespread use in the schools only when, in the 1920s, group administrable forms of the tests were developed. These tests grew out of the World War I experience with the group-administered Army Alpha test and came into school use at a time when the public was concerned with efficiency in the schools and with promoting higher academic achievement standards. (The nation had been shocked to discover that nearly thirty percent of army recruits could not read well enough to take the written form of the army tests, and most of these had attended school!) These pressures, taken together with the then prevalent belief in a fixed IQ that set limits on learning, set the stage for a massive program of tracking and streaming *within* the educational mainstream. Homogeneous grouping by mental ability was seen as the way to make instruction efficient; IQ tests were proposed as a method for accomplishing this tracking. The tests had the further advantage of giving the schools a scientific image just when the educators were attempting to establish themselves as professionals and when standards of scientific management were being imposed in both the private and public sectors of the economy. IQ tests came to be used—although we don't really know the extent of this practice—for assigning children to fast or slow classes within a given age-grade, for admission to special accelerated programs, and for other tracking decisions.

Although these tracking procedures came into question, and, in some instances, even disfavor, after World War II, a considerable amount of tracking (within schools or even within classrooms) persists today. Are IQ tests needed to make this tracking system work? Or, to put the question differently, would removing IQ tests change the way children are treated in school? The evidence is slender, but research on grouping decisions in the elementary school (Rist, 1970) suggests that IQ tests are quite subsidiary to other kinds of evidence (largely teacher judgment or actual classroom performance) in the grouping and tracking process. If this is the case, it seems likely that virtually all current tracking decisions could be made on the basis of achievement tests, school grades, and the like. IQ tests could be dropped entirely with very little effect on formal and informal grouping practices. If this hunch is correct, then we can envisage the IQ test in mainstream education "withering away," without any major change in grouping and tracking practices at all. Thus, group IQ testing could disappear from schools by the year 2000 without affecting children, positively or negatively, very much. Unless, that is, certain social forces which I will now discuss produce a new and compelling social function for IQ tests.

IQ TESTS IN ASSESSING THE OUTCOMES OF INSTRUCTION: THE GRADING FUNCTION

IQ tests do not play a direct role in assessing the outcomes of instruction. Achievement tests are the main vehicle for outcome testing, which meets both instructional management and accountability functions. There is a set of forces, however, that could lead school people to value IQ tests highly, in more or less their current form, as part of the outcome assessment process. I am referring to pressures to make schools legally responsible for children's failures to learn. Much recent pedagogical theory (e.g., Bloom, 1976; Glaser, 1977) has argued that *all* children can be taught the basic skills, and that the responsibility for failures to learn must be shifted from the child to the instructor. Instead of "writing children off" as unteachable, schools must invest extra effort in instructing the hard-to-teach. Implicit in this shift of responsibility is the belief that schools must not only offer instruction, but also ensure that learning takes place. For obvious reasons, these pedagogical theories have been warmly welcomed by groups interested in the educational welfare of poor, minority, and other children who have traditionally done poorly in school.

Today, the schools have no legal obligation to ensure that learning takes place; they are required only to offer instruction of a kind that is commonly considered appropriate to the age and population in question (Abel & Conner, 1978). But there are recurrent challenges to this position, in the form of court suits against schools that have failed to teach an individual or a class of students. Cases attempting to establish the legal obligation of schools to ensure that students learn literacy and other basic skills have now been brought in several states. The cases can be thought of as educational malpractice suits. Thus far, all court decisions have denied that the schools have an obligation to see that every child learns. But new cases are being brought and new arguments tested. Should some of these cases succeed in shifting the legal burden of responsibility to the school, it is easy to imagine that school boards everywhere will rush to establish the limits of their responsibility. An easy limit to seek would be one that sets up expectations for how much a given child ought to be able to learn, with the schools held responsible only for failures to meet these expectations. Where would the expectations come from? Re-enter the IQ test—now in the guise of insurance against malpractice.

This scenario is not particularly bizarre, nor do I believe that it would be hard to get the courts to accept the IQ, or its equivalent, as a limit. Popular wisdom generally believes in some limits to learning capacity, and people are willing enough to call those limits intelligence. Nor has scientific research on intelligence and learning yet been able to prove anything different. Furthermore, some test companies have been successful in the last few years in marketing to schools testing packages that include individual expectancy scores based on what are essentially IQ tests. Thus the stage seems to be set for a revival of interest in group IQ tests, not for scientific reasons, and not because they can help the schools do their instructional job, but because they will provide a publicly acceptable explanation of differential rates of success in instruction and thus protect the schools from external pressures that they could not otherwise deal with.

IQ TESTS FOR MONITORING AND ADAPTING INSTRUCTION: THE MONITORING FUNCTION

I turn now to the testing function toward which most of the newest scientific research on the nature of intelligence is implicitly directed. This is the function of monitoring instruction so that the process can be adapted to individual differences and to changes in competence over the course of instruction. The present state of the art in testing for instructional monitoring can only be called primitive. Despite a long-standing ambition of psychologists and educators to match instruction to specific cognitive abilities or cognitive styles, we have virtually no tests that have proven practically useful in guiding and monitoring this process. That is the essential message to be drawn from the extensive review of aptitude–treatment interaction research by Cronbach and Snow (1977). Disordinal interactions (interactions that establish that treatment X is best for one type of student and treatment Y for another type) are rare and inconsistent. Ordinal interactions, the more frequent, suggest mainly that while high ability students do well under most kinds of teaching, highly structured forms of instruction can often benefit those of generally low mental ability. Even on this point, however, the evidence is less than conclusive. More detailed assessments of ability that could be used to prescribe very different instructional treatments for different individuals do not exist. The best we can do in instructional monitoring at this time is to test mastery or nonmastery of specific curriculum-related knowledge or skill, and then pace instruction accordingly. This is the essence of the "mastery learning" strategy, and it is today's best practical way of adapting instruction to individual differences.

Is it likely that new forms of intelligence or aptitude testing will be developed that may substantially refine the process of instructional adaptation? It is striking how little intelligence tests have changed in half a century, and how difficult it has been to arrive at a precise, scientific definition of the term intelligence. In the years since Binet's pioneering work and the development of the first group tests, work on intelligence tests has been of two major kinds: (1) attempts to refine the procedures of test construction in order to perfect the technological instrument; and (2) attempts to refine the definition of intelligence, by identifying its components or analyzing its dimensions. It seems fair to say that the task of refining the technology has been more successful than the task of refining the definition. With respect to the latter, the various factor-analytic research programs of Spearman, Thurstone, Guilford, and others have succeeded in identifying a number of more or less separate factors of intelligence. But the factor analyses have not been successful, by and large, in explaining what underlies differences in test performance, and they have been notably unsuccessful in helping to develop a precise science of adaptive instruction. Of course, specific intelligence "factors" can predict relative likelihood of success in various content domains (e.g., high quantitative factor scores predict good performance in engineering courses), but these tests are not helpful in prescribing differential forms of instruction within a subject matter. Thus, they can serve as instruments only in the entry-point sorting process, not in instructional monitoring.

Recently, new approaches to analyzing intelligence have emerged, approaches designed to analyze performance on intelligence tests in terms of the parameters and constructs of cognitive psychology. The long-term goal of research programs of this kind is often to analyze performance both on tests and on school subject matter in terms of the same underlying processes. It is hoped that in this way it will become possible both to *explain* why IQ tests have been so successful in predicting school performance and to *prescribe* modes of instruction that will either teach important cognitive skills or adapt to individuals' characteristic cognitive processes. The adaptation to individual differences that may become possible as a result of this work will depend at least in part on new forms of testing—forms that allow assessment of key processes involved in school learning.

I believe that this line of scientific work on intelligence has a real possibility of providing us with a more powerful means of monitoring and adapting instruction—although we may not have moved very far toward practically useful tests within the short space of two decades. For this important scientific development in our understanding and, perhaps, testing of intelligence to take place, however, I believe there will need to be some important shifts in the focus of cognitive research on intelligence. An important part of current work is what may be called task analysis of intelligence test items (see Pellegrino & Glaser, in press). The goal of this analysis is to identify and describe the cognitive processes called upon as an individual performs tasks that are directly drawn from the tests or closely mirror the test items. The assumption appears to be that these processes will be, in the main, the same ones called upon in performing important school tasks. I believe this assumption may be largely incorrect.

Let me explain why. It seems probable that it is not *performance* on IQ tests that involves the same processes as learning in school. Rather it is *learning how* to perform well on IQ tests that involves the same processes. That is, people who do well on IQ tests are people who have *learned easily* during prior learning opportunities. They know the information required by the tests or can perform particular tasks that the tests present because they have learned easily in the past, and it is reasonable to predict that they will continue to do so in the future. They will do well on school tasks for the same reason—because they learn easily. It is the shared *learning processes* that make performance on IQ test tasks predict performance on school tasks. Although it is not at all difficult to find psychologists who find this hypothesis credible, I know of no program of research that is directly addressed to it. I am not aware, for example, of research on how people *learn* to do analogies, or how they *learn* vocabulary, or how they *learn* to do the kinds of quantitative reasoning that show up on tests. Cognitive analyses of school subject matter suffer from the same limitations. They have focused almost exclusively up to now on characterizing skilled performance, sometimes contrasting it with "novice" performance, but virtually never studying the process of *acquiring* knowledge and skill. Although the need to study cognitive processes of learning is now widely announced among cognitive scientists, there is little to point to in the way of achievements. There are a few artificial intelligence programs that learn to do a few tasks; there is an occasional study of how people transform their procedures in the course of practicing complex tasks; there are the beginnings of research on long-term acquisition of certain school subjects such as reading or mathematics. But all of these are struggling for appropriate methods, and even for appropriate formulation of their questions. Nevertheless, two decades is a relatively long time in the life of a modern science, and it is not unreasonable to hope that in twenty years we will know a great deal about the cognitive processes involved in learning, and that much of that knowledge will be couched in terms that allow us to distinguish among individuals.

To translate this knowledge into new kinds of tests useful for instructional monitoring and adaptation we will have to look for ways of assessing learning capabilities efficiently (i.e., with relatively little effort in a short period of time). If the "test" is not efficient in this economic sense, it will be just as useful to monitor the actual course of learning and adjust instruction to processes observed as it will be to give a test in order to decide what kind of treatment to use. Thus, new tests will be useful to the extent that they assess the specific processes to which adaptation must be made in a very efficient fashion. I think it is highly unlikely that current IQ tests, even with the reinterpretation that may be possible in light of the cognitive task analysis that is now proceeding, will be able to do this. Instead, we will need tests that are more direct measures of the processes involved in *learning* to perform test and school tasks. I think these tests are likely to be actual samples of learning, on tasks chosen to display the relevant processes as directly as possible. This would contrast with present IQ tests, which measure mainly information that has already been acquired.

One important advantage of this learning-oriented approach to testing may be the possibility of distinguishing, particularly among socially and educationally disadvantaged populations, between those who are normal or even above average in learning ability and those who truly learn with difficulty. By substituting learning tests for performance tests, we ought to be better able to distinguish between weak test and school performance due to lack of specific acquired knowledge or skills and weak performance due to general learning processes. At the present time, we are quite unable to establish whether a poor IQ test performance indicates a lack of opportunity to learn the kinds of tasks that appear on the tests, or whether it indicates a slow rate of picking up information from the environment. Since current tests are unable to make this distinction, there is no clear way to use them to identify learning talent among the educationally disadvantaged. Tests that would more directly observe learning processes might allow such identifications to be made.

SUMMARY

I have examined two major questions in the course of this essay. First, what is the likelihood that IQ tests as we currently know them will still be in use in the schools at the turn of the century? Second, what new kinds of tests of aptitude and intelligence can we reasonably look for?

With respect to the first question, I have suggested that IQ tests, or some very similar kind of assessment instrument, are likely to be functionally necessary in the schools as long as the present form of special education for the mentally handicapped remains with us—or until we are prepared to spend substantially more public resources on education for all children than we are now doing. Further, I have suggested that there is a very real possibility of a *revival* of interest in IQ tests in the educational mainstream as a protective response by school people threatened with legal responsibility for ensuring that all children, even the very hard-to-teach, learn. I believe these two areas—special education and the school's legal responsibility—are the things to watch over the next twenty years for new developments in global IQ measurement.

With respect to the second question (What new kinds of tests can we expect?), I have suggested the possibility of a serious shift in the science and therefore the technology of intelligence testing. Aptitude tests useful for monitoring instruction and adapting it to individual differences are essentially nonexistent today. Current work on the cognitive analysis of intelligence and aptitude tests may be able to provide the basis for much more systematic and refined matching of instructional treatments to aptitudes within two decades. We can particularly look forward to this development as work on the cognitive components of intelligence shifts attention from performance on the tests themselves to the *learning* processes that underlie both skillful test performance and skillful performance in school subject matters.

REFERENCES

Abel, D. A., & Conner, L. A. Educational malpractice: One jurisdiction's response. In C. P. Hooker (Ed.), *The courts and education: The seventy-seventh yearbook of the National Society for the Study of Education* (Part I). Chicago: NSSE, 1978.

Bateman, B. Teaching reading to learning disabled and other hard-to-teach children. In L. B. Resnick & P. Weaver (Eds.), *Theory and practice of early reading*. Hillsdale, N.J.: Lawrence Erlbaum Associates, 1979.

Bloom, B. S. *Human characteristics and school learning*. New York: McGraw-Hill, 1976.

Cronbach, L. J., & Snow, R. E. *Aptitudes and instructional methods: A handbook for research on interactions*. New York: Irvington, 1977.

Glaser, R. *Adaptive education: Individual diversity and learning*. New York: Holt, Rinehart and Winston, 1977.

Hobbs, N. *The futures of children*. San Francisco: Jossey-Bass, 1975.

Leinhardt, G. *The impact of innovative grouping and instruction on achievement* (LRDC publication 1978/13). Pittsburgh: University of Pittsburgh, Learning Research and Development Center, 1978.

Pellegrino, J. W., & Glaser, R. Components of inductive reasoning. In R. Snow, P. A. Federico, & W. Montague (Eds.), *Aptitude, learning and instruction: Cognitive process analyses.* Hillsdale, N.J.: Lawrence Erlbaum Associates, in press.

Rist, R. C. Student social class and teacher expectations: The self-fulfilling prophecy in ghetto education. *Harvard Educational Review,* 1970, *40*(3), 411–451.

Salmon-Cox, L. *Some information on standardized testing in the Allegheny Intermediate Unit: A report to participating schools.* Unpublished manuscript, University of Pittsburgh, Learning Research and Development Center, May 1978.

Tyack, D. *The one best system: A history of American urban education.* Cambridge, Mass.: Harvard University Press, 1974.

11

The Zone of Potential Development: Implications for Intelligence Testing in the Year 2000

ANN L. BROWN

AND

LUCIA A. FRENCH

University of Illinois

The emphasis of this paper is the practice and interpretation of intelligence testing of educable retarded children. The current and future state of intelligence testing are discussed in terms of three criteria: their predictive, diagnostic and remedial functions. In the first section we consider individual testing formats within a framework of Vygotsky's theory of potential development and the underlying assumptions of that theory concerning task analysis and transferring of training. In section two, we consider the social nature of the testing situation and the degree of contextual support provided for the learner. In the final section we consider Neisser's distinction between academic intelligence and everyday thinking with particular reference to the life adjustment of mildly retarded citizens.

This paper forms part of a series concerned with the general topic of the nature of intelligence (IQ) tests, and the purposes they will serve in the year 2000. As there is by no means consensus on the nature and form of IQ tests in the year 1979, such a broad topic invites speculation. We address the topic from the general viewpoint of theories of cognitive development and instruction, and from the particular perspective of the influence of IQ testing on the prediction, diagnosis and remediation of mild mental retardation.

At present, IQ tests serve one function exceptionally well, they predict academic success or failure. As the tests were designed originally to fill the pragmatic need of predicting school success, they are composed of items that are representative of the kinds of problems that traditionally dominate school curricula. Children who perform adequately on school tasks also perform adequately on the very similar IQ test items—a tautology we should not find surprising (Brown & French, 1979; Sharp, Cole, & Lave, 1979).

The preparation of this paper was supported in part by Grants HD 06864, HD 05951, and a Research Career Development Award HD 00111 to the first author, from the National Institutes of Child Health and Human Development, and in part by the National Institute of Education under Contract No. MS-NIE-C-400-76-0116.

Controversy concerning the efficacy of IQ tests arises when they are either overinterpreted or called upon to fulfill functions they were never designed to meet. Overinterpretation commonly takes the form of interpreting IQ measures as indices of "general intelligence," a form of idealized cognitive efficiency that somehow transcends the particular tasks and contexts of schools and other testing environments. Functions frequently demanded of IQ tests, which they were not designed to meet, are that they predict adaptations other than school assimilation, and that they serve an essentially diagnostic function.

Consider first the problem of diagnosis; a major function that we would optimally like any form of intelligence assessment to perform is diagnostic, for the eventual aim of those concerned with instructional psychology is to improve school performance rather than just to predict its course. In the first section of this paper we will consider possible mechanisms for improving the diagnostic functions of testing situations with an eye to possible remediation. We place our discussion of diagnosis and remediation in the framework of Vygotsky's (1978) theory of a zone of potential development. To illustrate the distinction between prediction and diagnosis we compare the basic philosophies underlying Soviet and American testing procedures (Section I). In Section II we consider the social nature of the testing situation and the degree of contextual support provided for the learner. The influence this might have on the prediction and diagnosis of cognitive status is examined.

Next, consider the predictive function of IQ tests from the standpoint of the identification of mildly retarded students. While it is true that current IQ tests serve a useful function in predicting the almost inevitable school failure of this population, there are some severe limitations to the predictive power of existing tests.

The first problem is that given our existing battery of IQ tests, we are generally unable to predict the academic failure of mildly retarded children prior to its occurrence. Roughly speaking, the existing tests provide valid prognostic information at the time when even the least astute teacher or parent will have noted the child's school difficulties. Referral to special education classes is still predominantly based on IQ measures, but referral to the testing situation that reveals the low IQ is usually based on teachers' identification of an existing school learning problem. One obvious need for future test development is that we improve our understanding and measurement of significant early indices of cognitive delay, so that we can identify (and hopefully alleviate) some of the problems of mildly retarded children before they fail in school. We will not address this topic further here, but it is a major concern in our program of research on the diagnosis and remediation of the slow-learning child (Brown & DeLoache, 1978; DeLoache & Brown, work in progress).

The second major limitation to the predictive power of current IQ tests is that within the mildly retarded range of ability (IQ 50–80), IQ does not relate in significant ways to successful adaptation after the school years. Mild retardation has been designated a school disease, for many who are diagnosed as retarded during the school years lose their school-imposed label and merge into adult society (Edgerton, 1967). In Section III, we will consider the nature of academic intelligence and everyday thinking in terms of the feasibility of designing intelligence tests to predict the real-life adjustment of mildly retarded adults.

I. THE ZONE OF POTENTIAL DEVELOPMENT

A. *Basic description of the Soviet testing philosophy:* For a variety of historical and social reasons standardized intelligence tests have been criticized, and at times officially banned, in the Soviet Union (Brozek, 1972; Wozniak, 1975); at the same time, however, an essential feature of Soviet social policy is a major commitment to special education (Vlasova, 1972). In recent years there has been a growing interest in the development of reliable methods for the differential diagnosis of learning disabilities, or temporary retardation, and more serious and permanent mental impairment (Vlasova & Pevzner, 1971; Zabramna, 1971). Given the unfavorable climate for the establishment of standardized testing, the Soviets have concentrated on the development of clinical batteries of diagnostic tasks to serve the purpose of evaluating differences in learning potential. Perhaps surprisingly, the content of the clinical batteries does not seem to vary greatly from our standardized psychometric tests, but the methods of testing and the data of prime interest reflect the different testing philosophies of the two approaches.

The method of clinical assessment is based on Vygotsky's theory of a zone of proximal (Vygotsky, 1978) or potential development (Luria, 1961). The distinction is made between a child's actual developmental level, i.e., his completed development as might be measured on a standardized test, and his level of potential development, the degree of competence he can achieve with aid. Both measures are seen as essential for the diagnosis of learning disabilities and the concomitant design of remedial programs (Egorova, 1973; Pevzner, 1972).

A child's standardized test performance is regarded as providing at best a quantitative index of current developmental status, or actual developmental level. Although informative concerning what the child knows now, it provides only indirect evidence about how he arrived at this state. Vygotsky claims that such measures also fail to provide any information about:

> those functions that have not yet matured but are in the process of maturation, functions that will mature tomorrow but are in the embryonic state. These functions could be termed the 'buds' or 'flowers' rather than the 'fruits' of development. The actual developmental level characterizes mental development retrospectively, while the zone of proximal development characterizes mental development prospectively. (Vygotsky, 1978, pp. 86–87)

The zone of proximal development is used as an indication of learning potential; children with the same current status on an IQ test item may vary quite widely in terms of their cognitive potential. It is claimed that a major difference between learning disabled and truly retarded children lies in the width of their potential zone. Given the central place of this concept in both clinical diagnosis and remedial training (Egorova, 1973), it is informative to consider exactly what the Soviets mean by the notion of proximal development and how they set about measuring its width.

A typical testing session consists of the initial presentation of a test item exactly as it would occur in an American IQ test with the child being asked to solve the problem independently. If the child fails to reach the correct solution, the adult progressively adds clues for solution and assesses how much additional information the child needs in order to solve the problem. The child's initial performance, when asked to solve the test item independently, provides information comparable to that gained with standardized American IQ testing procedures. The degree of aid needed before a child reaches solution is taken as an indication of the width of his potential zone. Once solution on a particular test item is reached another version of the original task is presented and transfer to the novel item is considered by calculating if the child requires fewer cues in order to reach solution.

The following is a concrete example of the testing materials and procedures. The problem presented to the child is a common IQ test item, usually referred to as pattern matching or geometric design. Such items occur on many standard tests, including the Binet, the WPPSI, and the WISC. The child is given a model (picture) of a silhouette shape and he must copy this model by combining a subset of wooden geometric forms. In the Soviet version of this task, however, there is an interesting trick; some of the requisite shapes are not included in the set of available wooden pieces but must be constructed by joining two wooden pieces together.

The first step in the testing procedure is to present a small model picture and ask the child to copy it with his wooden shapes; if he fails, he is given a life-size representation of the to-be-copied shape. There are a series of additional prompts, including a model that has one composite geometric shape (corresponding to one of the wooden pieces) clearly delineated in the picture. If this does not lead to solution the child is given a further detailed model that clearly shows the join (trick) necessary to create the missing form. If all else fails the tester constructs the figure and then encourages the child to go through the construction with him.

Of particular interest to us were the "transfer" tests. Following solution of Problem 1 (provided by the tester if all else failed), the second problem is immediately presented, with the same series of aids if so needed. Problem 2 is a new picture problem where it is necessary to construct (by joining) two of the composite forms. One of the required joined shapes is identical to that required in Problem 1, the other is a new construction. It seemed to us that these features of Problem 2 tapped two kinds of transfer. Specific transfer would be measured by the recognition that the subpart constructed to solve Problem 1 was again required for Problem 2 solution. More general transfer would be the knowledge that joining shapes in general would be a requirement of the pattern-copying task, and this knowledge should be reflected in the facility with which the child attempts to construct the new joined subpart. We would like to emphasize that this is our assessment of the transfer tests, and is not necessarily shared by our Soviet colleagues.

The Soviet diagnostic testing method provides invaluable information concerning the child's starting level of competence and an estimate of the width of his zone of potential development, the level of competence he can reach with aid. In addition we gain information of the child's ability to profit from adult assistance, his speed of learning, and the facility with which he transfers the new skill across tasks. Of prime importance for the diagnosis of the cause of school failure is the Soviet claim that whereas learning disabled (developmental backward) and mildly retarded children tend not to differ greatly in terms of their starting competence on a variety of cognitive tasks, the two groups differ dramatically in terms of their ability to benefit from the additional cues provided by the tester. Learning disabled children need fewer prompts than retarded children before they arrive at a satisfactory solution. They are also more proficient at transferring the result of their brief learning experience to new variations of the task within the testing situation and in subsequent independent class performance. In studies where comparisons with normal children were included, the average children were even more effective at initial learning and subsequent transfer than were the two clinical populations (Egorova, 1973; Lubovsky, personal communication).

In common with many second-hand reports of Soviet psychology, this description is notable for its lack of specificity. Although some examples of the specific test batteries are available to American readers (Wozniak, 1975), these examples must be only fragmentary illustrations of the type of test battery needed to fulfill the functions claimed for it, i.e., the differential diagnosis of fine degrees of retardation based on estimations of cognitive potential.

B. *Task analysis and transfer of training:* Quite explicit in the Soviet description of their testing program is the role of Vygotsky's theory of a proximal zone of development; the Soviets emphasize the place of graduated aids in uncovering the "readiness" of children to perform competently in any task domain. Also entailed by this position, and at least as important to contemporary theories of cognition, is an implicit theory of task analysis and transfer of training. Although the sample of tests we viewed clearly showed an implicit dependence on task analysis, our Soviet colleagues appeared to regard this aspect of their work as secondary, indeed almost as a serendipitous outcome of their considerable experience in devising clinically sensitive tasks.

We would like to argue that testing the zone of potential development as a means of diagnosis requires a detailed task analysis of a suitable set of cognitive tasks and detailed task analysis of possible transfer probes (Brown, 1978; Campione & Brown, 1978). Without this information it would be difficult to select either the series of graduated aids for the original learning task, or suitable methods for assessing the speed and efficiency of transfer. The importance of this point should not be lost in the rhetoric surrounding Vygotsky's theory of cognitive potential. In the diagnostic sessions, what is being measured, or at least the factor the Soviets claim is essential for differential diagnosis, is the efficiency of learning within any one task domain. The assessment of the width of a child's zone of potential development actually translates into the assessment of how many prompts he needs to solve Problem 1, versus Problem 2, versus Problem 3, etc. A child judged to have a wide zone of potential development is one who reduces the number of prompts needed from trial to trial, i.e., who shows effective transfer of a new solution across similar problems. As one of the traditional definitions of intelligence is the ability to learn then "estimates of it (intelligence) are, or at least should be, estimates of the ability to learn. To be able to learn harder things, or to be able to learn the same things more quickly, would then be the single basis of evaluation (Thorndike, 1926, pp. 17–18)." The Soviet attempt to measure directly the ability to learn is of more than casual interest.

We hope that even this informal look at the Soviet testing method makes obvious how great a reliance on careful task analysis and transfer measurement such a testing procedure would demand. It is in these domains that contemporary American instructional psychologists have devoted a great deal of attention and expertise (Glaser, 1978). Research programs based on anything from enlightened intuition to detailed computer simulations have formed the base of a growing interest in providing rigorous task analyses of basic cognitive skills. Of particular interest in this paper is the extensive work that has been conducted with facsimiles of IQ test items (Estes, 1974), e.g., the series completion task (Holzman, Glaser, & Pellegrino, 1976; Kotovsky & Simon, 1973; Simon & Kotovsky, 1963), geometric and verbal analogies (Mulholland, Pellegrino, & Glaser, 1977; Pellegrino & Glaser, 1978; Sternberg, 1977; Pellegrino & Glaser, this volume) and the Raven's (1938) progressive matrices items (Hunt, 1974; Jacobs & Vandeventer, 1971, 1972; Linn, 1973).

The aim of detailed task analyses is very similar to that of the Soviet testing program. Feasible rules for solution are specified explicitly and the tasks engineered in such a way that the particular rules used by a child can be detected. When this is done well, errors produced by the novice can be just as informative as correct responses produced by the proficient. With a well-designed task analysis it is often possible to detect not only the presence or absence of a desired piece of knowledge or skill but intermediate stages of understanding as well. Such a program of task analysis provides optimal information for those who would attempt any form of instructional intervention and the Soviet testing method is in many ways a mini-instructional format.

In order to assess how well the child has benefited from instructional aids it is necessary that we have a battery of appropriate transfer tests. This again demands careful attention to the underlying processes being tapped by any one task so that suitable varieties of surface formats can be selected that tap the same underlying rules (Brown & Campione, 1978). In the process of constructing batteries of suitable task domains that permit transfer, careful attention will have to be paid to the difficulty of "problem isomorphs" (Simon & Hayes, 1976), but hopefully tasks can be adapted or constructed that vary in surface structure, but at the same time demand identical processes for their solution. On initial inspection, tasks such as series completion, geometric analogies, and matrices problems all seem ideally suited to provide near and far transfer tests (Brown, 1978). For example, near transfer items might consist of a set of distinct problems demanding the same rules of solution (e.g., movement in a matrices problem). Intermediate transfer items might be those that demand the same rule in two tasks differing somewhat in their surface format, e.g., movement in a matrices problem and in a geometric analogy problem (Hunt, 1974; Sternberg, 1977), or the backward next rule in series completion items (Simon & Kotovsky, 1963) and in the Binet Letter-number decoding task (Stanford-Binet revised version 1964, Superior Adult II). Even farther transfer, between quite disparate tasks, might be implicated if Greeno (1978, p. 243) is correct in asserting the generality of the "psychological process of solving any analogy or series extrapolation problem involving identifying relations among components and fitting the relations together in a pattern."

Ideally what would be required for a systematic consideration of zones of potential development would be a series of well-analyzed task domains with near, intermediate, and far transfer items well defined. In addition one would need a series of relatively unrelated constellations of tasks where direct transfer from one to the other would not be expected. This would enable us to consider whether a child is adept at benefitting from graduated learning aids in one domain or in almost all domains. If there appears to be consistency in the width of an individual's zone in a variety of disparate domains, one might use the width as an index of his general "learning to learn" effectiveness, a measure of his "speed and efficiency" of new learning (Estes, 1974; Thorndike, 1926). If, on the other hand, the child's zone width varies as a function of the specific task constellation, this might indicate specific areas of learning disability. We realize that this must sound rather reminiscent of the age-old search for a separation of g and s factors (Spearman, 1927), and we will not reiterate the pitfalls of such a search here (Sternberg, 1977; Tuddenham, 1966). We would like to emphasize, however, that our approach would be based on process theories of learning rather than on a factor analytic determination of task clusters. We would also like to emphasize that the field of instructional psychology is still a long way from completing the theoretical work and empirical verification necessary for devising such transfer domains (Brown & Campione, 1978). Considerable advances have been made in recent years, however, and by the year 2000 perhaps such a technology shall be within the grasp of cognitive process theories of academic intelligence.

The development of a systematic battery of well-analyzed learning and transfer domains would be particularly useful for improving our diagnostic procedures for detecting and remediating the learning problems of academically marginal children. The current picture we have of such children can be summarized briefly. They perform poorly on a variety of problems that demand the use and control of strategies for adequate solution. With intensive, well-designed training they improve their performance dramatically, particularly when such training concentrates on both inculcating the specific strategies and providing detailed instructions concerning self-regulation (Brown, 1978). Such children experience difficulty primarily in transferring the results of any training to new situations, and this diagnostic transfer failure is particularly likely to occur if explicit instruction in self-regulatory mechanisms is not provided (Brown & Campione, 1978; Brown, Campione, & Barclay, 1979; Meichenbaum, 1977—see also Section II this paper). Because the Soviet method of testing the zone of potential development consists of a mini-training series, followed by well-designed probes, it should be particularly sensitive to the characteristic learning problems of educable retarded children. We are currently examining the transfer efficiency of retarded children, using a format similar to that used by the Soviets to uncover the zone of potential development. We hope that such a research program will provide guidelines for the development of tests of cognitive efficiency with greater diagnostic power than current standardized testing procedures.

II. INTERPERSONAL AND INTRAPERSONAL THINKING

A.   *Vygotsky's theory of internalization:*   In the preceding section we were primarily concerned with the problems associated with the selection of a suitable battery of tasks with which to test the width of a child's zone of potential development. Here we will consider another direction for research implied by the theory. Vygotsky's (1978, p. 86) definition of the zone of proximal development is "the distance between the actual developmental level as determined by individual problem solving and the level of potential development as determined through problem solving under adult guidance or in collaboration with more capable peers." To put this statement into historical perspective it is necessary to consider briefly the concept of internalization, so important to Vygotsky's thinking (Vygotsky, 1978; Wertsch, 1979). Vygotsky argues that all psychological processes are initially social, shared between people, particularly between child and adult, and that the basic interpersonal nature of thought is tranformed through experience to an intrapersonal process. Thus, for Vygotsky, the fundamental process of development is the gradual internalization and personalization of what was originally a social activity.

> We propose that an essential feature of learning is that it creates the zone of proximal development; that is, learning awakens a variety of developmental processes that are able to operate only when the child is interacting with people in his environment and in cooperation with his peers. Once these processes are internalized, they become part of the child's independent developmental achievement. (Vygotsky, 1978, p. 90)

From Vygotsky's viewpoint it is essential to consider a child's problem solving abilities in situations other than traditional testing milieux, situations such as mother–child dyads (Wertsch, 1978), children tutoring children (Allen, 1976), and group problem-solving situations (Kelley & Thibaut, 1954). In the basic clinical testing situation described previously, it is a supportive adult who leads and guides the child to the limits of his current ability. But other social settings could also serve the function of uncovering the uppermost level a child can reach with aid. In that the use of a social setting to uncover learning potential mimics the normal process of development—i.e., the social becoming internalized as the individual progresses—interpersonal situations might prove especially effective at revealing previously untapped learning potential.

Traditional theories of group problem solving are especially interesting in this context because they often parallel Vygotsky's thinking. For example, Bales (1950) contends that individual problem solving and group problem solving are necessarily similar, as the one (individual) is born of the other (social).

> Individual problem solving is essentially in form and in genesis a social process: thinking is a re-enactment by the individual of the problem-solving process as he went through it with other individuals. (Bales, 1950, p. 62)

Similarly, Kelley and Thibaut also put forward a theory of interalization similar to Vygotsky's when they suggest that an individual:

... acquires his thought and judgmental habits largely through interaction with other persons. It is by no means entirely fanciful to suppose that he 'internalizes' certain problem-solving functions that are originally performed for him by others. For example he may internalize a 'critic' role in the sense of learning to apply to himself the same standards and rules of critical evaluation that another person has previously manifested in interaction with him. (p. 738)

Whether the "critical other" is the mother, the teacher, a peer or an older child, a consideration of the effects of dyadic/group problem-solving in children would seem to have great potential for: (1) assessing the effects of situational variables on task performance, (2) uncovering a child's zone of potential development, and (3) acting as a learning vehicle for improving a child's performance.

Firm evidence to support this suggestion is, unfortunately, not yet available. Although there exists a considerable literature concerning such relevant areas as group problem solving (Davis, Laughlin, & Komorita, 1976; Kelley & Thibaut, 1954), and cross-age tutoring (Allen, 1976), the emphasis of prior research has been somewhat different from the one we would like to see, i.e., a concentration on group influences on individual learning. For example, in cross-age tutoring programs we know that the tutor tends to be the major beneficiary of the tutoring process (Allen & Feldman, 1974), but even when the tutees do show noticeable gains, improvement is measured against vague, global criteria, such as teacher ratings of general reading or arithmetic improvement (Horan, DeGirolomo, Hill, & Shute, 1974), rather than on the specific material that was the subject of tutoring. Similarly, the main concern in studies of group problem solving has been group effectiveness compared with individual performance (Kelley & Thibaut, 1954) rather than the influence of group activity on the learning of the individual child (Bos, 1937; Klugman, 1944).

B.   *Other-regulation and self-regulation:*   What kinds of influence would we expect social interactions to have on the child's learning ability? While it must be true that task-specific strategies can be demonstrated by the expert and imitated by the novice within a social medium, this would not necessarily lead to the durable and generalized learning gains that Vygotsky's theory would demand and that current Soviet psychologists claim they achieve. A consideration of the little data we have concerning the dynamics of group/dyadic problem-solving situations suggests that one of the major classes of cognitive activies that the group assumes initially (which may then be internalized by the child) are varieties of self-regulation skills (Brown & DeLoache, 1978; Meichenbaum, 1977).

Consider first a social psychologist's description of the major function of a problem-solving group.

Qualitatively group discussions seemed to be adequately characterized by the traditional analyses of individual thinking, e.g., stated by Dewey as: 1) motivation by some felt difficulty, 2) analysis and diagnosis, 3) suggestion of possible solution or hypothesis, 4) the critical tracing out of their implications and consequences, and perhaps 5) an experimental trying out, before 6) accepting or rejecting the suggestion. (Dashiell, 1935, p. 1131)

Most of these activities seem to be variants of the basic transsituational regulatory skills of predicting, checking, monitoring, and reality testing (Brown, 1978; Brown & DeLoache, 1978). Similarly, Bales (1950) describes the early stages of group interaction as being concerned with a variety of regulatory activities including: asking for, giving, repeating, and clarifying information, asking for and giving directions, and asking for and suggesting ideas or plans for possible lines of action. Shaw (1932) also noted that one major function of the group was that it acts as a form of executive to its individual members. For example, the initiator of a suggestion will reject his own plan only one-third as often as will other members of the group. The group members function together to reject inadequate plans that escape the notice of individuals working alone. Thus a major function of the group is that it makes overt many of the executive functions that are usually hidden when an individual works alone on a problem. Kelley and Thibaut (1954) suggest this essential role of critic and evaluator, first learned in interpersonal setting, becomes internalized as self-regulatory skills.

This genesis from other-regulation to self-regulation is the major focus of Wertsch's (1979) research with mother–child dyads. The basic situation is that mothers and their young children are given the task of copying a wooden puzzle (a truck) with a set of identical composite pieces. The mother is encouraged to help the child if necessary. The following is a sample of a videotaped interaction between a mother and her 2½-year-old daughter:

(1) C: Oh (glances at model, then looks at pieces pile). Oh, now where's this one go? (picks up black cargo square, looks at copy, then at pieces pile)

(2) M: Where does it go in this other one (the model)? (child puts black cargo square back down in pieces pile, looks at pieces pile)

(3) M: Look at the other truck (model) and then you can tell. (child looks at model, then glances at pieces pile)

(4) C: Well (looks at copy then at model)

(5) C: I look at it.

(6) C: Um, this other puzzle has a black one over there. (child points to black cargo square in model)

(7) M: Um-hm.

(8) C: A black one (looks at pieces pile)

(9)   M: So where do you want to put the black one on this (your) puzzle? (child picks up black cargo square from pieces pile and looks at copy)

(10) C: Well, where do you put it there? Over there? (inserts black cargo square correctly in copy)

(11) M: That looks good.

Here we can see the mother serving a vital regulatory function, guiding the problem-solving activity of her child. Good examples of the mother assuming the regulatory role are statements 2, 3, and 9 where she functions to keep the child on task and to foster goal relevant search and comparison activities. This protocol represents a mid-point between early stages, where the mother and child speak to each other, but the mother's utterances do not seem to be interpreted by the child as task relevant, and later stages, where the child assumes the regulatory functions herself, with the mother functioning as a sympathetic audience.

We would like to argue that social interactions between supportive "experts," such as mothers in Wertsch's example, master craftsmen in apprenticeship systems (Brown & French, 1979), and more experienced peers in tutoring studies (Allen, 1976) serve a major function of initially adopting the regulatory role of the group's activities. These regulatory roles are thereby made overt and explicit. This serves the diagnostic role of drawing out the novice's full capabilities, thus mapping his zone of potential development. It also serves a learning function that proceeds via the mechanism of internalization from other-regulation to self-regulation (Vygotsky, 1978).

In summary, in order to improve the predictive and diagnostic power of our tests by the year 2000 we will be forced to consider both the child's initial ability and learning potential in a variety of testing formats quite unfamiliar to today's standardized procedures. For example, a child's ability in any one task domain could be considered first in an individual problem-solving format and then in a supportive social setting. This should provide valuable information concerning the situational specificity of cognitive abilities. Michael Cole and his colleagues (personal communication) have already made some headway with this approach. They videotaped a group of children solving traditional IQ-like items in a a one-to-one formal testing setting and the same children solving the same items in a competitive social situation, i.e., a group IQ bee that involved animated discussion of the correct solutions. Another potentially illuminating testing procedure would be to consider individual performance before and after experiences intended to uncover zones of potential development, experiences that could include supportive adult/child cooperation, and group activities. We are currently initiating a program of research to examine the feasibility of such an approach. By the year 2000, we may have a battery of techniques for considering the situational specificity of cognitive competences and the learning potential of individual children. Armed with such information we should be able to form a far more balanced picture of the child's capabilities than can be revealed by his score on standardized tests.

III.   ACADEMIC INTELLIGENCE AND EVERYDAY THINKING

In several recent papers (Brown, 1978; Brown & Campione, 1978), we have considered the problems of intelligence and school performance from the particular perspective of the mildly retarded citizen, or "nonacademic" members of our society. Although we have covered quite different topics in these papers, the basic organizational format is constant. In the first half of each paper we deal with methods of improving the diagnosis and remediation of the academic problems of slow-learning children and then, in the remainder of the paper, we raise doubts concerning the utility of the whole enterprise. This format is repeated here. The basic dilemma concerns the predictive and diagnostic functions of our current tests. As regards school success, we are quite confident that extant IQ tests do an adequate job of predicting the performance of slow-learning children. The problem is that this prediction is essentially negative; we can predict school failure. A concern for the general welfare of this group of students leads us to call for the development of tests that do more than predict, tests that diagnose more sensitively and suggest areas where remediation is both necessary and possible. Thus, in the preceding section of the paper we have been concerned with methods of improving the diagnosis and remediation of academic problems.

When one considers the success of IQ tests for predicting adaptation outside of school settings, however, one must be less sanguine that existing tests provide any useful information concerning critical life experiences of the nonacademically inclined citizens. In order to enhance our ability to predict and diagnose everyday cognitive efficiency, we must consider the limitations of the types of tasks that traditionally constitute our tests and curricula. In the preceding sections we have been concerned with academic intelligence, i.e., performance on closed system (Bartlett, 1958; Cole, Hood, & McDermott, 1978), typical academic problems that have fixed goals, fixed structures and known elements. In consequence, we have neglected the importance of the contrastive class of open system problems that predominate everyday thinking. In a recent monograph, Cole, Hood, and McDermott (1978) have considered this distinction at length, and Neisser (1976, and this volume) has also contrasted academic intelligence with general intelligence, so we will make the point only briefly here. Academic intelligence is the type of thinking that is fostered by the schools and measured by IQ tests. It is characterized by attitudes toward information, problems, and problem solving peculiar to the school experience. There is an emphasis on abstractness and speed of solution, an overriding goal of reaching the correct solution, and an attitude that there is one best answer that can be reached through rational processes based just on the information given in the problem. Contrast this description with everyday reasoning. Speed is often irrelevant and a concrete solution is more appropriate than a general abstract rule. Also in contrast to academic problem solving, where there is little emotional commitment to any one answer, in everyday thinking there is a considerable investment in a particular answer, so much so that facts are often manipulated to support a desired conclusion. Everyday problems are open in the sense that one seldom has all the necessary information for solution and one does not weigh the available information rationally and evenly. Personal motivation is clearly involved in the selection and weighing of pertinent facts.

Traditionally the main concern of cognitive psychology has been the problems of academic intelligence. Similarly, it is understandable that intelligence tests, which were developed to predict the ability of students to profit from school experience, measure primarily academic intelligence. For the mildly retarded, however, problems that tap academic intelligence are the primary source of intellective difficulties, failure to perform effectively in an academic setting is, of course, the reason they were diagnosed as retarded. But a case could be made that in many "everyday life" contexts, academic intelligence is either inappropriate or irrelevant for successful adaptation. Consider in this light epidemiological surveys of the prevalence of mental retardation; prevalence increases from birth until 16 years and then declines. In addition, when one considers the rate of successful adaptation to adult life of those in the mildly retarded range (IQ range 50–80), IQ level does not predict successful adaptation (Edgerton, 1967).

The implication of the age dependence of prevalence rates, and the lack of relationship between IQ and social adaptation, is that the environment partially determines when or whether an individual can be judged as mentally deficient. In some sense, schools "create" a class of retarded citizens because of the reliance on academic intelligence which is beyond the capabilities of many. Once outside the academic setting, many of those who as children were diagnosed as retarded lead successful, productive lives as adults. They are not considered retarded by their peers, or by authorities concerned with labeling retardation, hence the dramatic decline of the prevalence of retardation after the school years.

Reacting to the prevalence figures, Berkson (1978) called for an analysis not only of the abilities of the individual, but also of the environments to which he must adjust. While it is clearly reasonable to advocate measuring competence in relation to the demands of an individual's environment, so that we can either predict successful adaptation to adult life or diagnose areas where problems in adaptation may occur, there is a definite problem in carrying this out. Both cognitive and developmental psychologists have concentrated on academic intelligence, on the cognitive capabilities of the college sophomore. Most of our theories of adult cognition are notable for this bias. We have almost totally ignored the blue collar worker, both in terms of estimating his abilities on academic closed-system tasks, and in terms of defining the cognitive demands of various vocational occupations in which he might engage. There are, therefore, some fundamental questions that remain unanswered (or unasked!), e.g., what are the average capabilities of successful blue collar workers? what are the minimum demands of their everyday life? and therefore, for what end should education be preparing the children who must eventually join their ranks? In order to answer such questions we need to develop an understanding of the cognitive demands of everyday life based on a theory of cognition that includes a consideration of more than academic intelligence.

Tests of functional literacy and minimum competence are being developed nationally in response to a demand that schools foster skills of everyday cognition. But these tests, as currently constituted, are unlikely to help with the prediction and diagnosis of everyday thinking problems. One reflection of the weakness of existing tests of functional literacy is the wide disparity in the prevalency rates reported, a finding that suggests that there is no agreed upon criterion of just what functional literacy might be (Fisher, 1978). Far from being based on a coherent theory of everyday cognition, the test items are selected on the basis of two intuitive criteria. First, the skills are said to reflect the competency expected from "normal eighth graders." Second, the items are derived from a "common sense" approach to defining the composite skills that will be needed in adult life. Not only is there no theory of nonacademic adult intelligence to guide the selection of items, but there is also an absence of the fundamental ethnographic analysis that would describe the types of competencies necessary for success in everyday life and in various blue collar occupations. Some of the items selected for inclusion on tests of functional literacy may indeed turn out to be excellent examples of the minimum skills needed for survival but in the absence of a theory of nonacademic adult cognition, and/or ethnographic observations concerning basic skills, we do not know what cognitive competences are needed for everyday life success. As a result we are basically ignorant concerning what type of intelligent activities we should foster in our schools, and tap in our tests of "functional" literacy.

We would like to argue that it is imperative for us to determine the types of everyday reasoning engaged in by the average "man in the street," not just to advance our knowledge of the kinds of capabilities the mildly retarded must possess to "pass" in the adult world (Edgerton, 1967) but also to expand our basic theories of psychology so that they can go beyond the cognitive capabilities of the academic elite. As we develop a psychology of mundane cognition, focusing on how ordinary people cope with the demands for reasoning in everyday life, we will be better prepared to predict the ability of the mildly retarded to adapt to everyday life in accord with their performance on "tests of mundane cognition."

If we are to predict, diagnose, and maximize the learning potential and life success of mildly retarded persons, both the approaches described in this paper will be necessary. We need to refine and extend the diagnostic procedures we use to estimate academic intelligence so that we may alleviate school problems for as many as possible. In addition, we must also consider the "end point" of cognitive development for those not academically inclined. We need to know what the minimum cognitive competencies demanded by everyday life situations are, so that we can predict who will fail, diagnose the source of failure, and attempt to prepare the less able child to meet the demands of everyday life more adequately.

IV. CONCLUSION

We have discussed the current and future state of intelligence testing in the light of three criteria: the predictive, diagnostic, and remedial functions they perform. Existing IQ tests perform the function they were designed to fulfill; that is, they predict academic success. By the year 2000 we would like to see an extension of the predictive power of intelligence tests so that we are able to (a) predict school failure prior to its occurrence and (b) predict potential adult competence by a consideration of performance on tests of everyday reasoning. To achieve these ends we will need to invest considerable energy in ethnographic surveys and experimental testing programs directed at improving our scanty knowledge in two main areas. First we need sensitive indices of early cognitive (in)competence that are related to subsequent academic intelligence. Secondly we need theories and measures of functional literacy, minimal competence, and mundane cognition, so that we can begin to predict life adaptation as well as academic success.

We would also like to see an increased emphasis on the diagnosis and remediation of cognitive deficits, of both the academic and everyday variety. We argue that Soviet theory and practice regarding the clinical diagnosis of learning disabilities provide a useful framework in which to examine the child's learning potential. In addition, a variety of interpersonal testing formats should be employed to examine the situational specificity of any cognitive ability, as well as the child's potential for benefiting from expert aid. Considering the current limited service to the identification and treatment of the retarded provided by IQ tests in the year 1979, any evidence of improvement by the year 2000 would be welcomed.

ACKNOWLEDGMENTS

The development of many of the ideas expressed in the manuscript was greatly influenced by discussions with Michael Cole, who, of course, cannot be held responsible for their present instantiation. We would like to thank Joseph Campione and Judy DeLoache for their feedback, both positive and negative, concerning various ideas expressed in this manuscript, and Roberta Jones and Pat Laughlin for guiding us to pertinent references concerning group problem solving.

We would like to express an especial appreciation to our colleagues at the Institute of Defectology in Moscow, V. I. Lubovski and T. V. Rozanova, for their hospitability and generosity in demonstrating the tests and procedures of defining zones of potential develoment.

REFERENCES

Allen, V. L. *Children as teachers: Theory and research on tutoring.* New York: Academic Press, 1976.

Allen, V. L., & Feldman, R. S. Learning through tutoring: Low-achieving children as tutors. *Journal of Experimental Education,* 1974, *42,* 1-5.

Bales, R. F. *Interaction process analysis: A method for the study of small groups.* Cambridge, Mass.: Addison-Wesley, 1950.

Bartlett, F. C. *Thinking: An experimental and social study.* New York: Basic Book, 1958.

Berkson, G. Social ecology and ethology of mental retardation. In Gene P. Sackett (Ed.), *Observing behavior: Theory and application in mental retardation.* Baltimore: University Park Press, 1978.

Bos, M. C. Experimental study of productive collaboration. *Acta Psychologica,* 1937, *3,* 315-426.

Brown, A. L. Knowing when, where, and how to remember: A problem of metacognition. In R. Glaser (Ed.), *Advances in instructional psychology.* Hillsdale, N.J.: Lawrence Erlbaum Associates, 1978.

Brown, A. L., & Campione, J. C. Permissible inferences from the outcome of training studies in cognitive development research. *Quarterly Newsletter of the Institute for Comparative Human Development,* 1978, *2,* 46-53.

Brown, A. L., Campione, J. C., & Barclay, C. R. Training self-checking routines for estimating test readiness: Generalization from list learning to prose recall. *Child Development,* 1979, in press.

Brown, A. L., & DeLoache, J. S. Skills, plans and self-regulation. In R. Siegler (Ed.), *Children's thinking: What develops?* Hillsdale, N.J.: Lawrence Erlbaum Associates, 1978.

Brown, A. L., & French, L. A. The cognitive consequences of education: School experts or general problem solvers. Commentary on "Education and cognitive Development: The Evidence from Experimental Research" by Sharp, Cole, and Lave. *SCRD Monographs,* 1979, in press.

Brozek, J. To test or not to test: Trends in the Soviet views. *Journal of the History of the Behavioral Sciences,* 1972, *8,* 243-248.

Campione, J. C., & Brown, A. L. Toward a theory of intelligence: Contributions from research with retarded childen. *Intelligence,* 1978, *2,* 279-304.

Cole, M., Hood, L., & McDermott, R. *Ecological niche picking: Ecological invalidity as an axiom of experimental cognitive psychology.* Unpublished manuscript. Laboratory of Comparative Human Cognition and Institute for Comparative Human Development. Rockefeller University, 1978.

Dashiell, J. F. Experimental studies of the influence of social situations on the behavior of individual human adults. In C. Murchison (Ed.), *Handbook of Social Psychology.* Worchester: Clark University Press, 1935.

Davis, J. H., Laughlin, P. R., & Komorita, S. S. The social psychology of small groups: Cooperative and mixed-motive interactions. *Annual Review of Psychology,* 1976, *27,* 501–541.

Edgerton, R. B. *The cloak of competence.* Berkeley and Los Angeles: University of California Press, 1967.

Egorova, T. V. *Pecularities of memory and thinking in developmentally backward school children.* Moscow: Moscow University Press, 1973.

Estes, W. K. Learning theory and intelligence. *American Psychologist,* 1974, *29,* 740–749.

Fisher, D. L. *Functional literacy and the schools.* Washington, D.C.: National Institute of Education, 1978.

Glaser, R. (Ed.). *Advances in instructional psychology* (Vol. 1). Hillsdale, N.J.: Lawrence Erlbaum Associates, 1978.

Greeno, J. G. Natures of problem-solving abilities. In W. K. Estes (Ed.), *Handbook of learning and cognitive processes* (Vol. 5). Hillsdale, N.J.: Lawrence Erlbaum Associates, 1978.

Holtzman, T. G., Glaser, R., & Pellegrino, J. W. Process training derived from a computer simulation theory. *Memory and Cognition,* 1976, *4,* 349–356.

Horan, J. J., DeGirolomo, M. A., Hill, R. L., & Shute, R. E. The effects of older-peer participant models on deficient academic performance. *Psychology in the Schools,* 1974, *2,* 207–212.

Hunt, E. B. Quote the raven? nevermore! In L. W. Gregg (Ed.), *Knowledge and cognition.* Hillsdale, N.J.: Lawrence Erlbaum Associates, 1974.

Jacobs, P. I., & Vandeventer, M. The learning and transfer of double classification skills by first graders. *Child Development,* 1971, *42,* 149–159.

Jacobs, P. I., & Vandeventer, M. Evaluating the teaching of intelligence. *Educational and Psychological Measurment,* 1972, *32,* 235–248.

Kelley, H. H., & Thibaut, J. W. Experimental studies of group problem solving and process. In G. Lindzey (Ed.), *Handbook of social psychology* (Vol. 2). Reading, Mass.: Addison-Wesley, 1954.

Klugman, S. F. Cooperative vs. individual efficiency in problem solving. *Journal of Educational Psychology,* 1944, *35,* 91–100.

Kotovsky, K., & Simon, H. A. Empirical tests of a theory of human acquisition of concepts for sequential patterns. *Cognitive Psychology,* 1973, *4,* 399–424.

Linn, M. C. The role of intelligence in children's response to instruction. *Psychology in the Schools,* 1973, *10,* 67–75.

Luria, A. R. Study of the abnormal child. *American Journal of Orthopsychiatry,* 1961, *31,* 1–16.

Meichenbaum, D. *Cognitive behavior modification: An integrative approach.* New York: Plenum Press, 1977.

Mulholland, T. M., Pellegrino, J. W., & Glaser, R. *Components of geometric analogy solution.* Paper presented at the meeting of the Psychonomic Society, Washington, D.C., November, 1977.

Neisser, U. General academic and artificial intelligence. In L. Resnick (Ed.), *The nature of intelligence.* Hillsdale, N.J.: Lawrence Erlbaum Associates, 1976.

Pellegrino, J. W., & Glaser, R. *Components of inductive reasoning.* Paper presented at the Office of Naval Research/Navy Personal Research and Development Center Conference on Aptitude Learning and Instruction: Cognitive Process Analysis, San Diego, March, 1978.

Pellegrino, J. W., & Glaser, R. Cognitive correlates and components in the analysis of individual differences. *Intelligence*, 1979, this volume.

Pevzner, M. S. Clinical characteristics of children with retarded development. *Defektologiia*, 1972, (3), 3–9.

Raven, J. C. *Progressive matrices: A perceptual test of intelligence*, 1938 individual form. London: Lewis, 1938.

Sharp, D., Cole, M., & Lave, C. Education and cognitive development: The evidence from experimental research. *Society for Research in Child Development Monographs*, 1979, in press.

Shaw, M. E. A comparison of individual and small groups in the rational solution of complex problems. *American Journal of Psychology*, 1932, *44*, 491–504.

Simon, H. A., & Hayes, J. R. The understanding process: Problem isomorphs. *Cognitive Psychology*, 1976, *8*, 165–190.

Simon, H. A., & Kotovsky, K. Human acquisition of concepts for sequential patterns. *Psychological Review*, 1963, *70*, 534–546.

Spearman, C. *The abilities of man.* New York: The Macmillan Company, 1927.

Sternberg, R. J. *Intelligence, information processing, and analogical reasoning: The componential analysis of human abilities.* Hillsdale, N.J.: Lawrence Erlbaum Associates, 1977.

Thorndike, E. L. *Measurement of intelligence.* New York: Teacher's College, Columbia University, 1926.

Tuddenham, R. D. The nature and measurement of intelligence. In L. Postman (Ed.), *Psychology in the making.* New York: Alfred A. Knopf, 1966.

Vlasova, T. A. New advances in Soviet defectology. *Soviet Education*, 1972, *14*, (1–3), 20–39.

Vlasova, T. A., & Pevzner, M. S. (Eds.), *Deti s vremennymi zaderzhkami razvitiia* (Children with temporary retardation in development). Moscow: Pedagogika, 1971.

Vygotsky, L. S. *Mind in society: The development of higher psychological processes.* (Eds.), Cole, M., John-Steiner, V., Scribner, S., and Souberman, E. Cambridge, Mass.: Harvard University Press, 1978.

Wertsch, J. V. Adult–child interaction and the roots of metacognition. *Quarterly Newsletter of the Institute for Comparative Human Development*, 1978, *1*, 15–18.

Wertsch, J. V. From social interaction to higher psychological processes: A clarification and application of Vygotsky's theory. *Human Development*, 1979, in press.

Wozniak, R. H. Psychology and education of the learning disabled child in the Soviet Union. In W. Craikshank & D. P. Hallahan (Eds.), *Research and theory in minimal cerebral dysfunction and learning disability.* Syracuse: Syracuse University Press, 1975.

Zabramna, S. D. (Ed.), *Otbor detei vo vspomogatel'nye shkoly* (The selection of children for schools for the mentally retarded). Moscow: Prosveshchenie, 1971.

12

Intelligence Testing
in the Year 2000

WILLIAM W. TURNBULL

President, Educational Testing Service

The future evolution of intelligence tests is likely to move them in the direction of measuring multiple aspects of ability. Tasks will be less abstract and closer to the life experiences of the individual. Parallel tests will be available in a variety of languages and dialects. The metric will change from the present formula to a separate score for each measured ability, normed in relation to a variety of cultural and linguistic backgrounds. The dominance of environment will be firmly established and the "constancy" issue will be buried. The scores will be used for short-term predictions and decisions, related especially to schooling, and the idea of making "life" predictions or sorting children according to long-term "tracks" will fade. Will we still call them intelligence tests?

"The Year 2000" has been used as a surrogate for "the distant future" for so many years that we may not have noticed how close it is coming. It now lies as far ahead of us as the post-Sputnik year 1958 lies behind us. Taking the title of this symposium literally, then, and assuming that the past is one reasonable guide to the future, I was tempted, in writing this paper, to suggest that intelligence testing will probably change about as much in the next twenty-one years as it has in the twenty-one just past.

Since that line of thought did not help me a great deal, I decided instead to look back to the turn of the last century, to see if one could contrast the state of the art around 1900 with the probable or possible state of the art around the year 2000.

The approach of the 20th century found James McKeen Cattell experimenting with "mental tests" which he gave to college students. Anastasi (1976, p. 9) summarizes the tests used—"measures of muscular strength, speed of movement, sensitivity to pain, keenness of vision and of hearing, weight discrimination, reaction time, memory and the like," noting that

In his choice of tests, Cattell shared Galton's view that a measure of intellectual functions could be obtained through tests of sensory discrimination and reaction time. Cattell's preference for such tests was also bolstered by the fact that simple functions could be measured with precision and accuracy, whereas the development of objective measures for the more complex functions seemed at that time a well-nigh hopeless task.

And, of course, Cattell had illustrious company in his school of thought.

I invoke this bit of history for a purpose. We continue in 1979 to see the modern descendants of the psychological approaches of the turn of the last century, albeit their theory and their methodology in most cases is vastly improved. I'll say just a few words about this line of inquiry, which I shall call the "neural efficiency" approach, then consider briefly the second main strand today, sometimes called the "information processing" approach, and finally devote most of my remarks to the third line of attack, which might be termed the "psycho-educational" approach. This last set of procedures is the one toward which I would look for the greatest help in producing tests that are useful in schools and colleges for a few decades to come.

The "neural efficiency" approach, alive and well in laboratory settings, is of course the attempt to find physiological measures that tap directly into the speed or quality of functioning of the neural network. Examples are the evoked potential work of Ertl (1971) in Canada and of the Hendricksons (1978; 1978) in England, or the latter-day reaction time experiments of Jensen (1978) on which he reported at last September's meeting of APA. With the advances in theory and technology in this century, one may hope for some success in these efforts by the year 2000.

The discovery of more sophisticated neurological bases for Spearman's "g," or the development of simple behavioral measures of neural efficiency such as response time, may, if they prove valid, lead us to especially useful tests for very young children, as in screening for retardation or other handicap. As the child grows older, however, he or she experiences progressive differentiation in psychological functioning, in the range of tasks confronted, and in the broader environmental conditions in which development takes place. By the time the child is in school, where most intelligence testing is done, the differentiation has progressed sufficiently that behavior is more situation-specific. It is my thesis that for tests to be most useful in academic settings—the environment in which I propose to discuss them—they should reflect responses to the varied tasks posed in school, demanding performance of increasing depth of understanding and involving a progressively broader array of attributes that are called into play to produce a successful, adaptive response to tasks and environments that become more and more complex as the child grows older.

The second approach I mentioned, well represented on this panel, is the "information processing" approach, which Sternberg (1977) has explored impressively especially in relation to verbal analogies. This work may, I believe, be of enormous value not only to the understanding of intelligence but also to the development of tests that draw in the most efficient combinations upon the "components," as Sternberg calls them—the cognitive microprocesses—that the individual employs in solving the tasks comprising the test, or rather the test item. Information processing approaches have made notable contributions to theoretical psychology. In relation to academic testing, I see them as likely to contribute to the more precise formulation of test questions in the familiar psychometric or educational formats. I do not believe it likely that they will give us separately measured components that stand themselves as the variables of utility in the schools.

The third approach to intelligence testing, the "psycho-educational" approach, is of course the basis for most of today's standardized testing. It is conceptually imprecise and it deals in phenomena—especially classroom-related phenomena—that are extraordinarily hard to analyze with precision, although Scandura (1977) and others are opening up new fields of analysis. To a degree, the present tests work because they mirror in themselves the complexities of the classroom behaviors that constitute the criteria of interest.

As we all know, the early breakthrough in testing—useful in relation to schooling—came just after the turn of the century in Binet's work. He was successful precisely because he accepted the difficulties of measuring complex functions, and instead of concentrating on simple responses presumed to yield indices of efficient neural functioning, created tasks that simulated real-world problems or posed classroom-relevant questions to be answered. My belief is, in short, that at least for the rest of this century the most promising avenues for the development and improvement of "intelligence" tests that are to find utility in the classroom will owe more to Binet than to Galton.

What will intelligence tests be like in the year 2000? Instead of an IQ they will yield scores that reflect separately the various aspects of ability that are of interest, will express those abilities in a more manageable metric, and will report them in terms of greater educational utility. The learning tasks confronting the child will be multifaceted, and will yield scores that reflect separately the various pertinent aspects of developed ability.

In recent years we have moved away from the original ratio metric from which the IQ was derived—the ratio of "mental age" to chronological age—and toward the substitution of a standard score as the measure of intelligence. This is a step very much in the right direction. Roger Lennon (1978), speaking about the IQ at the annual meeting of AERA and the National Council on Measurement in Education in 1978, said "A persuasive case can be made for elimination of this term [IQ] on the grounds that it now carries, in professional and lay minds alike, an insupportable freighting of emotional and otherwise irrelevant connotations." In this regard, I would agree with him completely. Lennon goes on, however, to say "But it is sensible to wonder whether it can that easily now be exorcised from the language, or whether the terms invented to replace it will be more accurately interpreted." As usual, Lennon has a point.

I would suggest that in the attempt to rid our society of the term "IQ," exorcism is unlikely to be effective but that "benign neglect" may at least be a term for which an appropriate use could be found. I believe we should stop using IQ as an appellation. When we have just succeeded in substituting a standard score for a ratio, it seems counterproductive to continue using the term "quotient" or its abbreviation in describing intelligence. In response to Roger Lennon's query as to what terms might be used to replace "IQ," I would suggest that we could do worse than to use a list supplied earlier in his same paper. He said

> To be sure, the content of most intelligence tests, from Binet to the present, has been drawn heavily from about a dozen types of tasks: vocabulary, general information, analogical reasoning, series or sequence manipulation, perceptual acuity, spatial abilities, quantitative skills, classification, syllogistic reasoning.

Moving toward use of those terms, and toward measurement of the child's development with regard to those skills separately rather than in the aggregate, would mark a considerable advance in intelligence testing.

Even better than using the language of factor analysis to describe test content would be the further demystification of the tests by substituting, for the psychological terms we tend to use, words that are more common to the classroom and to the home. If a test is in fact a test of addition, for example, or more broadly of arithmetic, it doesn't help the teacher or the parent to call it a test of "quantitative skills." To have a child who can't add is one thing—regrettable but understandable and, one may hope, remediable. To have a child who is "deficient in quantitative skills" is, to most people who deal with children on a daily basis, only marginally intelligible but distinctly ominous, as if all hope for a complete child must be abandoned.

In effect, in designing tests we have used psychological constructs to provide the basic architecture, but in their development we have drawn heavily upon classroom behaviors that have been found valid in relation to those constructs. We have then named the test scores for the constructs rather than for the behaviors. To stick with my example of "quantitative skills," or "numerical ability," or "N" we have used this construct or cluster of constructs to help lay out what we want the test to include. We have then asked what manifestation of that factor one can expect to observe in children at a certain grade level, and concluded that problems involving addition and subtraction would be appropriate. The children taking the test have duly added and subtracted. But then we have called the test score not a measure of addition and subtraction but of quantitative skills—a respectable part of intelligence.

To the psychological or educational research person, that escalation of vocabulary conveys a broader and richer sense of the variable in question, provided the facet of behavior or attainment tested is indeed an adequate basis for generalizing to the construct. But in the escalating process, we tend to lose altogether the people who are trying to make sensible decisions on the basis of the scores, and who would have a chance of doing so if the names placed on them were close to the operations that generated them. This process finds its apotheosis in the terms intelligence and IQ.

One of the most unfortunate side effects of our use of the terms for constructs rather than for classroom-observable behaviors is the apparent justification it provides for basing long-term judgments and decision on test scores. In the case of young children, especially, ascribing long-term implications to the scores derived from tests as they are today is hazardous business. The tests measure abilities and skills that are learned by children at a period of dynamic development, in the first place, and under highly differentiated conditions of exposure to opportunities to learn the skills being measured in the second. The scores can be very helpful indeed in indicating how well a child can perform the specific operations required by the test, and consequently what that child is ready to do next. This kind of interpretation is encouraged by test titles and score reports that sound like the language of the classroom. By contrast, the generic construct titles inevitably suggest enduring characteristics of the individual. That suggestion in turn produces a temptation to extrapolate present performance into the future, to classify students rather than teach them.

Whereas the use of test scores for short-term assignments to new learning tasks is eminently sensible, the tendency toward long-term assumptions or predictions may be the most pervasive negative aspect of testing in the schools today.

There must be, I think, a law that says the validity of the inference drawn from a test score varies inversely with the remoteness of the criterion. This law holds not only for test scores but for any information about people, and especially about young people. The point to be made here is that we encourage long-term prediction when we escalate the terminology we apply of abilities we have measured from classroom skills to factors and from factors to eternal verities like IQ, presumed in our society to encompass much of the person's permanent intellectual equipment—if not total worth.

With tests that are geared recognizably to the kinds of questions to be resolved in the classroom, some long-standing issues may be less vexing. The more situation-specific the test, the less one is tempted to expect that performance will be invariant over time, ascribable to heredity, and generalizable to a large domain. The limitation on generalizability must be recognized as a loss, but the trade-off for the virtue of greater validity for the decision at hand is likely to be highly worthwhile. Tests of this kind are likely to be very much the product of the learning environment, and it is difficult to see that the nature–nurture issue will burn as brightly as it has in the past in relation to single-score tests often of more abstract content.

The problem of labels has, of course, been of particular concern in relation to people whose cultural and linguistic backgrounds are not those of the mainstream. Two principal approaches have been proposed to the problems involved in interpreting the scores of pupils whose dominant language is other than English. The two approaches are separate norms or separate tests.

The solution through separate norms is probably a transitional step. Separate norms may be seen as useful if one is interpreting scores in terms of factors rather than in terms of the specific operations required by the test itself. The question being asked, in this case, is "What is this child's verbal ability?" The observation is that the child has made a low score on a test of reading passages in English. Immediately someone will point out that this child began speaking a different language at home and has had less exposure to the English language than have others in the norms group, and therefore his or her verbal ability cannot be judged in relation to the performance of the others in the group. *Ergo*, we need norms based on other children who have had limited opportunity to learn English so that we can infer this child's verbal ability in relation to pupils of similar background.

The picture changes entirely if you ask, not "What is this child's verbal ability?" but "How well can this child read English?" If the child has a low score, and if the learning task to be predicted or assigned in the classroom is reading English, the teacher's main problem after seeing the test results is to make sure that the pupil is next given reading exercises at the proper (easy) level of difficulty. No assumption about the child's generic verbal ability is involved. It may be of some interest and even of some value to know that most other children from non-English backgrounds have equal, more, or less difficulty with the material, but such a discovery is largely immaterial to the classroom decision to be made about the child in question.

At present, since tests and scores carry factorial labels rather than operational ones, and since those who interpret and make decisions on the basis of scores are caught up in the escalation of inference to higher levels of abstraction, we probably need separate norms. The need for differential norms will tend to fade as we label and interpret tests more modestly. Whether or not the need will have disappeared by the year 2000 is a moot point.

Another approach, of course, is to provide parallel tests in a variety of languages. This is a costly procedure but one that is, of course, technically feasible. With parallel tests available, children can be tested in their dominant language, achieving scores that more nearly reflect their abilities assuming that their opportunities to develop their competencies in the language of the test have been about equal. This solution has some utility if the question being asked is ability in the factor: a child who reads well in Portuguese and who is tested in Portuguese can demonstrate skill in reading and hence verbal ability, or "V." If the ensuing instruction is to be in Portuguese, the finding also is relevant to the academic decision to be made.

The situation is different if the ensuing instruction is to be in English. In such an instance, a high score on a reading test given in Portuguese tells you nothing about where the child is ready to begin the program of teaching and learning in English. In order to make that decision, you need a reading test in English, although of course it would be folly to interpret the latter score as indicating the child's standing on "the verbal factor." The score on the Portuguese-language version might not be without utility, however. If you had two children of comparable background, both with low reading scores in English, but one with high scores in Portuguese and the other with low scores, you might infer a greater developed reading skill in the former that could transfer to the learning of English. But the proof of the pudding would still be how well each of the two children did indeed acquire the English-language reading skill.

CONCLUSION

My view, then, is that over the next twenty years or so we are likely to see evolutionary rather than quantum changes in intelligence tests, at least as they are used in academic settings. We are likely to see tests that provide separate scores on a variety of abilities. They are likely to be standard scores. The ratio defining the IQ may by then have been abandoned everywhere and the term IQ may have disappeared into psychological and educational history.

The new terms to replace IQ may well be drawn from factor theory at first but increasingly may refer rather to the skills required daily of the children in the classroom. The testing itself may likely be seen to draw its relevance and hence its utility more from the tasks of teaching and learning than from psychological theory, although the development of the test may draw importantly on psychological as well as educational theory.

With the movement toward rather concrete tasks embedded in the flow of learning, it is likely that those who interpret the scores will be more inclined to use them to make near-term decisions about the next problems to give the child and to refrain from assumptions about his or her long-term potential. Perhaps our most severe problems of test score misuse come from decisions that cannot be modified or reversed in the near future on the basis of further evidence. Hence the development of a mode of test use that ties the scores to decisions with proximate consequences, if it comes about, will be of inestimable value. The same new emphasis on a variety of test scores as part of a dynamic system of instruction is likely to resolve the heredity-environment issue, for these tests in these circumstances, in the direction of environment.

Since the schools will still be dealing with pupils whose backgrounds of language and culture have provided differential opportunities to learn the tasks that make up their academic environment, we will need differential norms as long as people persist in relating the scores to psychological constructs rather than to classroom tasks. A more satisfactory solution will be at hand when parallel tests of the same abilities are available to describe the child's competencies in both the dominant language and the language of instruction.

If all these changes come to pass by the year 2000—as I believe they will— three questions remain. Will we then call these tests intelligence tests? If not, will we need still other measures to call intelligence tests? If the answer to either of those questions is "yes," why?

REFERENCES

Anastasi, A. *Psychological testing* (4th ed.). New York: Macmillan, 1976.

Ertl, J. P. Fourier analysis of evoked potentials and human intelligence. *Nature*, 1971, *230*, 525–526.

Hendrickson, A. *The biological theory of intelligence.* Paper presented at the meeting of the International Congress of Applied Psychology, Munich, 1978.

Hendrickson, E. *The physiological measurements of intelligence.* Paper presented at the meeting of the International Congress of Applied Psychology, Munich, 1978.

Jensen, A. R. *g-Outmoded theory or unconquered frontier?* Paper presented at the meeting of the American Psychological Association, Toronto, 1978.

Lennon, R. T. Perspective on intelligence testing. *NCME Measurement in Education*, 1978, *9* (2), 1–8.

Sternberg, R. J. *Intelligence, information processing, and analogical reasoning: The componential analysis of human abilities.* Hillsdale, N.J.: Lawrence Erlbaum Assoc., 1977.

Scandura, J. M. *Problem solving: A structural/process approach with instructional implications.* New York: Academic Press, 1977.

13

A Job Half Done:
The Road to Intelligence Testing
in the Year 2000

DOUGLAS K. DETTERMAN
Case Western Reserve University

After a brief historical review of the development of the intelligence test and the study of individual differences, it is suggested that the major impediment to an understanding of human intelligence is the fragmented way it is studied. This fragmented approach is in contradiction to the very factors which make the intelligence test successful. An orientation is suggested which integrates the various aspects of the study of human intelligence. If this approach, or one like it, is adopted and applied until the year 2000 it is suggested that intelligence tests will have a very different appearance than they do today. They will be an integral, but indiscriminable, part of a systematic theory of the acquisition of knowledge.

I am not sure who said it but I am in full agreement with the statement that those who do not know history will repeat its mistakes while those who do will be free to make new mistakes. Before telling you where I think we should go—what new mistakes we should make—I must first describe to you where I think we have been. To begin with, I believe that the idea that human behavior is understandable from a scientific perspective is the most important philosophical development of this century. More importantly, I believe that the measurement of human intelligence is the most advanced development so far to arise from an application of this philosophy.

The events which led to the invention of intelligence tests have been thoroughly summarized by Matarazzo (1972). I will be more concerned with the interpretation of these events than with the events themselves since they are familiar to most introductory psychology students. Damaye had been working with Blin to attempt to develop a test which would differentiate mentally retarded individuals on the basis of mental ability. The test devised contained questions like, "Is a week longer than a month?" In fact, the questions were similar to those presently used by physicians to assess neurological status after a head injury. There were twenty questions on the test, each scored from zero to five depending on the quality of the answer. The

TABLE 1
Damaye's Test

		T_1	T_2	...	T_m	
	S_1	X_{11}	X_{12}	...	X_{1m}	$X_1.$
Mental	S_2	X_{21}	X_{22}	...	X_{2m}	$X_2.$
Ability =	:	:	:	:	:	
	S_n	X_{n1}	X_{n2}	...	X_{nm}	$X_n.$
		$X_{.1}$	$X_{.2}$	...	$X_{.m}$	

subject's score was total number of points. This test can be represented by the matrix shown in Table 1. Test items, or tasks, form the columns and subjects form the rows. As can be seen from this matrix, a subject's score represented only variation due to his mental ability since all subjects were given a common set of tasks and average performance on these tasks was not taken into account in reporting individual scores. Another way of putting this is that each subject's score reflected only row means. Damaye's test ordered only subjects (the rows).

Binet's early career had been spent investigating problems which have a very modern flavor. For example, he had studied the development of perception and of memory for sentences in children and had attempted to relate measures of memory to academic achievement. When faced with the task of developing a test which would predict academic skill, Binet's varied research interests produced the substantial insight that any successful test would have to measure a conglomerate of mental skills. This contribution has been well recognized.

Binet's second insight was a stroke of pure genius. It was the simple notion that the ability to perform mental tasks is related to age. He realized that Damaye's test scores were meaningless because they failed to reflect differences in mental ability as a function of age. How Binet went on to develop the concept of mental age is a story often told but seldom appreciated.

An item of particular mental age was defined as one which half of the children of that chronological age passed and half failed. More generally, what he did was to order the items of his test according to difficulty in a sample of subjects representative of the full range of ability and then to transform these item difficulties to an age scale. Table 2 shows Binet's modification of Damaye's test. If Binet had stopped here he would have

TABLE 2
Binet's Test

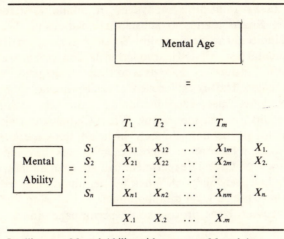

Intelligence = Mental Ability with respect to Mental Age

accomplished nothing. Note that adding up the number of items each subject gets correct to produce the row sums is what Damaye had done. The difference was that Binet's items formed a meaningful metric. It was possible to report *row means in relationship to column means* as mental age. Thus, a single measure represented both subject and task sources of variation. This is the essential genius of Binet's contribution.

Binet had two hopes for his test. First, he hoped that it would be predictive of academic achievement. It was. Despite what critics have said about IQ tests, it is an institutionalized fact that they predict about 25% of the variance in grades and about 50% of the variance in number of years of education, among other things. Binet's second hope was that his test would be prescriptive. Given a prediction of poor academic achievement, interventions could be prescribed which would alter the predicted outcome. This hope was never realized. In fact, I make the flat assertion that given a low IQ score there is no scientifically supportable intervention which could be undertaken to alter the expected outcome. An analogous situation would be having a test which would predict if a person was going to get a fatal disease for which there was no treatment.

American psychologists shared Binet's hope for the development of prescriptive measures for poor academic achievement. Tuddenham (1963) has described how the pioneers of the study of individual differences attempted to relate basic processes to academic achievement. There were two studies which had a particularly profound effect on American psychology.

These were the Sharp and Wissler studies. Sharp was a student of Titchner who was interested in mental tests. She tested seven graduate students on a number of tasks including measures of memory, attention and discrimination. Sharp found no substantial relationship between these measures and indices of academic ability. Wissler was a student of Cattell also interested in mental tests. Cattell had collected data on freshmen at Columbia with the intention of relating these data to their college performance when they were graduated. The tests given were of basic processes such as auditory reaction time, letter span, reproduction of a ten-second interval, and maximum rapidity of arm movement. While Cattell was waiting for his subjects to graduate he unfortunately included the experiment and its expected outcome in his lectures. Since Columbia was the center of teacher education of the day, Cattell's experiment had acquired a reputation before any of the data had been analyzed. When Wissler finally analyzed the data in 1901, it must have been a great disappointment to Cattell to find only small correlations between basic processes and performance in various college subjects.

According to Tuddenham, the Sharp and Wissler studies had a tremendous impact on the study of individual differences in the United States. They convinced the academic community that attempts to account for higher intellectual processes in terms of more basic processes were doomed to failure. Besides that, since they were done before Binet's work reached this country, they set the stage for the attitude adopted by academic psychologists, and still largely prevalent among them, that IQ tests represented some sort of shoddy sleight of hand which offered no real opportunity for understanding higher mental functioning. This attitude persists even though those few scientists who continued studying the problem later found that many of the processes studied by Sharp and Wissler have a significant relationship to intellectual functioning.

And so that is how the study of human intellectual processes stood seventy years ago and that is about how it stands today. There is no primary focus on the topic. If a researcher studies the topic, he will have as his primary identification some other area of psychology or education. The participants in this symposium and the authors who publish in *Intelligence* can be identified with education, developmental psychology, information processing, cognition, mental retardation, precocity and genius, or physiological psychology, to name only a few.

The effect of what might euphemistically be called diversification is that those few who study human intelligence use methodologies unique to their area of primary identification. While this diversity might be viewed as a strength, in actuality it produces a multifaceted science with no two researchers concentrating on the same facet. This has left us with a hodge-podge of findings which we are unable to integrate into a common theoretical approach.

There are several good examples of the kind of thing I am talking about. Scarr and Weinberg (1977) found that black children adopted by white families showed a gain in IQ even though their ordinal position in the distribution was largely unchanged. All of the children who were adopted showed a uniform increment from the new environment. Thus, depending on the way the data were examined, different conclusions could be drawn. Mean pre- and post-adoption performance would indicate an overall improvement in IQ while the correlation between the scores would indicate little or no change.

Royer (1977) has studied the block design test but in a manner quite different from the majority of researchers who have examined this test. Rather than investigating subject characteristics which produce good or bad scores on the test he investigated stimulus characteristics which affected performance. In his research, he found several stimulus factors which controlled task difficulty for all subjects.

These examples illustrate a major problem in the study of human intelligence. It seems that researchers concentrate either on subject or task variables. There are few, if any, examples of models which attempt to take both sources of variation into account. This is particularly ironic since the major strength of intelligence tests is that they capitalize on both sources of variation. We have ignored Binet's major insight much to our detriment.

Cronbach (1957) pointed out this problem in a slightly different way some time ago. Unfortunately, his solution was to consider the interaction of subject and task variables as the datum of primary concern. What he hoped to find were treatments which had differential effects across the range of ability. This was certainly a commendable goal but premature. Before it will be possible to understand interaction effects of a small class of variables that behave in certain ways it will be necessary to understand the seemingly much larger class of subject and task variables and their interaction effects (though not of the form required by Cronbach) which constitute the major sources of variability in human intelligence.

What I am calling for, then, is the integration of the study of human abilities. We must develop more eclectic approaches. And if we do not take Binet's fundamental insight of simultaneously considering subject and task variance to heart, we will have made little or no substantial progress by the year 2000. If, however, we are able to capitalize on the lesson Binet has given us and what we have learned ourselves since then, I believe we will not only make real progress in understanding human intelligence but that the methodologies we develop will be the major ones in use by social scientists in the year 2000.

Having painted a picture of the two roads before us to the year 2000—one leading to a stagnation and the other to a golden age—I should now give specific directions on how to travel the better of the two paths. While I do have some ideas of my own about how to get there, I suspect there are many alternate routes and so I will only map out the terrain in a general manner and hope that I can tell you enough to allow you to find your own way.

Any successful approach to the study of human intelligence must include at least five components. These are the (1) dependent variables, (2) subject-independent variable, (3) task-independent variables, (4) methodology for combining task- and subject-independent variables to predict the dependent variable, and (5) a test for determining the adequacy of the empirical and/or theoretical results of 4. I assume the goal of this approach is to understand human intelligence in terms of more basic processes, or more specifically to understand why intelligence tests are capable of doing what they do.

THE DEPENDENT VARIABLE

The obvious dependent variable of interest is a score on an intelligence test. However, it has become clear that this dependent variable is too complex to understand as a whole. Factor analysis has given some good leads about which sorts of tasks or parts of intelligence tests might be most productively studied. These are tasks which are as nearly univocal as possible; so-called marker tests which have minimal intercorrelations with tests representing other factors. At the same time it should be kept in mind that factor analytic studies have demonstrated, in the opinion of most, that there are no truly univocal tests. All mental abilities are more or less related to all others. Since we are dealing with a complex system, the human mind, this is just what should be expected. The dilemma is that we will have to attempt to understand a complex, integrated system by studying its parts behaving, at times, as if they were independent. You have to start some place when you are eating a plate of spaghetti.

Selection of a task to study is actually a minor problem. Far more serious is the imprecise measurement provided by most of the tests. Since progress in any science is often equated with the precision of measurement achieved, a first priority should be to improve the precision of the dependent variable employed. As an example of the imprecision which exists take vocabulary tests. I estimate that even the best vocabulary test available, used with large groups of subjects, would require a change in vocabulary size equivalent to that produced by over a year of college for the change to be statistically detectable. It would be impossible to detect the relatively subtle effects which would result from the standard experimental treatments usually employed by using such insensitive tests.

Classical psychometrics would suggest item selection and lengthening the test to increase reliability. These measures would be useful but they would not result in the sort of sensitivity required. The problem is that a test of sufficient sensitivity might be so long that nobody could take it. There are several alternatives. First, a greater effort should be made to exactly specify the theoretical or normative distributions of the knowledge domains being measured. Taking vocabulary as an example, it is presently impossible to be certain that any set of words composing a vocabulary test is a representative sample of words in English because the words were arbitrarily selected by a test maker. If it were possible to specify the distribution of words in English it would then be possible to obtain a representative sample of those words. A test constructed from such a sample would approach ratio measurement. Further, if it were possible to exactly specify the distribution of, say, words in English a second alternative for improving the precision of measurement would be available. This is tailored testing in which a test is contructed as it is being taken on the basis of the subject's last response or set of responses. For example, it is presently technically possible to have a very large, representative sample of words in English stored on a device accessible to a reasonably inexpensive computer. The computer might be programmed to initially give the subject a short test composed of a representative sample of the stored words. Based on his performance on these words, a new test would be constructed using any one of a number of strategies. The purpose of the second test would be to obtain results of greater precision than the first test. Selection of items for the second test could be based on traditional psychometric considerations such as item difficulty, or better still, on a well developed theory specifying the dependent variable with respect to task independent variables. Vocabulary is a particularly good example to illustrate the possibilities which exist for more precise measurement of the dependent variable, but with a little imagination this same line of reasoning can be extended to almost all of the tests of abilities which compose human intelligence.

Regardless of the specific course taken there are two points that must be kept in mind. First, the complexity of the system of abilities called intelligence requires that it be analyzed in parts at the same time keeping in mind these parts compose an integrated system. Second, the quality of knowledge concerning these parts of the system will be a direct function of precision of measurement. To the dictum that anything which exists can be measured, I would add that anything that can be measured, can be measured precisely. I do not believe that it is possible to overemphasize this last point.

TASK-INDEPENDENT VARIABLES

Given current practices in the study of human intelligence, there is no simple way for determining the difference between subject- and task-independent variables. Two experimenters may use the same variable for entirely different purposes, one as a subject variable and one as a task variable. For example, an experimenter might use subject-rated frequency of words on a vocabulary test as a method of classifying items or as a method of classifying subjects. Classification of a variable as a subject or task-independent variable, then, depends on the intention and methodology of the experimenter.

As a general rule, anything which clarifies the relationship between columns (tasks) in Table 2 will be regarded as a task-independent variable while anything which clarifies the relationship between rows (subjects) will be considered a subject-independent variable. This rule leads to a classification not in accord with current thinking. For example, factor analysis, as traditionally practiced, is considered to be a technique for studying individual differences or, in other words, subject-independent variables. it has gotten this reputation primarily because it is based on correlations. However, the principal focus of most factor analytic studies is to simplify the classification of tasks or items. For example, if a large set of vocabulary test items were factor analyzed, the results might specify a set of basic words known to a greater or lesser degree by everyone in the population and sets of "specialized" words known only by certain segments of the population. This process would tell us a good deal about the relationship between items but nothing at all about why a particular subject obtains a particular score (row–means). It should be remembered that it would be possible to rotate the matrix 90 degrees and repeat the factor analysis using subjects as "variables." This would tell us something about subjects.

The tradition has been to label any methodology which employs correlational techniques as one concerned with individual differences and any technique which uses group means as one concerned with group differences or general laws. What this distinction emphasizes is an inability to devise a statistic which summarizes relationships between scores and mean level of performance simultaneously. It does not clearly define the intention of the investigator.

Application of the general rule about what is a task- and what is a subject-independent variable cited previously reveals that many researchers who claim to be interested in individual differences are actually interested in task variables. For example, the investigations of Royer concerning the block design test were clearly directed toward task-independent variables and even used standard analysis of variance statistics. Another example is Sternberg's (e.g., 1979) investigations of analogy problems directed at understanding the component processes involved in the solution of such problems. Using mainly correlational techniques, he has broken this task into more basic subtasks. Because the major focus of these investigators has been on task variables does it mean that they are not really studying individual differences? That conclusion is only half right. They are studying one aspect of the topic, and a very important one at that. However, from my point of view, or perhaps more accurately from Binet's point of view, their models will not be complete until they include subject-independent variables in them. This deficiency does not reduce the importance of what they have discovered about tasks which most would agree are good indicants of some aspect of human intellectual functioning. In fact, as nearly as I can determine the only rule for determining if someone is a member of individual differences–human intelligence fraternity is the kind of task they investigate. If the task is one traditionally used to measure intellectual functioning, he is a member regardless of how he investigates it.

What sorts of task variables will be included in theories of intellectual functioning in the year 2000? I suspect that there will be two basic types: structure and content variables (Sternberg, 1979). Content variables are those which specify the knowledge domain. In the case of vocabulary some might be frequency of a word in the language, number of meanings the word has, or if the word has a meaningful root. Structure variables are those which specify the relationship between items or tasks. Again for vocabulary tests, structural variables might be those variables which describe the differences between recognition and recall tests of vocabulary, variables which describe the general process of how subjects go about selecting a synonym for a given word, or variables which describe the semantic relationship between words. It is structural task variables which have been given the greatest attention by cognitive psychologists and are often prefixed by the word meta-.

A full list of task-independent variables is not possible because there is only now beginning to emerge a sense of what sorts of variables will be needed to provide a general account of the tasks employed to assess intellectual functioning. What is clear is the test which sets of such variables integrated into a theoretical framework will have to meet. The basic test is a simple one. Not only will these variables have to predict performance on the test they were originally designed to predict but on all other tests of that class. Once again using vocabulary as an example, not only would a theory relating independent task variables have to predict, say, the ordering of item difficulties for all items on the test used to originate the theory, but also on all extant vocabulary tests, and in fact, on any conceivable vocabulary test that could be developed. This prediction must be *a priori*. It must be based only on knowledge of task-independent variables for the test to be predicted. As nearly as I can determine all predictions of vocabulary test scores from other vocabulary test scores are done *post hoc*. That is, it is first necessary to obtain scores on both tests before making a prediction of one test score from another. This is much different from the test I am proposing.

A more advanced test of the adequacy of theories about task-independent variables involves the capability of the theory to specify the relationship between the kind of test in question and tests of other sorts of ability. As an example, a good theory about task-independent variables for a vocabulary test should also specify the relationship between vocabulary and verbal fluency or vocabulary and analogies. In fact, the more inclusive this predictive power, the better the theory. This second test will move us toward general theories of human intellectual functioning.

SUBJECT-INDEPENDENT VARIABLES

As previously stated, subject-independent variables are those which clarify the relationship between subjects. Far less systematic attention has been given to subject than task-independent variables. However, there also seem to be two classes of subject-independent variables: capacity and process variables. Capacity variables specify a limit on performance. An example might be the lower limit of reaction time for a subject or the amount of information that could be held in short-term memory. There has been a tremendous hesitancy to speculate about what variables might place limits on human intelligence even though it is fairly clear that there must be some. Capacity variables are closely related to the concept of biological power which in turn seems related to heritability. Perhaps this chain of relationships is why there have been few speculations concerning capacities.

Processes, on the other hand, have received a fair amount of attention. Processes which have been investigated are quite easily confused with task-independent variables. For example, Campione and Brown (1978) discuss the processes which compose metamemory. Unlike many other meta-investigators, their interest is in discovering processes which are employed by subjects of average intelligence but not by retarded subjects. Thus, primary interest is in discriminating among ability levels, in sorting subjects out. Process variables may be generally defined as those variables which describe differences between subjects in the way information is processed. This would not only include differences in learned strategies or plans but also differences in processing dictated by differences in capacity.

As for task-independent variables there is a test for determining the adequacy of a theory integrating subject independent variables. Such a theory should predict interventions and specify the limits of those interventions. It will tell us what can and cannot be done to change an individual's score on a particular test. It will be diagnostic and prescriptive. When we are able to do this we will have accomplished Binet's hopes for intelligence tests.

COMBINING SUBJECT- AND TASK-INDEPENDENT
VARIABLES TO PREDICT
THE DEPENDENT VARIABLE

So far the discussion has proceeded as if it were possible to refine the dependent variable and develop theories about subject- or task-independent variables as if they were independent activities. That is not the case. Unless we are capable of integrating all of these aspects in a single theoretical statement we will not have capitalized on Binet's major insight. Further, the ability to precisely specify any one set of variables will depend on the ability to specify the others. In the final analysis, any one of these three variables, whether it be the dependent variable, task-independent variables, or subject-independent variables must be specified with respect to the other two components just as they are in Binet's test.

Reinspection of Table 2 will show that the situation I have been discussing is identical to Binet's test. For mental age one need only substitute task-independent variables and for mental ability substitute subject-independent variables. All of the variables studied in an effort to obtain a better understanding of human intelligence can really be regarded as refinements of Binet's and Damaye's original operationalized constructs of mental age and mental ability. The same reasons that required Binet to express mental ability as a function of mental age require us to express subject-independent variables in relation to task-independent variables.

Unfortunately, there are no good methodologies for doing this. The approaches which come closest are the aptitude by treatment, analysis of variance approach and analysis of covariance, but neither is completely adequate. I do not believe that the lack of adequate approaches is because they would be impossible to devise but rather because no one has been looking for them very hard. Developing such methodologies should be a first priority.

TESTS FOR DETERMINING
ADEQUACY OF RESULTS

Tests of adequacy have been presented at appropriate points but they are worth summarizing since, if passed, they would determine the form of intelligence tests in the year 2000. First, the dependent measure must be precise. Development of this precision will probably require computers. Second, a good theory integrating task-independent variables will not only predict, *a priori*, performance on other tests but will also suggest the relationship between the task under study and other tests of intellectual ability. Third, a good theory encompassing subject-independent variables will be prognostic, diagnostic, and prescriptive. Fourth and most important, an adequate account of any intellectual test must express subject- and task-independent variables in relationship to each other as predictors of the dependent variable.

INTELLIGENCE TESTS IN THE YEAR 2000

A test of any mental ability which passed the above tests would satisfy the wishes of almost everyone studying human intelligence. However, if it met these objectives it probably would not be a test anymore. It would be a theory of education or cognition or information processing or development or of any or all of the areas now studying human intelligence. It would be a proscribed theory, but nonetheless a theory. What we presently call tests would probably cease to exist. They would become an indistinguishable part of a systematic scheme for the acquisition of optimum amounts of knowledge.

What I am calling for, then, is an integrated science of the study of intellectual ability. While my predictions about what will happen if such a synthesis is accomplished may seem proposterous, bear in mind that reality constantly outdoes science fiction. Footprints on the moon were difficult to imagine 21 years ago.

REFERENCES

Campione, J. C. & Brown, A. L. Toward a theory of intelligence: Contributions from research with retarded children. *Intelligence,* 1978, *2,* 279–304.

Cronbach, L. J. The two disciplines of scientific psychology. *American Psychologist,* 1957, *12,* 671–684.

Matarazzo, J. *Wechsler's measurement and appraisal of adult intelligence* (5th ed.). New York: Oxford University Press, 1972.

Royer, F. L. Information processing in the block design task. *Intelligence,* 1977, *1,* 170–191.

Scarr, S. & Weinberg, R. A. Intellectual similarities within families of both adopted and biological children. *Intelligence,* 1977, *1,* 170–191.

Sternberg, R. J. The nature of mental abilities. *American Psychologist,* 1979, *34,* 214–230.

Tuddenham, R. D. The nature and measurement of intelligence. In L. Postman (Ed.) *Psychology in the Making.* New York: Knopf, 1963.

14

A Review of
"Six Authors in Search of a Character:"
A Play about Intelligence Tests
in the Year 2000

ROBERT J. STERNBERG
Yale University

Six points of view regarding the future of intelligence testing are considered, and a combined, "prototypical" point of view is synthesized that seems to represent a consensus of authors regarding the directions in which intelligence testing and research on intelligence are going. The past history and present status of intelligence testing and research are briefly considered, and then their future is discussed. The future seems to include assessment of various kinds of components of intelligence—performance components, acquisition components, retention components, transfer components, and metacomponents. The distinction between academic and everyday intelligence is discussed, as are the cultural and temporal limits of any one notion of intelligence. Finally, the usefulness of the notion of intelligence as a prototype of people's beliefs is considered.

I am pleased to have the opportunity to review the world's premiere performance of *Six Authors in Search of a Character,* a play about intelligence tests in the year 2000. The plan of the play is clear and simple, although it is only now, as a prelude to the final act, that the plan can be revealed: Put together an outrageous assemblage of six authors and see whether a character emerges. The character is an important one, because it is he (which I use in a generic sense to include she as well) who will rule the Land of Intelligence. As you know, most inhabitants of this land are required to take written tests demonstrating their competency in the laws of the land, and the ruler largely determines what forms these tests will take, and what functions they will serve.

As a critic of this particular play, I am happy to announce that, in my opinion, a character has emerged. Before introducing you to this character, however, I would like to reintroduce you to two of his progenitors. These progenitors were creations of earlier plays and earlier times. In retrospect, we may wonder how these earlier rulers ever ascended to their respective thrones.

Preparation of this article was supported by Contract N0001478C0025 from the Office of Naval Research to Robert J. Sternberg.

But we must be cautious in our criticisms of earlier playwrights, lest we, too, be ridiculed by the authors of a play on intelligence tests in the year 3000, or even 2100.

Let me remind you first of Factorman, believed by some to have been created by parthenogenesis. Factorman first appeared near the turn of the century, and at times has seemed to have the staying power of Methusaleh. Factorman divided the Land of Intelligence into a series of governing districts called "factors," no doubt in honor of Factorman himself. A general factor contained the highest governing body, which passed and enforced laws relevant to all of the factors considered collectively. Specific factors passed and enforced laws relevant to each of them individually.

Factorman encountered serious problems during his rule. One of these was that within a few years a host of pretenders to the throne emerged, all of whom claimed to be the true Factorman. All of these putative Factormen agreed that the factorial organization of government was the proper one; but they disagreed as to how many factors there should be, how these factors should be organized, and what these factors should be called. One "Factorman" disdained the near-autocracy of the general factor, and argued for a system of states' rights, according to which each of seven or so factors would be viewed as equally primary. Another "Factorman" was a federalist, and believed that a strictly hierarchical arrangement of factors served best. Another "Factorman," believed by some to harbor anarchist sentiments, argued for as many as 120 independent factors, each responsible only to itself. And the worst problem of all was that after a while, it was clear neither who was the true "Factorman," nor how one could even devise a way of telling who this individual was. A desperate attempt was made to reveal the true Factorman by having the whole bunch of "Factormen" appear on a television show, *To Tell the Truth,* but when the emcee asked the true Factorman to stand up, all chairs were vacated instantly. A system was suggested whereby each Factorman would rule in rotation, but no one could agree as to what rotational plan to use: There seemed to be no good criterion for choosing one over another. Most seriously, the governmental structure was not accompanied by a well worked out governmental process: The system seemed not to provide for a clear way to execute and enforce laws once they were made.

During the 1960s and 1970s, the "Factormen" were overthrown by a young and hearty challenger for the throne, Componentman. The relative present strength of Componentman, and the concomitant weakness of Factorman (whoever he may be) is shown by the fact that Factorman has received only passing references during the course of this play, whereas Componentman has been a central figure, and seemingly, at times, the villain: Neisser seems to have intimated that Componentman should be overthrown; Horn, Resnick, Brown, Turnbull, and Detterman seem to have agreed that Componentman should be demoted to a position of lesser influence, and I find myself in agreement with these authors. Who is this Componentman, whose rule is in such jeopardy?

Componentman organized a government that differed in a key respect from the government of Factorman: The new government emphasized the processes of governing rather than the structure of government. Componentman divided the Land of Intelligence into a set of components, again, no doubt, in honor of himself. Each component was to be responsible for a separate governmental process. Since single components would clearly be insufficient to carry out laws of any complexity, components were allowed to engage in cooperative ventures called "strategies." These strategies were able to solve complicated problems that no single component could have solved alone.

At one time, Componentman seemed to offer a nearly complete package of government. Through him it became possible to identify the elementary information processes (components) that carried out intelligent behavior. It became possible, moreover, to specify the representations upon which these components act; to estimate the latencies, difficulties, and probabilities of component execution; to identify the strategies into which components combined; and to assess how consistently these strategies were executed (see Sternberg, 1977, 1978a, 1979). Why, then, are even some of the strongest former backers of Componentman, including some of the authors of this play (and certainly myself), backing off? The reason seems to be that although Componentman has offered a nearly complete package of government, what is missing is fundamental, and perhaps more fundamental to good government than what Componentman has to offer. What is missing is the set of higher-order processes that decide what lower-order processes should be used to solve problems. Components provide the means by which the laws of the Land of Intelligence can be carried out and enforced. But how are decisions made as to what laws to enact in the first place? How is it decided what components, representations, strategies, and speed-accuracy tradeoffs to use? Componentman remains embarrassingly silent on these issues.

Enter Metacomponentman. If there is any consensus at all among the authors of this play, it is that Metacomponentman is the legitimate heir to the throne, and that he should take it over as soon as possible. Metacomponents supplement components by supplying the decision-making and planning that are necessary for the components to carry out their functions. Whereas components solve problems, metacomponents decide how the problems will be solved, and even what problems need to be solved in the first place (Sternberg, 1979).

When a new challenger seeks ascension to the throne, initial bursts of enthusiasm often substitute for empirical research. Some of this substitution has occurred in the study of metacomponents. Nevertheless, there has been at least some initial solid progress on the metacomponential front, which I will note here.

The work of Brown and her colleagues, cited in Brown and French's contribution to this play, represents one direction in which work on metacomponents is likely to progress. Comparing various kinds of atypical performance to more typical kinds of performance makes one aware not only of what particular decisions are made, but of what decisions actually need to be made. As ethnomethodologists have so ably pointed out in the sociological realm, it is often not until norms are violated that we become aware of what the norms are. Markman's (1978, in press) work on comprehension monitoring seems to fall into the metacomponential domain, as does some of the work that has been done on metamemory (see Flavell & Wellman, 1977, for a review). My own work on the development of intelligence (see Sternberg, 1979b) also addresses issues in the metacomponential domain. In this work, as in Brown's, the contrast between more and less able groups provides a basis for understanding just what decisions need to be made in intelligent functioning.

The problem in metacomponential research (however it has been called) has been that metacomponents have resisted experimental isolation in much the same way that components once did (see Sternberg, 1977, 1978b): We have been no more able to isolate metacomponential decision times or difficulties than we were once able to isolate componential execution times and difficulties. As a result, we talk about metacomponents in a rather fuzzy way, identifying them in indirect ways that do not permit systematic study of their properties. Bill Salter and I have devised two methods we believe enable one to isolate these metacomponents, however, and thus to go beyond somewhat obscure references to homunculi, control processes, or executive processes. We are studying these metacomponents in the laboratory now, in the hope that by the year 2000 plus or minus, we will be able to isolate them in practical settings. I will describe these two methods here for the first time.

The method of structural precueing is a development emanating from the original method of precueing, which is used to isolate information-processing components (Sternberg, 1977, 1978b). In the method of structural precueing, each test trial occurs in two parts. In the first part, the subject receives some advance (precueing) information that may or may not be helpful in solving the test item; in the second part of the trial, the subject receives the full problem and solves it. The first part of the trial can vary in the amount of advance information presented. In one condition, subjects receive no advance information: The first part of the trial consists merely of the presentation of a blank, lighted field. As soon as they are ready, subjects press a button indicating their desire to see the full problem. In another condition, subjects receive the structure of the problem, but not its content. For example, if the problem consists of a standard analogy with three answer options, subjects would see the structure, X : X :: X : (X, X, X), with each X indicating a word whose identity has yet to be disclosed. Subjects take as long as they need to view this structure, understanding that their task is to do as much strategy planning as is possible on the basis of this structural information. When a subject is ready to see the actual problem, he presses a button, and the actual analogy (with content) appears; for example, LAWYER : CLIENT :: DOCTOR : (MEDICINE, PATIENT, NURSE). The problem latencies of primary interest are contrasts between the two conditions of precueing for each part of the trial. The facilitation obtained on account of structural precueing is viewed as strategy-planning time. The facilitation can be measured either by taking differences between the first parts of the trials under each of the two conditions, or by taking differences between the second parts of trials under each of the two conditions. The second difference measure is probably of greater interest, since it involves actual solution of the full problem. In order to use this method, it is necessary that problems vary in their structures and in the strategies that can be employed to solve the problems of varying structure. In the analogies study, for example, problems vary in the number of locations in which variable options occur (one, two, or three), in the number of options at each location (two or three), and in the particular locations in which options rather than given terms occur. Thus, one item might be a standard analogy such as the one presented earlier; another might be a nonstandard analogy of the form exemplified by LAWYER : (CLIENT, JUDGE, JURY) :: DOCTOR : (MEDICINE, PATIENT, NURSE). Each of the twenty structural variations used in our experiment requires at least some change in strategy, and each subject receives each variation under each condition of structural precueing. Note that it is essential that each structural variation require a different strategy: If each successive problem required the same strategy, the precueing would serve no purpose. This fact forms the basis for the second method Bill Salter and I are using to isolate strategy-planning time.

The method of mixed-versus-blocked trials eliminates the need for precueing. Subjects receive full analogies (or other kinds of problems) with varying structures requiring varying strategies. Problems are presented either in blocked form or in mixed form. When presented in blocked form, all trials in a given set of items involve problems with identical structures. Once the subject has formulated a strategy for the first item, he can use that strategy for each successive item in the set. When presented in mixed form, each trial in a given set of items involves a problem with a different structure that requires a different strategy. The strategy used for a given problem is not applicable to the next problem, so that it is necessary to formulate a new strategy on each successive trial. Metacomponential time for strategy planning is obtained by subtracting for each subject mean blocked-trial time from mean mixed-trial time.

Although all authors of this play seem to agree that Metacomponentman should ascend to the throne as soon as possible, the authors seem determined not to repeat past mistakes, which have allowed essentially autocratic rule by a single individual. The authors have specified other governmental roles as well, and although these roles are subordinate ones, they are important in their own right. Let us consider these roles now.

The role of learning in the government of the Land of Intelligence has been a variable one over the years. Some years, Learningman is to be found in the government; other years he's not. This year, apparently, he's been elected by a unanimous vote: All of the authors have mentioned the importance of learning to the theory and testing of intelligence, noting also that its importance has been ignored of late. Turnbull refers to the importance of short-term prediction of learning. Resnick has observed that although much recent research has been devoted to isolating components of performance on intelligence-test items, virtually no research has been devoted to understanding the acquisition of these components. Horn contrasts learning in different modalities. Brown and French have introduced to us the Vygotskian concept of a "zone of potential development," which seems to refer to latent capacity of some kind. Detterman notes the importance of learned "content" variables as measures of intelligence, an example of which is vocabulary.

Still another representative in the government of the Land of Intelligence would seem to be Transferman. The importance of transfer to the government of the land is mentioned by several authors of this play: Horn discusses the importance of transfer between sensory modalities; Brown and French discuss the role of transfer in their learning tasks; Turnbull notes the problem of transferring measured ability from a primary language to a secondary one, or vice versa. And we cannot ignore yet one more representative: Retentionman. Learning without transfer is not of much use, since the learning will never be carried beyond the original situation in which it occurs. But one cannot have transfer unless one retains the original learning long enough to apply it to a new setting. Learningman, Transferman, and Retentionman form a trinity within which there is unity: You can't have one in a theory without having the others. Fortunately, the three cooperate rather than compete.

Can learning (and possibly transfer and retention) be broken down into a set of elementary components, and if so, how can these components be isolated? Brown and French suggest one way of isolating possible components of acquisition. In their method, based upon that used in Soviet psychology, subjects receive successive cues in a problem task, with the zone of potential development estimated on the basis of the number (and perhaps types) of cues needed before the subject can proceed to solve the problem on his own. This method resembles my own method of precueing in some respects, and the resemblance leads me to question whether the method suggested by Brown and French really isolates acquisition components, or whether instead it isolates performance components, as does the method of precueing. Suppose that a task requires information-processing components a, b, c, and d for its solution, and suppose that the components are executed in that order. Suppose further that each of two subjects would be able to solve the problem, but for the lack of one component. Subject 1 lacks component a, and Subject 2 lacks component d. If cues are presented in a successive order, allowing problem solution from beginning to end, then one cue may be sufficient to enable Subject 1 to pursue solution independently; Subject 2, however, might need as many as three cues before being able to solve the problem in its entirety. There may be ways of getting around this problem, but whatever they may be, the method still seems like one for isolating components of performance rather than components of acquisition. It functions much the way the method of precueing does in componential analysis, removing certain components from information processing to allow isolation of other components. The results reported by Brown and French are consistent with this type of analysis. If, for example, learning-disabled subjects are able to solve problems with fewer prompts than are mentally retarded subjects, it could well be because they lack fewer components, or are able to access these components with less precueing.

Janet Powell and I are currently engaged in attempting to isolate components of acquisition, transfer, and retention, in one of the tasks mentioned by both Resnick and Detterman—vocabulary. It is not surprising that vocabulary items have been neglected in the current wave of research on information-processing components of performance on intelligence-test items: The items simply provide no basis for the analysis of task performance. But they do seem to provide a basis for the analysis of what we call acquisition components. We believe that these acquisition components are responsible for vocabulary's being the best single measure of intelligence available.

In our current research, subjects are presented with a series of narrative passages of the kind found in newspapers, textbooks, magazines, and other everyday sources of information. The passages are typical in every respect except that they contain embedded within them one or more words of extremely low frequency in the English language. A given low-frequency word can occur one or more times within a given passage, or can occur multiple times across passages. After reading each passage, subjects answer certain questions about it. One of these questions requires them to provide a written definition of one of the low-frequency words. Structural variables in the narrative passages are used to predict the relative difficulties of learning, transferring, or retaining the various words as they occur in the context. At the end of the experiment, subjects are presented with a long list of words, some but not all of which have appeared in the passages. They are asked to rate their confidence of having seen each word previously, and to define those words that they have previously seen.

The first possible test on the meaning of a given word is at the end of the passage in which the word first occurs. At this time of test, the subject can look back at the passage to try to figure out what the word means. Results from this test are used in the estimation of difficulties of acquisition components. The second possible test on the meaning of a given word is at the end of a passage in which that word occurs for the second time in a second and new context. In this test, as in the preceding one, the subject is allowed to look back at the passage that was just read for help in defining the word. The subject is not allowed to look back at the preceding passage in which the word occurred, however. Improvement in the quality of this second definition relative to the quality of the first definition serves as the basis for estimating difficulties of transfer components. The same procedure applies to the third and fourth possible tests. The last possible test on the meaning of a given word is in the final recognition and definitions test. In this test, there is no supporting context, other than that of the other low-frequency words that are being tested (some of which have not previously appeared). Subjects are not allowed to look back at the previous passages. Quality of definitions given in this final test is used as the basis for estimating difficulties of retention components.

Judy Sprotzer and I have been investigating transfer components in a rather different context, that of reasoning by analogy. Trials of analogy solution are presented in pairs. In the first trial of the pair, subjects are presented with a standard analogy, such as LAWYER : CLIENT :: DOCTOR : (MEDICINE, PATIENT, NURSE). In the second trial of the pair, subjects receive an analogy that overlaps with the first analogy in some subset of analogy terms, for example, LAWYER : PARALEGAL :: DOCTOR : (PATIENT, MEDICINE, NURSE). In fact, for each base analogy, there are fifteen other analogies that differ in all possible subsets of terms (including the null set). It is possible to construct a set of linear equations that provides the basis for estimating components of transfer for the different operations used to solve analogies (see Sternberg, 1977); for example, encoding of analogy terms, inference of the relation between the first term of the analogy and the second, or mapping of the relation between the first term of the analogy and the third. These transfer components measure the time saved by the subject's ability—in the second analogy of the pair—to profit from having already performed an operation. For example, in the pair of analogies above, five of the six terms to be encoded in the second problem have already been encoded in the first problem; the inference between the first and second terms of the second analogy is new (that is, different from the inference in the first analogy); the mapping between the first and third terms is the same as in the first analogy. Isolating transfer components should enable us to determine the loci of transfer of training in reasoning tasks.

The idea of a distinction between academic and everyday intelligence appears explicitly in two acts of this play—those of Neisser and of Brown and French—and implicitly in other acts as well. The idea of a distinction between academic and everyday (or social) intelligence has long been an appealing one, and has even made its way into some theories of intelligence (e.g., Guilford, 1967). The problem with the distinction is that evidence in support of a separate unified construct of everyday or social intelligence has been practically nonexistent (see, for example, Keating, 1978). It is hard to know what to make of the lack of evidentiary support for the construct. Tests of everyday intelligence, like those of creativity, are so inadequate to the construct they seek to measure that one cannot decide the theoretical issue on the basis of the operational measures currently used to address the issue. The issue is unlikely to die, anymore than the issue of creativity and how to measure it has died. Despite the inadequacy of the tests that are presently available, it is difficult to believe that there are not forms of everyday intelligence (and creative intelligence) that differ from what standard intelligence tests measure. It may be that there is no one unified construct of everyday intelligence, but several constructs. Such multiplicity of constructs would explain why no one trait has emerged in the research that has been done to date. The problem seems to remain one of finding appropriate tests to measure the trait or traits.

Another theme common to several acts of this play—particularly to those of Neisser, Horn, and Turnbull—is that of cultural relativity in the meaning of intelligence. Horn supplements this theme with one of temporal relativity—what we call intelligence at a given time in a given culture may not be the same as what we call (or should call) intelligence at a different time in (ostensibly) the same culture. This change may occur in part because of subtle changes in the culture that we are only barely aware of. Previous research certainly reinforced the notion that what is viewed as intelligent behavior in one culture may be viewed as quite unintelligent in another (see, for example, Cole, Gay, Glick, & Sharp, 1971; Goodnow, 1976). To the extent that intelligence is defined, stipulatively, in terms of behaviors that are adaptive within a given culture, there can be no doubt that intelligence must be defined relatively, that is, within a given cultural context. However, this divergence in stipulative definitions of intelligence should not obscure communalities in basic processes that probably do exist cross-culturally: The same performance components, acquisition components, transfer components, and metacomponents seem likely to be used by all people, regardless of their culture. What probably differs across cultures is the importance of these components in adapting to everyday life, and it is for this reason that the nature of intelligence is variable across cultures.

A major source of change in the structure and content of the intelligence tests of the future may well be in the uses to which they are put. Some of the authors, most notably Resnick, Brown and French, and Turnbull, have questioned the educational uses to which the tests have been put in the past, and have suggested ways in which the tests might better be utilized. If there is any agreement at all among these authors, and I believe that there is, it is in the conviction that the tests of the future will serve more and more for short-term prognosis and diagnosis and less and less for long-term planning. The notion of intelligence as a fixed, immobile trait that remains invariant over the years no longer finds many advocates. Tests should stimulate innovative educational planning, not serve as a substitute for it.

I have saved for last a discussion of what I believe to be one of the most interesting ideas to have emerged from this play—the idea of intelligence as a prototype, as suggested by Neisser. My agreement with this framework for viewing intelligence could not be expressed any more strongly than by my pointing out that this entire review has consisted of an attempt to form a prototype representing the collective views of the six authors who have contributed to the play. The techniques used by Rosch (see, for example, Rosch, 1978) for studying prototypes, plus new techniques, might open up new avenues of research on intelligence. I think a few caveats need to be stated, however.

First, the idea of intelligence as a prototype, as the idea now stands, is a point of view rather than a theory. I find it useful heuristically in much the same way that I find the notion of scripts (or frames) useful. In the case of the present notion, the theoretical content needs to be filled in, and empirical demonstrations are required to show that the point of view really does have interesting researchable implications. Such research, I think, is most worthy of further pursuit, and likely to be profitable.

Second, because the notion of intelligence as a prototype is a point of view, it is not inconsistent with my own or other theories of intelligence. Society has created an essentially arbitrary concept, and society's prototype would seem to give us a fair representation of what that stipulative concept is. But I believe that there are fundamental aspects of human cognition that are nonarbitrary—namely, the performance components, acquisition components, transfer components, retention components, and meta-components of human information processing. And a useful purpose would be and has been served by trying to relate these various kinds of components to intelligence as it is defined by society. Today, the intelligence test seems to serve this reference function, at least for what Neisser refers to as academic intelligence. Perhaps one direction in which Neisser's thoughts might lead is toward better reference criteria; but for the time being, there seems to be no well worked out alternative to intelligence tests.

Finally, as Neisser points out, the existence of a "positive manifold" for intelligence tests argues in favor of a prototype, or underlying unitary construct, of intelligence. This construct has often been referred to as *g*. Calling this general factor or common something a prototype seems like a good first step toward understanding it. Discovering people's intuitions regarding what behaviors characterize the prototype seems like a good second step. But there is a third step that must follow these two, namely, the seeking of understanding of the psychological mechanisms underlying the objects of people's intuitions. If one of the characteristics of an intelligent person is (according to Cornell undergraduates) that he or she is "able to think logically," then we must understand how people do logical thinking. As it happens, this has been a major goal of my own research program directed toward the understanding of intelligence. I believe, therefore, that Neisser's notions complement, rather than contradict, many of my own regarding the nature of intelligence.

I would like to conclude by thanking the authors of this play for not taking its title too seriously. If they had, a one-liner might have sufficed for any given act: "Intelligence Tests in the Year 2000: They're Here!" Instead, the authors have pointed out multifarious directions in which intelligence testing might move, if not by the year 2000, then by some years thereafter, hopefully, not too many. My interpretation of their suggestions is that we will see more, not less, of what I have called componential analysis. But the scope of componential analysis will have to be expanded to include kinds of components other than the performance components I and others have concentrated upon to date. We will seek to understand as well the components of acquisition, transfer, and retention, as well as the metacomponents that control componential activities. This is now the main thrust of my own research. It is not clear to me, as it is not clear to Turnbull, that componential types of tests will replace refinements of the tests now in existence. But if our ultimate goal is to understand as well as to measure intelligence, it seems that as a bare minimum, componential tests will be wanted to supplement what we already have.

ACKNOWLEDGMENT

I am grateful to Bill Salter, whose coining of "Componentman" in another context led me to pursue Componentman's family tree.

REFERENCES

Cole, M., Gay, J., Glick, J. A., & Sharp, D. W. *The cultural context of learning and thinking.* New York: Basic Books, 1971.

Flavell, J. H., & Wellman, H. M. Metamemory. In R. V. Kail, Jr., & J. W. Hagen (Eds.), *Perspectives on the development of memory and cognition.* Hillsdale, N.J.: Lawrence Erlbaum Associates, 1977.

Goodnow, J. J. The nature of intelligent behavior: Questions raised by cross-cultural studies. In L. B. Resnick (Ed.), *The nature of intelligence.* Hillsdale, N.J.: Lawrence Erlbaum Associates, 1976.

Guilford, J. P. *The nature of human intelligence.* New York: McGraw-Hill, 1967.

Keating, D. P. A search for social intelligence. *Journal of Educational Psychology,* 1978, *70,* 218–223.

Markman, E. M. *Comprehension monitoring.* Paper presented at the Conference on Children's Oral Communication Skills, University of Wisconsin, October, 1978.

Markman, E. M. Realizing that you don't understand: Elementary school children's awareness of inconsistencies. *Child Development,* in press.

Rosch, E. R. Human categorization. In N. Warren (Ed.), *Studies in cross-cultural psychology.* London: Academic Press, 1978.

Sternberg, R. J. *Intelligence, information processing, and analogical reasoning: The componential analysis of human abilities.* Hillsdale, N.J.: Lawrence Erlbaum Associates, 1977.

Sternberg, R. J. Componential investigations of human intelligence. In A. Lesgold, J. Pellegrino, S. Fokkema, & R. Glaser (Eds.), *Cognitive psychology and instruction.* New York: Plenum, 1978(a).

Sternberg, R. J. Isolating the components of intelligence. *Intelligence,* 1978(b), *2,* 117–128.

Sternberg, R. J. The nature of mental abilities. *American Psychologist,* 1979(a), *34,* 214–230.

Sternberg, R. J. *The development of human intelligence.* (Cognitive Development Technical Report No. 4) New Haven: Department of Psychology, Yale University, 1979(b).

Author Index

Page numbers in *italics* indicate where complete references are listed.

Abel, D. A., 210, *214*
Allen, V. L., 225, 226, 228, *233*
Allison, R. B., 117, *135*
Anastasi, A., 237, *244*
Anderson, J. R., 52, *58*
Anderson, N., 95, *103*
Atkinson, R. C., 20, *30,* 37, *59,* 63, 70, *86, 87,* 117, 126, 127, 128, 131, *135,* 142, *161*
Atwood, M. E., 49, 50, *58, 59*
Averbach, E., 121, 125, *135*

Baddeley, A. D., 91, 93, *104*
Bales, R. F., 225, 227, *233*
Barclay, C. R., 150, 153, 154, *162,* 224, *233*
Bartlett, F. C., 229, *233*
Bateman, B., 207, *214*
Becker, J. D., 152, *161*
Belmont, J. M., 71, 85, *86,* 146, 147, 149, 151, 156, *161, 162*
Berkson, G., 230, *233*
Bever, T. G., 94, *104*
Bisanz, J. H., 64, *86, 88*
Bloom, B. S., 209, *214*
Bobbitt, B. L., 64, *88,* 157, 158, 160, *163*
Bobrow, D. G., 95, *104,* 152, *161*
Boies, S., 63, *88,* 157, *163*
Boring, E. G., 180, *189*
Borkowski, J. G., 146, *161*
Boruch, R. F., 13, 14, 22, 23, *31*
Bos, M. C., 226, *233*
Boyes-Braem, P., 181, 183, *189*
Bray, N. W., 147, *162*
Breitmeyer, B. G., 126, *135*
Brelsford, J. W., 117, *135*
Brown, A. L., 85, *86,* 142, 145, 146, 147, 148, 149, 150, 151, 152, 153, 154, 155, 161, *162,* 217, 218, 222, 223, 224, 226, 227, 228, 229, *233,* 254, *256*

Brozek, J., 219, *233*
Bruner, J. S., 184, *189*
Burke, D., 70, 71, *87,* 157, 160, *163*
Butterfield, E. C., 71, 85, *86,* 146, 147, 149, 151, 156, *161, 162*

Calfee, R. C., 45, 46, *58, 135*
Campbell, D. T., 23, *30,* 128, *135*
Campione, J. C., 85, *86,* 142, 146, 147, 148, 149, 150, 151, 152, 153, 154, 155, *162,* 222, 223, 224, 229, *233,* 254, *256*
Cantor, N., 184, *189*
Carpenter, P. A., 36, *59,* 65, 74, *86, 87, 88,* 91, 92, *104*
Carroll, J. B., 10, 27, *30,* 34, 56, 57, *59,* 68, 69, *87,* 89, 97, *104;* 113, *135*
Carroll, J. M., 94, *104*
Case, R., 142, *162*
Catlin, J., 94, *104*
Cellerier, G., 142, *162*
Chase, W., 36, *59,* 65, *87,* 89, 90, *104*
Chi, M. T. H., 70, 71, *87,* 142, 143, 156, 160, *162*
Chiang, A., 37, *59,* 63, *87,* 126, 128, 131, *135*
Clark, H. H., 36, *59,* 65, *87,* 89, 90, *104*
Cliff, N., 18, *30*
Cohen, R. L., 6, 19, 20, *30*
Cole, M., 217, 229, *234, 235,* 265, *267*
Conner, L. A., 210, *214*
Cooper, L. A., 72, 75, *87*
Corcoran, S. K., 7, 20, *31*
Coriell, A. S., 121, 125, *135*
Craik, F. I. M., 143;, *162*
Cronbach, L. J., 85, *87,* 89, *104,* 105, 107, 108, 110, 117, 134, *135,* 211, *214,* 249, *256*

269

Subject Index

A

Ability, *see* Mental abilities
Accountability, 205
Achievement, 107, 205, 247
Achievement tests, 199, 204, 209
Acquisition, *see also* Learning, 146, 212, 245, 256, 262
Additive-factor method, 41, 44–46
Analysis of covariance structures, *see* Covariance structure analysis
Aptitude, *see also* Intelligence, Mental abilities, 84, 105–112, 116–117, 134
Aptitude-treatment interaction, 85, 105–106, 111, 113, 116, 134, 169, 211

C

Cognitive component approach, 1, 2, 62, 68
Cognitive correlates approach, 1, 2, 62–63, 66–67
Cognitive dependency analysis, 44–45, 48
Cognitive development, 66–67, 70, 85, 142, 144, 157–158, 198, 217, 232
Cognitive psychology, *see also* Information processing, 33, 89–90, 103, 106, 108, 111, 116, 160, 172, 180, 192, 197–198, 201, 211, 236, 253
Compensatory education, 207
Componential analysis, 24, 38, 42–44, 79, 114–115, 263, 267
Components, 42–43, 259–260, 263, 266–267
  acquisition, 262–267
  metacomponents, 259–267
  performance, 263–267
  retention, 263–267
  transfer, 263–267
Comprehension, *see* Verbal comprehension
Computer simulation, 41, 48–50, 68, 77, 111, 113, 147, 222

Concepts, 181–182
Content, 27, 211, 253, 260, 266
Control processes, *see* Executive processes; Components, metacomponents
Correlational psychology, *see* Differential psychology
Correlation, 5, 10, 96–97, 168, 170
  canonical, 18, 28, 170
Covariance structure analysis, *see also* Factor analysis, maximum likelihood, 11, 38–39
Creativity, 265
Culture, 175, 177, 191, 193–194, 265

D

Differential psychology, *see also* Psychometrics, 33, 89, 92, 98, 101, 103, 106–108

E

Education, *see also* Instruction, 61, 85–86, 194, 203, 205, 214
Errors, 9
Executive processes, *see also* Components, metacomponents, 66–67, 70, 139, 141–146, 153–154, 160–161, 174, 260
Experimental psychology, *see* Cognitive psychology

F

Factor analysis, 3–4, 7–13, 17, 22, 24, 27, 29, 35, 39–40, 98, 113–114, 121, 168–169, 211, 224, 240–243, 250, 252, 258
  interbattery, 17

273

I

M